Martin Simonson

The Lord of the Rings and the Western Narrative Tradition

2008

Cormarë Series No. 16

Series Editors: Peter Buchs • Thomas Honegger • Andrew Moglestue • Johanna Schön

Editors responsible for this volume: Andrew Moglestue and Johanna Schön

Library of Congress Cataloging-in-Publication Data

Simonson, Martin
The Lord of the Rings and the Western Narrative Tradition
ISBN 978-3-905703-09-2

Subject headings:
Tolkien, J. R. R. (John Ronald Reuel), 1892-1973 – Criticism and interpretation
Tolkien, J. R. R. (John Ronald Reuel), 1892-1973 – Language
Fantasy fiction, English – History and criticism
Middle-earth (Imaginary place)
Literature, Comparative

Cormarë Series No. 16

© Walking Tree Publishers, Zurich and Jena, 2008

All rights reserved. No portion of this book may be reproduced, by any process or technique, without the express written consent of the publisher

Copyright: Martin Simonson 2008
Cover illustration: Anke Eissmann 2008

Set in Adobe Garamond and Shannon by Walking Tree Publishers
Printed by Lightning Source in the United Kingdom and United States

For Cristina, Lucía and Gabriela

Preface

The Lord of the Rings and the Western Narrative Tradition is a long-desired though maybe rather unexpected answer to one of the great puzzles (or, depending on the point of view, irritations) of Tolkien criticism: the question of the genre of *The Lord of the Rings*. Its defiance of traditional critical categories and the critics' difficulties to link it to a definite genre seems to lie at the heart of many a dismissive response. The seemingly protean nature of the text, which opens with an idyllic description of the Shire but then undergoes various changes in tone and style, is – unlike *Ulysses* – not self-referential and marked enough to provide the literary critic, who has been traditionally trained in the canon of modernist works, with sufficient clues. The narrative tone seems to change in a haphazard way without a clear overall development. This impression was further strengthened by some well-meant attempts of comparison between Malory's rambling style or the identification of a host of 'sources and analogues', both medieval and modern, so that *The Lord of the Rings*, not unlike *Beowulf,* became a quarry for source-hunters and analogy-gatherers more interested in the individual building-stones (to use Tolkien's metaphor of the Tower) than in the work itself. Even the realisation that *The Lord of the Rings* should be more appropriately placed within a 20th century context (see also Margaret Hiley's forthcoming study *Aspects of Modernism in the Works of C.S. Lewis, J.R.R. Tolkien and Charles Williams*) has not changed this widespread attitude. Thus, although the consideration of the modern(ist) framework has widened and deepened the critical appreciation of Tolkien's work, it does not provide a sufficiently wide scope for an adequate view of all the constitutive elements and, most importantly, of how they interact. Martin Simonson's radical decision to include the entire Western narrative tradition can be seen as the surprising yet logical response to this critical deficit. Only by means of opening up the field of possible literary models and exemplars has it become possible to overcome the particularising tendencies of former studies into classical, medieval and modern sources and analogues. Yet even so the project would not have succeeded if Martin Simonson had not also convincingly illustrated the 'mechanics' and the dynamism of this highly complex conglomerate of elements within the framework of *The Lord of the Rings*.

I had the pleasure of meeting Martin in person at the ESSE (European Society for the Study of English) conference in Zaragoza (Spain) in 2004 where he gave a paper on Tolkien and thus got to know him and his approach 'in person'. Since then, he has presented his ideas in several articles (most recently in *Tolkien Studies* 3), but it is only now in this book-length study that he has the necessary scope to develop them to the full and illustrate the often intricate processes at length. I am convinced that this volume is going to provide a new impulse to Tolkien studies and that his theory will prove able to develop and evolve by means of incorporating new insights and discoveries. I thus wish this book a warm and attentive reception by its readers.

Thomas Honegger
Zurich, January 08

Contents

Chapter 1
The Lord of the Rings and the Quest for a Meaningful Context — 13

Chapter 2
The Western Narrative Tradition: A Matter of Constant Fusion — 19
2.1 Main characteristics of epic poetry
2.1.1. The evolution of epic literature: from Homer to Beowulf — 25
Homer 25 / The *Argonautica* of Appolonius Rhodius 29 / The *Aeneid* 35 / *Beowulf* 39
2.2. Romance — 42
2.2.1. Romance from the Middle Ages to the 19th century — 43
Medieval romance 43 / Romance and Epic blended: chanson de geste – narratives and Renaissance epics 48 / Epic romance and the novel 54
2.3. The modern novel — 56
The gothic novel and supernatural fiction 57 / The romantic imagination and the novel: the Legend in broad daylight 60 / New worlds, old traditions: the fantasy novels of MacDonald and Morris 62
2.4. Myth and the Western narrative traditions — 67

Chapter 3
The Lord of the Rings and Ironic Myth — 73
3.1. The Great War — 75
The War Poets 76 / High Modernism: T.S. Eliot, Pound and Joyce 79
3.2. Ironic myth — 82
The cases of *In Parenthesis* and *Four Quartets* 87
3.3. Tolkien, Modernity and *Ironic Myth* — 93
The Lord of the Rings and the Great War 93 / *The Lord of the Rings* and Modernism 99 / The Secondary World in context 102 / A different dialogue 106

Chapter 4

The Exploration of the Limits of the Inter-traditional Dialogue
in *The Lord of the Rings* 113

4.1. Leaving the Shire 119
The elves in the Shire 132

4.2. The Tom Bombadil-digression: from myth-making to map-making 137
Dreams, mists, hedges, tunnels and gates: the borders of romance 140 / Trees and sleep: romance space consolidated 141 / Tom Bombadil and Goldberry: nature and myth 144 / More dreams, fog, and gates: romance and myth in the Barrow-downs 147 / The road: novel on the way back to Bree and Middle-earth 148

4.3. Aragorn's heroic evolution 151
Aragorn in Bree: Epic and the Adventure Novel 152 / Rivendell: Romance and Epic 158 / Lórien: Romance 162 / From Amon Hen to Fangorn: Novel, Epic, and Romance 163 / Meduseld and Helm's Deep: Epic 167 / Isengard: Novel 170 / Minas Tirith: Epic and Romance 171 / Victory: Romance 173

4.4. Rivendell: narrative mélange 174
A border rehabilitated 174 / Defining the heroes 178

4.5. The Mines of Moria: generating applicability 183
The Mines of Moria and the twentieth century 184 / The intrusion of the novel 185 / Novel and myth in dialogue 186 / The Bridge of Khazad-dûm: the meeting between Christian and pagan traditions 189

4.6. Gandalf: messenger of the Valar 190
Gandalf in Fangorn: romance wizard 191 / Rohan and Gondor: Christian virtues, pagan courage 193

4.7. Frodo and Sam: journey to the end of the Third Age 199
The adventure novel 200 / The dystopic romance of the Great War 202 / The Black Gate: Epic rejected 204 / Fusion: adventure novel and dystopic romance of the Great War 205 / Pseudomedieval romance 207 / The gothic novel 210 / Towards the mythic end of the Third Age 214

4.8. Back to the Shire: dismantling the intertraditional dialogue 218

Chapter 5
The Meta-Narrative Myth of Hope for the Twentieth Century   221

Bibliography
Primary Sources   227
Secondary Sources   229
    Literary genres, concrete works and literary theory 229 / Poetry of the Great War, Modernism and the Twentieth Century 233 / Monographs and studies on Tolkien and his works 236 / Dictionaries 243

Index   245

Parts of this book previously appeared in the following publications:

Sections 3.1. and 3.3:
Parts of these sections appeared in 'The Lord of the Rings and the Great War: War Poetry, Modernism, and Ironic Myth' in: *Reconsidering Tolkien,* Honegger, T. (ed.), Walking Tree Publishers, 2005, pp. 153-170.

Section 4.1:
This section appeared as 'Three Is Company: Novel, Fairy Tale, and Romance on the Journey Through the Shire' in: *Tolkien Studies,* vol. III, Anderson, D. et al. (eds.), West Virginia University Press, Morgantown, WV, 2006, pp. 81-100.

Section 4.3:
Parts of this section appeared as 'An Introduction to the Dynamics of the Intertraditional Dialogue in The Lord of the Rings: Aragorn's Heroic Evolution' in: Honegger, T., Weinreich, F., (eds.), *Tolkien and Modernity II,* Walking Tree Publishers, 2006, pp. 75-114.

Acknowledgments

The author would like to express his gratitude to Eduardo Segura of Instituto de Filosofía Edith Stein, Granada, who directed the dissertation that later developed into this book – thank you also for your friendship, Edvard. José Miguel Santamaría, Eterio Pajares and Vicky Olsen of Universidad del País Vasco, Vitoria, have generously offered assistance with matters both academic and bureaucratic. He would also like to thank Thomas Honegger of Walking Tree Publishers for his patience and invaluable advice; Birger Simonson for his tireless support; Cecilia Bergil and Jan Olov Nilsson for providing the weary with shelter and encouraging thoughts; Honorino Casado and Irene Julia Gil for being there, always; and the members of *Los Exploradores del Crepúsculo* for their adventurous spirit and good example.

He also thanks his wife Cristina, for her solid faith in the seaworthiness of this vessel, that proved its captain wrong and made it to the shore in spite of all the heavy weather. Good steering, mate.

Martin Simonson
January 2008

Chapter 1

The Lord of the Rings and the Quest for a Meaningful Context

Ever since the publication of *The Lord of the Rings*, the critical approaches to Tolkien's masterpiece have been very varied, and over the years they have become more and more specialized. Apart from a multitude of papers, published in academic journals[1] and critical anthologies, the *corpus* of book-length studies dedicated to Tolkien's work has steadily grown and includes themes as diverse as descriptive grammars of Tolkien's invented languages, guidebooks to the places Tolkien visited and that supposedly inspired different aspects of Middle-earth, critical works attempting to disclose how the intellectual circles he frequented in Oxford influenced his linguistic philosophy, the presence of Christian aspects in his work, studies of how his experiences in the Great War triggered the development of his particular literary vision, narratological analysis[2], etc. The list could be made much longer and even include other areas of knowledge and fields of art.

When contemplating this overwhelming amount of approaches, it would seem difficult, at least at a first glance, to outline something like a common ground in Tolkien criticism. However, I believe that it is possible to discern three main branches. In the first place we have the analytical approach based on the disclosure of literary and, sometimes, remotely historical sources for different aspects of the work.[3] In the second place, the studies attempting to reveal the applicability of the story to the historical and cultural conditions of the 20th century.[4] Finally we have the critical works centered on more technical aspects of the narrative, such as the descriptive grammars, metrical and structural analysis, etc.

---

1 Some of the publications that have most frequently included articles on Tolkien are *Inklings: Jahrbuch für Literatur und Asthetik; Journal of the Fantastic in the Arts;.Mythlore; Mallorn; Studies in Medievalism*, among others.
2 Recent examples of these approaches include, respectively: González (1999), Lyons (2004), Flieger (2003), Wood (2003), Garth (2004), and Segura (2004).
3 See Chance and Day (1991); Clark and Timmons (ed.) (2000), and Day (2003).
4 See Veldman (1994), Curry (1998), Flieger (1997), Shippey (2002).

Roughly, the main part of this bibliography is made up of the first two groups. The problem is that these fields of research are often put in frank opposition: while the first group tends to emphasise the importance of the work as a catalyst for (mostly) medieval literary traditions, in the studies belonging to the second it is considered relevant insofar as it implicitly addresses the predominant political and cultural issues of the 20th century, such as the need for a stronger ecological commitment, or the dangers of totalitarianism.

Another question which has generated much debate and that involves all three branches, deals with literary genre – what type of literature is this? Most critics consider that it is not possible to attribute a single definition to the work, since such an approach would only refrain the reader from getting the full picture.[5] While the fact that many different genres are at work is beyond doubt, from my point of view, no Tolkien scholar has so far succeeded (or even attempted) in explaining the particularity of genre *interaction* in *The Lord of the Rings*; that is, how the dialogue between different literary traditions conditions both the writing and the reading of the story.

The main aim of the present study is to discover a common ground in Tolkien criticism, or at least to show one of the possible roads that may take us there. For this reason, my critical approach should be able to reconcile the two stances represented by the first two groups in Tolkien criticism, as outlined above. Both fields of research, viewed separately, are of course valuable and useful for the diclosure of certain implicit fields of meaning present in the text, but they are at the same time seriously (and necessarily) limited, and sometimes even *limiting*, as conductors towards a wider understanding of the work. A critical formula capable of combining and integrating both stances would neutralise many of the contradictions and incoherencies generated by their inherent academic provincialism.

The same formula should also be able to produce a new approach to the question of genre in Tolkien's work, without excluding any of the reasonably justified proposals previously made. In order to do so, I wish to verify the originality of the work as derived from its capacity to put a great number of different

---

5 The most influential critical work that represents this stance is Shippey's The Road to Middle-earth (2003, first published 1982). See also Segura (2004).

literary traditions in smooth dialogue, but within a concrete literary context, much closer to modernism than to the pseudomedieval romances of William Morris, or, for that matter, the misleadingly denominated 'fantasy' literature by writers such as C.S. Lewis or Ursula K. Le Guin. Hence, I consider that it is possible to defend the apparently paradoxical opinion that *The Lord of the Rings* is *sui generis* within a concrete literary context.

Apart from providing us with a foundation for the explanation of the dialogue between different literary traditions within Tolkien's masterpiece, this approach would also help us to legitimate its importance in the English – and universal – literary context of the twentieth century. This, in turn, would hopefully clear the way for a removal of much prejudice on behalf of mainstream literary criticism, which is often motivated by the apparent lack of a literary context in which to situate this work.

In the third place, our critical formula should disclose *how* the different narrative traditions interact in *The Lord of the Rings*. If we are able to analyse the different levels of generic interaction, we might also be able to explain a number of apparent contradictions regarding characters, descriptions of physical space, action, and focalisation, which may (or may not) depend on the *limits* of different traditions in dialogue with others.

The starting point for the present study was found in Shippey's (2003:210-211) discussion of genre in *The Lord of the Rings*. Here, Shippey highlights the work's capacity to express five of the literary modes, as outlined by Frye (1971) in his influential critical study *Anatomy of Criticism* – myth, romance, high mimesis, low mimesis and the ironic mode. I was struck by the fact that Shippey left out the mode of ironic myth, proper to the 20th century and the next phase in the cycle described by Frye, because in many of its expressions, this literature is characterised by an exhaustive incorporation of different literary traditions of the past on a simultaneous level. The exhaustive corpus of source-hunting studies on Tolkien's best-known work seemed to confirm that *The Lord of the Rings* fulfilled the criteria of this mode, too.

However, in many of these studies, references to different genres often become quite loose in context. What does it really mean to say that the War of the

Ring is epic, that Lothlórien is indebted to romance, or that Sam is a novelistic character? As soon as any given genre is mentioned in relation to an episode, or to a character, or to a physical space, I get the impression that something is lacking. From my point of view, there is no such thing as pure paradigms in this 'tale' (to use Tolkien's own, perhaps deliberately vague definition of what it was he had written), and I believe that this is so mainly because of the insistent, ever-present intertraditional dialogue that permeates all levels of the narrative. Hence, I consider that there is a real need in Tolkien criticism to find a formula that may fruitfully account for this.

In order to be able to confirm the presence of one genre or another, I will present the main characteristics of what I perceive as the four great Western narrative traditions in the following chapter with some rigour. These four paradigms are myth, epic, romance and the novel. This chapter will be used as a point of reference for the later comparison between the different branches of each of these traditions and *The Lord of the Rings*, which will be an important part of the analysis in the fourth chapter.

In the third chapter I will discuss the similarities and differences between Tolkien's work and some of the representatives, both war poets and modernists, of what Frye terms ironic myth, while the fourth chapter will be devoted to an application of the conclusions to a textual analysis of the dynamics of the intertraditional literary dialogue in *The Lord of the Rings*.

Apart from the selective use I will make of Frye and Bakhtin, I will consequently ignore the approaches of mainstream literary criticism, since none of the established methodologies has proved capable of providing me with relevant tools for the analysis. The need to design a unique methodology is an inevitable response to the work's particular characteristics, as I have had to analyse literary aspects previously unexplored by genre criticism in the context of comparative literature. This white spot on the official map (as drawn by critics who have, so to speak, tried to avoid the monsters) is probably due to the (to many) 'monstrous' originality of the work and the scarce appreciation of *The Lord of the Rings* on behalf of the scholars dedicated to this branch of criticism (the latter effect being potentially derived from the huge popular success the work has enjoyed).

In other words, the problem is largely the same as that which Tolkien outlined in his famous essay on the Old English epic *Beowulf* – the work is usually not considered a masterpiece by mainstream literary criticism due to a general refusal to accept the centrality of monsters. Tolkien's work is very clearly, and not only chronologically, at the centre of twentieth-century literature, in spite of its fantastic setting, as we shall see. That *Beowulf* was a source of inspiration for Tolkien is likewise beyond doubt, but the roots of *Beowulf* go back further than the feats of a Geat in Denmark, and the branches of the epic tradition reach all the way to twentieth-century modernism. *The Lord of the Rings* does so, too. In the following chapter we shall see what happened to European story-telling once Ulysses returned from Troy, and how the roots, stem and branches of Tolkien's best-known narrative all belong to one vast, fascinating tree of many hues and fibres.

Chapter 2

The Western Narrative Tradition: A Matter of Constant Fusion

In this chapter, I obviously do not pretend to offer a detailed study of the main narrative traditions since Homer and up to the nineteenth-century novel (the twentieth century will be left for the third chapter). What I pursue is rather to survey the general characteristics of each major genre – epic, romance, and novel, together with their most important variations – with the aim of establishing a foundation for the central analysis of the present study, which will deal with the particular applications and combinations of different elements from these traditions in *The Lord of the Rings*, and how they are related to the configuration of plot and character-drawing.

I will delve deeper into certain details, particularities and concrete works of the different subgenres in the fourth chapter, as long as they are relevant for the narrative situation under study – for example, the British adventure novel of the nineteenth century, the humoristic novel of Dickens and Jerome, and Hardy's rural novels are all relevant for the narrative construction of the Shire and will consequently be discussed in that section.

For this reason, the present chapter will provide us with an overview of the main generic traits, to which the mentioned works may adhere to a greater or lesser extent. In this showroom, we are mainly interested in the general features of each picture and in understanding the literary and historical relationship between them – to grasp the narrative continuity that links the previous traditions with *The Lord of the Rings* on a diachronic level. We will begin with the epic tradition.

2.1. Main characteristics of epic poetry

It is very complicated, if not impossible, to cover all the implications of epic literature in one single, brief definition. Hainsworth (1991:5) claims that "[t]he seed of epic is sown when myth and folktale are blended and cast into the narrative mode of heroic poetry". The statement as such will not bring us much closer to the definition we are looking for, but it may serve as a starting point for the understanding of the narrative exposition and the purposes of the literature that began taking shape towards the seventh century B.C.E.

The main function of myth could be said to be the explanation of the human condition and the revelation of ideal models of conduct by means of superhuman intervention in the natural world. As opposed to the folktales, whose heroes and fantastic animals are allegedly fictional and do not carry out actions of significant importance for the human race, myths have a paradigmatic value and are presented as fact, not fiction.[6]

On the other hand, the main function of heroic poetry is that of providing a community with a positive and encouraging image of itself, in order to inspire pride and hope in its members. Heroic poetry celebrates and confirms something, just like the epic, but, as Hainsworth (1991:6) points out, whereas the latter *explores and questions* while celebrating, the former does not. In this way, epic literature seems to arise when heroic poetry is expanded with inquiries into issues that are crucial to human existence, and with the intervention of supernatural elements of different kinds.

While the folk tale was used mainly to entertain the audience, the poets who composed heroic poetry pretended, among other things, to speak of heroes that the audience could identify with. For this reason, they portrayed a reality which was closer to human experience than that of the folktales. The epic narrative internalized the identifying and encouraging functions of heroic poetry, but the poets aimed at a greater coherence in their presentation of the world. However, as the epic narrative world involves an immense thematic, temporal and spatial amplitude, the authors had to modify their exposition of reality in order to fulfil their aims. The natural course of events is, as everyone knows, often marked by chance and decidedly unheroic – that is, a far too incoherent, prosaic and fragmented an affair for epic narratives.

---

6 Eliade (2000:21) discusses the pretension of veracity in mythic tales as opposed to the admitted falsehood of the folktale.

Since a portrayal of naked, unadorned reality is not the issue at stake in epic poetry, the solution was to use the heroic tale as the thread of the story, and expand it with secondary tales – fictional as well as historical anecdotes, tales, and facts.

In this way, the heroes and their actions remained at the centre, but there was also room for many other stories, which were incorporated into the main narrative at a subordinate level, by means of digressions.[7] These digressions, or subordinate stories, were not always used to explain in more detail some concrete aspect of the central action, but were frequently included to create temporal depth (Beye 1993:102). It was necessary to increase the temporal perspective in this way, since another consequence of the ambition to maintain a strict internal coherence was that the epic poets tended to compress the temporal span of the main story, which normally begins just before the dénouement of the most crucial events (for example, the main action of the *Iliad*, dealing with the last days of a ten-year-long war).

In order to convey the temporal depth, the thread of the story – the main heroic action – is frequently and inevitably interrupted by movements back (in the stories about events taking place before the main action) and forth (the main action, and even further on with the narrator's perspective telling of that past).[8] The effect of this is that the narrative almost always advances slowly and becomes very extended. Another reason for the incorporation of the secondary tales is the epic poet's pretension to offer a total vision, the sum of a culture, to his audience, and in this way to save it from oblivion. For this reason, the digressions tell of traditions, genealogies and historical as well as fictional events that relate, in one way or another, to a given cultural context; in other words, they take on an almost encyclopaedic function.

---

7 This is such a salient feature that most scholars consider it central to the idea of epic narratives. It is significant that Aristotle, the first scholar to produce written literary criticism concerning the epic tradition, should explain Homer's narrative technique by saying that he uses a central story as a starting point for other episodes that adhere to it (Aristotle and Horace 1991:86).

8 Goethe claimed in his correspondence with Schiller that this pendulous movement that continually postpones the main action is what makes epic different from tragedy, which is based on clarity and concentration (Hainsworth 1991:42). According to Ford (1993:41), it is this particular structure, in which the central action gives rise to all the secondary tales, that in the end evokes "the entire heroic world of the past, the deeds of gods and men".

The importance of the main heroic action, then, resides in its ability to generate a great abundance of secondary tales[9] that, taken together, transmit the cultural legacy of the past. It is not surprising that the backdrop for the central thread of the story often is a war, given that large-scale warfare necessarily involves the participation of different cultures – few things are as effective as an exterior threat to highlight the virtues of the proper culture – and individuals, each one with a story of his own. Furthermore, its consequences affect the lives and continuity of entire nations. At the same time, wars offer a generous setting for the affirmation and celebration of heroic deeds.

In the epic tale, the protagonists acquire a power and greatness unthinkable in other narratives (with the exception of myth) and this central position of the heroes, put on display for the critical scrutiny of the audience, carries a number of consequences related to their characterization. In the first place, the hero becomes a public character who represents the totality of his community,[10] but at the same time, he remains an individual with a proper name and history. It is yet another paradox in the long list of rhetorical contradictions that the epic narrative struggles to reconcile, this time as a result of the mélange between myth and heroic poetry. As a result, the epic hero is neither purely mythical nor exclusively human.[11]

The hero's actions are always a response to a series of situations that put his courage, strength or will-power to the test. These trials are often of such a magnitude that the entire community's fate comes to depend on their result. In order to defeat the opposing forces, the epic hero may accept help from supernatural sources, either from benevolent gods or by means of magic artfacts. However, it would seem that he reaches true greatness, prestige and dignity when relying solely on his own physical or mental strength.[12]

---

9 In Hegel's (1975:1044-45) opinion, epic narratives produce a complete vision of the past by using an event rich in meaning that puts on display the whole culture of a nation or an epoch.
10 Hardie (1993:4) uses Aeneas of the *Aeneid* as an example of this trait, saying that he is "a synecdochic hero," but his statement is also valid for the greater part of the important epic heroes. Moretti (1996: 12) goes even further and claims that the epic world as such is "a world that takes form thanks to a hero and recognizes itself in him."
11 For a more extensive discussion of the epic hero's double affinities, see Kerenyi (1974).
12 Epic heroes such as Achilles, Ulysses, Jason, Aeneas or Beowulf all receive help from supernatural objects or divinities, but in the end it is their own inherent strength, whether physical or moral, that brings them victory.

This human quality, and above all the hero's mortality, would seem to be inherited from previous heroic poetry.

Apart from the hero's mortality, his personal traits are often in the service of presenting a favourable portrait of the community that he represents. As a general rule, the epic hero is tall, handsome, aristocratic, muscular, courageous and skilful at anything he undertakes (Toohey 1992:9). Seen from a modern-day perspective, he also possesses other, less flattering qualities, being often cruel, vain, unfaithful, greedy and deceitful. However, all of these traits are powerful allies in the epic hero's pragmatic mission of manifesting the aristocratic society's masculine virtues of the age: to satisfy the needs of his ego by means of material or amorous conquests, to affirm himself in the face of adversity, and to make his name immortal by carrying out impressive feats.

Another consequence of this strange combination of mythological and human characteristics is that the action always takes place in a more or less remote past, generally in the so called Heroic (or Bronze) Age. The epic world as such is presented as a combination of the central heroic action, of great social and political importance for an entire culture and set in a semi-primordial age, and the events of the quotidian world, evoked in digressions and similes. These modifications of reality expand the world-vision, making it broad enough to include not only the world of men, but also the subterranean and divine worlds, so that the inclusion of myth and supernatural events becomes not only feasible but even inevitable. The semi-primordial temporal framework enables the poet to portray sublime characters and events without yielding completely to the folktale's more frivolous marvels, since the glorious past was conceived of as a time when the gods often interacted with elected humans. At the same time, a marked nostalgia for these lost days of glory is normally present, so that the stories often take on an elegiac character. The mourning for lost glory is also extended to the worries of the protagonists: Achilles is incapable of accepting his mortality, wishing to be immortal like his mother; Ulysses longs for his lost youth; Medea goes mad because of lost love; Aeneas dreams about recovering the presently ruined splendour of Troy, and the old Beowulf yearns for the faithful allies of his youth, now long dead.

On a stylistic level, the temporal setting brings about a diction considered archaic even by the poets' original audience, though Greene (1963:24) attributes this particularity to the fact that the main aim of the poet is to inspire awe and admiration for the prodigious yet human feat, and that the archaic tone would be a result of the poet's need to prepare the audience for a narrative that tells of accordingly prodigious, yet true, events and characters.

The notion of the past is thus crucial for the shaping of epic literature, both as a means of justifying the sublimity of the protagonists and the supernatural events, and as a way of providing the poet with a temporal framework that enables him to move back and forth in time, making the transmission of the cultural legacy more fluent. The two realities, the historical and the primordial, are brought together in this pseudohistorical past, and the outcome is an encyclopaedic narrative, covering beliefs and traditions while at the same time rescuing genealogies, events and places from oblivion.

At the same time, we must bear in mind that the internal coherence is just as important for the vitality of the epic narrative as the evocation and transmission of the cultural legacy. While the epic world needs thematic, temporal and spatial amplitude, the events, characters and places must conform to a strict internal coherence in order not to contradict other information related to the main action or to the digressions. This does not mean that the epic tale is *realistic*, at least not from the point of view of eighteenth and nineteenth-century standards of realism. The Greek people of Antiquity did not think that the concepts of veracity and credibility were necessarily related to the empirically demonstrable, but rather to narrative coherence. As Ford (1993:50) explains,

> [t]ruth in the archaic period is not the same as historical accuracy. In Homer, the word [*alêtheia*] is used of accounts by human speakers about matters of which it is difficult to know the facts [...] A 'true' speech was one that reported precisely and in detail, with scrupulous attention to what one has said before and the consequences of what one is saying.

Ford also mentions the concept of *enargês*, which would be translated more or less as "intensity" or "force", that was used to describe "something or someone appearing convincingly before one's eyes [...] The word is also used to describe poetry that puts its incidents clearly before the audience's eyes." (Ford 1993:54) For this reason, the supernatural elements – be they gods, monsters, places or artefacts – may abound in an epic narrative without ruining its credibility (*alêtheia*), as long as the poet makes them conform to the internal coherence.

Evidently, not all epic works express these traits in the same way, though it would seem that the characteristics and objectives outlined above are shared, to a greater or lesser extent, by the most important works of this narrative tradition, as we shall presently see.

2.1.1. The evolution of epic literature: from Homer to *Beowulf*

Homer

The works attributed to Homer, the *Iliad* and the *Odyssey*, were the first two epic narratives in Western literature to be put down in writing. As such, they have had an immense influence on later expressions not only of the genre, but on Western literature in general. However, it is important to bear in mind that the two works should not be grouped together as one and the same thing – in fact, there are many differences between them, which can be appreciated mainly in the selection of themes, the presentation of the heroes, and the representation of reality.

In the *Iliad* we might say that the overarching issue is war, and the exploration of how the moral code of the aristocratic warrior affects his relationship with the world he lives in. The strong emphasis on the presentation of the heroes and their conduct – virtuous as well as despicable – would seem to aim at portraying models which were left to the audience to abhor or embrace, though Toohey's (1992:9) view, that "[m]isuse of the heroic impulse is a generic theme of the epic", is perhaps nowhere as clear as in Homer's portrayal of Achilles.

There is also a tendency in the *Iliad* to create some sort of common identity for the different families and representatives of the many small Greek kingdoms that take part in the battle against the Trojans. Weber (1983:235), when alluding to the disciplined silence and unity of the Greeks, that stand out favourably against the cacophony among the Trojan ranks before the battles, even goes as far as to claim that "the aim is to present a common ethos for all Greeks."

The *Odyssey*, in which the theme of heroic honour is given a more superficial treatment, concentrates on other aspects of life, which not only affect the aristocracy. In this narrative, the undisputable protagonist is Ulysses himself, and the main themes are exemplified by his adventures and misfortunes. Among them is the dialogue that the hero struggles to establish with his environment in order to discover what really matters in the quest to lead a good life. The return to Ithaca involves a refusal to accept the immortality offered by Calypso, the material wealth of Circe, and the perennial sexual pleasures that both are willing to bestow upon him. The underlying idea running through the whole narrative is, quite simply, that temptation leads to trouble. Furthermore, the dialogue between the man and his environment underscores the need to resort to diplomatic skills rather than to arms, and displays the hidden powers of those who know how to manipulate reality by means of wit, lies and disguises.

A theme shared by both works is mankind's reluctance to accept its destiny, though the meaning of that concept varies from one narrative to another (Hainsworth 1991:71-72). In the *Iliad*, Zeus shares out Good and Evil arbitrarily to humanity, while in the *Odyssey*, the same god affirms that the mortals should not blame him for their lot, alluding to the idea that the deeds of each man shape his destiny. In any case, the characteristics of this elusive destiny are not very well defined in either of the poems; it is rather a matter of two different approaches to its inevitability. To me, it is the rebellion of the young and impetuous Achilles against the premonition that speaks of his premature death, and the stoicism of the mature and thoughtful Ulysses as he battles against certain gods and elements for a safe return to his home, that confer meaning and interest to these characters.

The *Iliad* (and, to some extent, the *Odyssey*) provides us with abundant examples of model heroes, according to the canon of the age of composition. However, as opposed to what might have been expected of a narrative that pretends to evoke the totality of a society, almost all protagonists are male and belong to the aristocracy. Apart from their sex and social class, they are usually handsome, intelligent, strong and relentless. In general, the Homeric hero will attach prime importance to the issue of investing his name with glory – that this should be the aim (indeed, the *duty*) of all heroes is taken for granted. Thus, the struggle, which is the essence of the hero's life, is related to the intention of flouting (even if it is only posthumously) the law that governs all mortals: every hero's goal is to survive death and oblivion, the great enemy of all, through spoken or sung memory.

This pragmatic attitude contributes to the effective exorcism of any existential or moral doubts in the protagonists (though the existential *conflict* is always very much present). In other words, apart from the accumulation of glory and property, which he achieves by means of ruthless deeds, the homeric hero usually lacks moral ideals and is seldom afflicted by internal conflicts.[13] This lack of moral doubts brings him closer to the primordial world and its god-prototypes,[14] though not in all cases. Ulysses, for instance, is more nuanced as a character compared to most other homeric heroes. He often resorts to his wit as a potent alternative to armed conflict, and he is capable of conceiving efficient stratagems that subvert the codes of heroic honour and decorum. This is mainly due to his particular vision of the world, not as an absolute and unbreakable entity, but as something which can be modified and manipulated by human intelligence. On numerous occasions, he appears disguised in order to deceive his enemies, and when he speaks, his great rhetorical skills turn the most improbable lies into something resembling truth.[15]

The adjective that best describes him is perhaps "cunning", but he has many other sides: he can be obnoxious, greedy, proud and cruel, and he is a lover of the pleasures of life. As a character he embodies the basic characteristics of the homeric heroes, as they appear in the *Iliad*. It would almost seem as if the poet, instead of concentrating on one or two particular features of his

---

13 Auerbach (1979:29) discusses this further.
14 This homeric hybrid is a result of the intimate relationship between the heroes and the gods, who frequently visit the world of the mortals to assist and help their favourites, or to punish those who have insulted them in one way or another. These elected mortals are often even related to the divinities by blood. Achilles, for instance, is the son of the goddess Thetis, while Hermes is the great-grandfather of Ulysses, to mention the divine origins of the two main protagonists of Homer's works.
15 Beye (1993:57) stresses Ulysses's capacity of reinventing himself in order to survive in a changing world. On the other hand, Ford (1993:54) considers that "Odysseus has *enargês*: he is someone appearing convincingly before the audience's eyes." Ulysses's capacity of transforming reality according to his will is present in most of his actions.

personality, allows Ulysses to exhibit them all. This is not very surprising, since the tales and adventures linked to his person dominate the major part of the narrative.

As for the representation of reality in the homeric poems, we might say that it largely follows the scheme that we have previously outlined. In the first place, the action takes place in a past considered remote for the audience of the 7th century B.C.E. – to be more exact, towards 1180 B.C.E.[16] In the *Iliad*, which aims to tell of events connected to the siege of Troy, the main action begins with the final stage of the war. Likewise, the directly referred action of the *Odyssey* covers only the very last stage of Ulysses's voyage, which, just like the Trojan war, has lasted for ten years. The previous events transcend through digressions and interviews, and in the shape of memories. These digressions include extensive catalogues of genealogies, places, objects and other cultural minutiae which widen and deepen the world presented to us, without necessarily providing information that is relevant for a fuller understanding of the conflict with the Trojans, or the initial stages of Ulysses's travels.

As for the presence of the supernatural, apart from the divine interventions it is true that, as Hainsworth (1991:33) points out, there is only one fantastic element in the *Iliad*, namely Xanto, the talking horse. The *Odyssey*, on the other hand, features an extensive section (books IX-XII) in which the 'historical' world gives way to an enchanted geography full of monsters, magic and marvels of the most varied kinds. From here on, epic poets will exploit the possibilities offered by the fantastic without hesitating, and to such an extent that it is currently considered a feature inherent to the genre. However, the marvellous elements of the second part of the *Odyssey* adds a strong flavour of what later will be called romance[17] to the narrative, and the integration of romance elements involves a serious narrative problem, given that the representation of reality changes considerably from one tradition to another. Hainsworth (1991:35) appeals to reasons of generic incompatibility

---

16 At about this time, a real battle was fought at the place where the remnants of Troy were found, though it was not of such a magnitude as Homer's work suggests. Apart from the citadel, the city was in ruins by the time Homer composed the Iliad. For an outline of the latest findings in Troy and its relationship to the Iliad, see *http://www.archaeology.org/0405/etc/troy.html* (25-10-2006 12.15). See also Latacz (2005).
17 See section 2.2.1 of the present chapter.

derived from different conceptions of reality when he claims that Ulysses's adventures in 'wonderland' were relegated to a subordinate level, distanced from the main action by a digressive device, because such a fantastic tale could never take up a vital space in an epic narrative (which he understands to be more realistic, at least in the homeric conception of the tradition). Be that as it may, the presence of the fantastic in the *Odyssey* also contributes to the establishment of generic interaction, which from now on becomes another important characteristic of the epic tradition.[18]

In short, taking off with Homer, the Western narrative tradition was given a powerful start, full of possibilities for further exploitation. What happened next testifies to its potential.

The *Argonautica* of Appolonius Rhodius

Apollonius Rhodius was born around the year 300 B.C.E. in the city of Alexandria, legacy of the conquests of Alexander the Great and home of the legendary Library of Alexandria, where research on Homer's text was carried out by editors and scholars such as Aristophanes of Byzantium and Aristarchus of Samothrace, among others. Apollonius, who also worked as an editor in the library (he is actually said to have become head of the library), was a well-known philologist of his time, with considerable knowledge of the Greek literature written up to date.

His mentor was the poet and scholar Callimachus, who professed the need for contemporary poets to use a style of poetry based on brevity, concentration, wit, elegance, and sophistication in order to make it palatable for the Alexandrinian audience. Apart from an abundant dose of elegance and sophistication, Apollonius broke with the rest of the rules laid out by Callimachus when he created the *Argonautica*, an epic poem based on the already famous story about Jason and

---

18 Toohey (1992:19), for instance, believes that an epic narrative "must contain generic play and variety" and insists on the importance of generic interaction in the genre. This generic play is much more present in the *Odyssey* than in the *Iliad*, the language and structure of which are much more inflexible. Beye (1993:145) explains that the overall structure of the *Odyssey* depends on several generic/thematic divisions. The first part, Beye says, is of the typical epic-heroic kind, while the second is marked by a fairy-tale atmosphere and the third is more similar to a domestic or social story.

Medea, using a number of technical and thematic aspects from Homer's works for inspiration.[19]

Apollonius shared with Callimachus the idea that it was necessary to bring contemporary literature closer to current life and taste, and, as a result, he strove to update Homer's themes. Hainsworth (1991:54) says that

> [t]he question of the Hellenistic poets was whether or not the ethos of Homer could be adapted to a civilized bourgeois world, keeping the form but changing the essense [...] [The *Argonautica*] was a mythical tale tricked out in archaic dress but contemporary in its ethos.

However, from my point of view, the question is rather if the ethos of Homer was incompatible with the civilized bourgeois world solely on the basis of social refinement. According to García Gual (1988:120-121), it is a matter of expanded perspectives:

> The epic hero represents ideals that nobody questions and everybody agrees are noble. This is possible in a small world, a closed society, in which concepts and ideals are standardized by uniform customs, traditions, faith and experience, and this ceased to exist in the times of Sophocles [...] The wider the world, the smaller Man is. This is what happened in the *Argonautica*.[20]

The Alexandrinian society was far more cosmopolitan than the one Homer composed his works for, and the literary taste had also changed.[21] However, whereas the old epic formulae were no longer efficient to give expression to the world, the pseudo-mythological plots were still appealing.

The *Argonautica* tells of the quest for the Golden Fleece, on the one hand, and of the love story between Jason and Medea, on the other. The story begins when Jason turns up at the court of Iolcos to claim the throne from his uncle Pelias, who had previously usurped it from Jason's father Aeson. Pelias says that he will yield the throne on the condition that Jason recover the legendary Golden Fleece, jealously watched over by a terrible dragon in Colchis, a land

---

19 For two full-length studies on how Apollonius used the previous narrative traditions in his own work, see Clauss (1992), and Knight (1995).
20 My translation.
21 García Gual (1985:119) considers that the main influences on the work of Apollonius were the Alexandrinian taste for sentimental and erotic scenes and the psychological approach to character-drawing in the tragedies of Euripides.

on the edge of the world. Jason accepts the challenge and sets out, together with fifty-four heroes, among others Orfeo and Heracles, in the ship Argo. After a number of adventures they reach Colchis, where Medea, the daughter of king Eetes, falls in love with Jason and helps him with her magic (against her father's wishes) to retrieve the Golden Fleece, escaping with him from her father's wrath. During the return trip they are followed by Apsirto, Medea's brother, whom they slay, and after a brief stop at Circe's palace they reach Tesalia, where the voyage ends.

The narrative is full of allusions, referring both to the Homeric poems and to other texts, and this generates a sophisticated blend of genres and literary traditions. However, the most direct and obvious relationship is established with Homer's works in general, and the *Odyssey* in particular. In fact, the structure is almost a calque of Ulysses's adventures in the enchanted archipelago (cantos IX-XII).[22]

In spite of all this, the thematic differences are important. While it is true that Appolonius explores certain aspects of the heroic code and its consequences, the return as a metaphor for the life cycle, and the ethic implications of hospitality, other topics are far more prominent in the *Argonautica*. Beye (1993:202) considers that the poem is about "the problematic, frightening, all-consuming, dangerous passion of a woman's love and the man's inability to understand it," whereas Clauss believes that the fundamental opposition in the story is between physical strength, represented by Heracles, on the one hand, and diplomatic skills and beauty, represented by Jason, on the other, with a favourable outcome for the latter.[23]

To be sure, the *Argonautica* is very different from the homeric epic narratives in its portrayal of the world and the characters. The change of ambience, involving a more humanized and sentimental approach to story-telling, makes

---

22 Knight (1995:32) offers a detailed account of the similarities between this section of the *Odyssey* and the corresponding episodes in the work of Apollonius.
23 Clauss (1992) dedicates the main body of his study *The Best of the Argonauts* to explain Applonius's new concept of the epic hero, highlighting his rhetorical skills and preference for amorous affairs instead of the perennial search for glory on the battlefield, which was the trademark of the previous epic heroes.

the characters more individualized: each hero now has his or her particular qualities and peculiarities, and they lack the ostensibly public character that marked the homeric heroes. This brings them closer to later literary traditions that enhance personal qualities compared to the epic prototypes. Perhaps as a result of the need to integrate this novelty within the framework of the tradition established by Homer, Apollonius tries to find a balance between particular and combined, or common, action.

The solution is to design the group of heroes as an organic unit, so that the audience conceives of each one as an important part of a well-defined and ideal community in which the different parts work together in relative harmony, creating a model based on combined efforts. In Apollonius's work, the hero acquires his true strength and significance not as an individual on his own, but as a part of a larger unit.[25]

As a consequence, it is difficult to find an absolute protagonist among the Argonauts, and even if Jason stands out above the rest, being the leader of the expedition and the object of Medea's love, he is, compared to the homeric heroes, much less authoritative and even insecure in his role as leader. Apart from this, when Medea enters the scene, the reader will find it even more difficult to define who the true protagonist of the story really is, partly because Appolonius grants her a very strong voice, but also because she is exposed to a moral dilemma that confronts her love for Jason with the loyalty to her father and her family, which is perhaps even more dramatic than the adventure of the Golden Fleece.

We might say that some aspects of Medea's character come close to the Ulysses-paradigm, but in a female version, since she combines the roles of virgin and witch, and assimilates characteristics of different female heroines of other

---

25 Knight (1995:11) stresses the idea of community as central to the conception of the *Argonautica* and claims that "[t]he Argonauts became the community against which all others are compared," while Clauss (1992:62) argues that "[t]he adventure is not about a man, but of men," adding that the importance of harmony was also present in the character of Ulysses (Clauss 1992:87). The perspective is thus inverted: while Ulysses is an individual who embodies all the virtues of his age, in the *Argonautica* individual virtues are considered secondary to that of the community – the heroes become complete only when accompanied by the others.

legends, tragedies, and epic works.[26] On the other hand, it is mainly Medea that Appolonius uses for his experiments with the introduction of a greater psychological realism in the epic framework.

Jason – albeit to a lesser extent – is also described with the ambition to create a psychologically credible character.[27] Contrary to the previous, homeric hero-prototype, who never doubts the correct course of action and embodies the ideals of his community with undisputable authority, Jason is frequently at a loss to decide what is best for the expedition, and his leadership is questioned from the very beginning. Also, his worries are more centered on how to manage Medea's passion than on figuring out the most adequate method for achieving immortal fame and glory. Love is inevitably an internal process, and as such, it requires a more complex narrative treatment, from the point of view of psychological credibility, than the purely heroic issues, which must always and necessarily be external and visible.

The story of the Argonauts gives us a more civilized picture of the Heroic Age, which corresponds to the changing literary taste and the wider horizons of the Alexandrine society it was originally written for. The characters of Jason and Medea are clear examples of a literary adaptation that modernizes a previous tradition, but they are not the only modification proposed by Apollonius. In the *Argonautica*, the presentation of the heroic world also changes.

While the fantastic episodes in the *Odyssey* are limited to books IX-XII, in the *Argonautica* the protagonists travel in a more or less enchanted world during almost the entire narrative. In this 'pseudoreality' Jason fights monsters and navigates the rivers Po, Danube and Rhine that, as if by magic, have become confluent; he visits places inhabited by supernatural and sometimes invented creatures (Knight 1995:31), and he receives a great deal of help from magical sources to carry out his quest.

---

26 Beye (1993:203) mentions Ariadne, Penelope, Circe in Homer's rendering and Aeschylos's Clytemnestra as models for Medea. Knight (1995:36) claims that the parallelism between Medea and Nausicaa (of chapter XIII in the *Odyssey*) is an example of creative allusion (in Knight's definition, creative allusions are characterized by being purely literary, and by showing no intention to parody or plagiate the original sources).
27 Hainsworth (1991:73) claims that Jason is the first novelistic hero for this reason.

The main difference compared to the corresponding adventures of Ulysses, is that the world evoked in the *Argonautica*, while decidedly enchanted, is much more detailed and coherent.[28] Hence, in spite of the abundance of supernatural elements, Appolonius invests his particular vision of the enchanted world with more realism.

The gods also interfere in the action. Compared to their role in the homeric works they have, in the *Argonautica*, an even more decisive impact on the action. For instance, it is actually the gods who establish, through their debates, discourses and actions, that the narrative should concentrate on the love story of Jason and Medea (Brioso Sánchez 1986:22). In this way, the divine intervention is centered on the desire to create entertainment out of an amorous passion, something which gives us an idea of the generally trivializing treatment Appolonius applies to the epic tradition in order to satisfy the taste of his times.

As for the encyclopaedic function of the epic, it would seem as if Apollonius were more bent on recreating and modernizing certain formulae of preceding literary expressions, than in recording the extraliterary past – the cultural legacy – of a community. As opposed to the unbiased encyclopaedic information given in the homeric catalogues, the different aspects of the lost world are now mainly used to adorn the narrative with elegant allusions.[29]

In my opinion, the *Argonautica* constitutes an important variation of the epic narrative that consolidates the romance potential previously glimpsed in the episode of similar characteristics found in the *Odyssey*. Generally speaking, the presence of romance paradigms in the *Argonautica* is more evident than in the *Odyssey*, and they are mainly seen in the romance ambience that now permeates the whole narrative, exhibiting a clear taste for the bucolic and exotic. This strain towards the pastoral is also evident in the minor epic poems of the Trojan War Cycle (the *Kypria*, the *Aithiopis*, the *Little Iliad*, the *Iliou persis*, the *Nostoi* and the *Telegony*), but I think that it is in the works of Appolonius

---

28 In Beye's (1993:194) opinion, the world evoked in the *Argonautica* is contemporaneous, though "so bizarre that it could be labelled fabulous."
29 Clauss (1992:7) claims that the prose of Apollonius deliberately directs the reader's attention towards the homeric texts in order to establish contrasts between both, while Knight (1995:18-19) concludes that compared to Homer's works, Appolonius's similes are more closely related to the main action and they do not include as many redundant details.

where the romance treatment of the epic finds its most suggestive and complete expression in this age.

Some critics believe that Appolonius takes the epic tradition so far towards romance that it is doubtful whether it should be labelled epic at all. Beye (1993: 198), for instance, says that with the *Argonautica*, "[r]omance begins to take shape as an overtly fictional prose narrative," while Greene (1963:73) dismisses its action as a "parody of heroic poetry". Hainsworth (1991:44) offers a more reconciliatory approach, though still rather negative, suggesting that Apollonius "blunted with fantasy and romance the keen edge of the heroic ideal." At the same time, he concedes that "it embodies the spirit of the Hellenistic Age too deeply not to have some echoes of the public voice of the epic." (Hainsworth 1991:73)

However far Apollonius moved from Homer's conception of the epic, the tradition did not die with the *Argonautica*. In the first century B.C.E., a Roman poet decided that it was time to recover the original epic stance and all it implied, lending his voice to the cause of a patriotic reformatory project. His name was Publius Vergilius.

The *Aeneid*

With the *Aeneid*, Virgil, as he is commonly called in English, redirects the evolution of the epic tradition back towards the grandiloquent discourse of the homeric tales. As we have seen, wars provide a suitable backdrop for epic poetry because of their heterogeneous social and cultural context and political transcendence, and in the *Aeneid*, Virgil makes full use of the theme. As in the *Iliad*, the narrative exploits the sceneries and action of big-scale warfare to a great extent, and like the *Odyssey*, the siege of Troy is used as the starting point for a fantastic Mediterranean voyage.

It was even an armed conflict that motivated the composition of the *Aeneid*. In the year 32 B.C.E. there was a civil war in Rome, in which Octavius (later named Augustus by the senate) triumphed over Marcus Antonius. In the face of the growing moral decadence that the new emperor perceived in the Roman society, he considered that one of his most important duties should be that of recovering the traditional Roman ideals, especially patriotism, reverence for the gods and love of the family. Augustus realized that poetry, which was in vogue among the Roman elite, could be an efficient vehicle to achieve his aims, so he asked Virgil, by then an already well-known and prestigious poet, to write a work that established the mythic origins of the Roman Empire in general, and of the emperor in particular, while paying special attention to the conveyance of the mentioned ideals.

The task must have seemed gratifying to Virgil, who was presented with a magnificent opportunity to inaugurate a Latin epic tradition in a society that had appropriated Greek literature, philosophy and mythology, and that was hungry for a proper cultural identity.[30] He responded to the challenge by composing a long, epic poem about the Trojan hero Aeneas and his struggle to establish the foundations for the Roman Empire.

The story begins after the fall of Troy. Aeneas, who had already in the *Iliad* been presented as one of the most important Trojan heroes after Hector, has abandoned the ruins of the fallen city and journeys with his men on the Mediterranean Sea without bearings. His mother, Venus, finally becomes aware of Aeneas's precarious situation and directs him towards Carthage, governed by the beautiful queen Dido. The queen falls in love with the hero who, pushed by destiny to continue his quest to seek out a new land for his people, renounces her love, and the queen commits suicide as Aeneas embarks on an adventurous voyage to seek guidance from the Sibyl of Cumae. The Sibyl sends him to the Subterranean World, where Aeneas's dead father explains the details of his destiny, urging him on to Italy, a land plagued by war and misfortunes, where King Latinus and a warlord named Turnus play the leading roles. Aeneas settles in Latium, on the spot which will later become Rome. He receives magic arms, wrought by Vulcan, and he recruits a great army in order to overthrow Turnus. A bloody war ensues, full of major and minor incidents described in great detail, that takes up the last four of the narrative's twelve books and culminates in the final scene in which Aeneas, infuriated by the murder of king Evander's son Pallas, kills his rival.

---

30 In Beye's (1993:224) view, "the inspiration for the *Aeneid* was the notion that the Roman Empire was destined to make the Greek ideals real."

The first part of the poem, that deals with Aeneas's complicated voyage to Italy, strongly recalls the *Odyssey* with its many adventures, strange meetings, sufferings and fantastic elements, while the second part, dominated by the war, is thematically closer to the *Iliad*. However, Virgil's focus is always on the foundation of Rome, which means that all levels of the narrative are intimately related to this central thread. In this, it is similar to the narrative stance of the *Argonautica*, where the main action and the digressions are much more closely related than in the homeric epics.

One of the novelties in Virgil's version of the epic is a variation of the duel between two heroes.[31] In previous epic narratives, this struggle was intimately associated to self-assertion and revenge, the idea of winning glory or achieving possessions, as in the battle between Achilles and Hector. While the duel between Aeneas and Turnus in the *Aeneid* may symbolize the continuity or dissolution of political and social systems – one of the central themes in the homeric epics – there is a big difference compared to the latter works, related to the implied magnitude of the struggle. In the *Aeneid*, the gods are so profoundly involved in the course of action that the fate of the whole world seems to be at stake, and the war between the two heroes is turned into a duel between constitutive and destructive forces operating on a global scale, light versus darkness.[32]

Aeneas, on the other hand, is an epic hero of the homeric school in the sense that he can be seen as a representative of his community who embodies multiple virtues and, as such, he is under no obligation to act in accordance with rules of psychological plausibility. However, Aeneas is different from Homer's models in that his actions are motivated not only by his wish to restore glory to the Trojan people, but also by more humane feelings, such as compassion. From this point of view he is similar to Jason, and in the end,

---

31 The idea of the double hero was insinuated in Homer – mainly reflected in the characters of Achilles and Héctor – and Virgil explores and exploits the idea, and in the end it seems almost as if Aeneas were fighting against himself (Hardie 1993:22). This idea would later be appealing to Renaissance poets and artists as inspiration for their own half-pagan, half-Christian interpretations of the Classical age, the underlying idea being that the *Aeneid*, in spite of its pagan context, can be read as an allegory of the struggle between Satan and God.
32 See Hardie (1993:57-58).

it is precisely the empathy of these heroes that brings them victory,[33] though the price they pay for it is a diminished heroic stature. As Hainsworth (1991: 103) points out: "civilized heroes such as Jason or Aeneas seem negative and colourless," adding: "But what is civilized behavior if not restraint on self assertion?"

The greatness of purpose in the *Aeneid* depends more on the implications of the battle between Aeneas and Turnus than on a successful portrayal of the characteristics of the heroes themselves, and this is paralleled by the description of the world. In my opinion, if there is anything in Virgil's art that stands out above all else, it is his capacity to display grandiose perspectives and ample scenery, selecting and incorporating the details so as to reinforce the power of the whole.[34]

The role of the gods also becomes less frivolous[35] than in previous epic narratives. The interventions of the divinities are no longer sporadic or limited to a single hero's fortune or disgrace, or to the unravelling of a game of love – rather they establish the guidelines for a battle of universal importance and control the action from the beginning to the end, as the main instigators of the conflict between Aeneas and Turnus.

While for Homer the presentation of the heroic world was mainly used to save persons, events and traditions from oblivion, Virgil portrays the past with a much more specific purpose, combining historical fact with mythology to establish the divine origins of Augustus and to highlight the manifest destiny of the Roman Empire. At the same time, he incorporates a great number of references to characters, themes and devices of the previous epic tradition. As a consequence thereof, the depth of the heroic world, as evoked in the *Aeneid*, relies to some extent on the reader's erudition and a general awareness of former

---

33 Greene (1963:89) correctly claims that "Aeneas survives because he gives up pride, willfulness and energy. Dido and Turnus don't give up these things and die for it." In Cuatrecasas's (1998: 25) opinion, the most conspicuous trait of Aeneas is his piety, a quality which in Virgil's time was considered the mother of all virtues.
34 From my point of view, the scene that best shows Virgil's skills of portraying ample sceneries is the one in which Aeneas contemplates an artistic representation – we are not informed of what kind – of the siege of Troy, at a temple in the forest of Dido.
35 At the same time, they are not wholly deprived of a certain degree of fancy. For example, what makes the goddess Juno conspire against Aeneas is the resentment she holds against him for not having considered her the most beautiful when he was given the choice.

expressions of this tradition. However, these references are not as self-conscious as in the case of Appolonius, and the result, as Beye (1993:232-234) correctly concludes, is that "[t]he allusions suggest rather than insist: the reader is free to fill in the tone or depth of each scene as he or she wishes".

This subtle approach to a literary encyclopaedic treatment within the framework of the epic tradition is interesting, because the style will not only inspire allegorical readings and a subsequent modernization of the genre among the Renaissance poets, it will also provide the foundations for the treatment of certain encyclopaedic aspects in the nineteenth-century fantastic novel.[36]

Beowulf

The anonymously written epic[37] poem *Beowulf* was composed in the 8th century, probably in the region of Northumbria or Mercia, in the northeast of what we today know as England. Like the homeric works, *Beowulf* was created for public recitals, and the written composition retains many features of the oral style (Alexander 1973:9-12).

The story as such is about Beowulf, a young hero from Gautland (more specifically, in the south of present-day Sweden) travelling to King Hrothgar's court in Denmark to kill Grendel, a monster that has been attacking the King's hall Heoroth for some time. After dealing with Grendel, Beowulf follows the monster's footprints to a lake, at the bottom of which he kills the monster's mother in its underwater den. The second part of the story takes place in Gautland. Beowulf, having now ruled the country for fifty years, seeks out a dragon that threatens his people. Both die as a consequence of the battle, and the poem ends with a prophecy that speaks of the end of the *gautar*.

The defence of a royal court is a frequent and even central theme in early germanic poetry, such as the legend of the battle of Finnsburg, the *Hrolf Kraki Saga* or the

---

36 See section 2.3 of the present chapter.
37 Not all scholars agree on this definition. Tolkien (1997:31), in his essay '*Beowulf*: The Monsters and the Critics', prefers the term "heroic-elegiac poem," alluding to the theme rather than to its formal characteristics. On the other hand, Alexander (1973:19-35), presents several arguments for labelling it epic. Personally I consider it to be an epic narrative without doubt, at least if we consider the general characteristics of epic poetry, as outlined in the first part of the present chapter, valid.

Nibelungenlied. However, in *Beowulf*, an epic poem, the action is extended by means of digressions and similes, so that the work ends up discussing questions of more universal significance than the mere details of a battle.

Again, we find ourselves immersed in a narrative with a solemn seriousness of purpose, that explores the theme of mortality[38] and how the passing of time destroys men and entire civilizations alike. The radically split structure of the poem – the juxtaposition of the hero's vigorous youth of the first part, with the old age of the second – powerfully emphasizes the theme. The main difference between *Beowulf* and the previous epic works lies in the blend of pagan and Christian elements and stances, which confers a very particular quality to the main hero. We have already seen how the *Aeneid* leaves room for Christian interpretations in spite of the strong presence of pagan culture and religion. In *Beowulf*, this vagueness is also present, but the perspective is inverted: while the narrator insists on the hero's Christian traits, the words do not really convince us, because Christian dogma lies only on the surface and does not really affect the actions or the heroic stance of the protagonists.[39]

Tolkien (1997:20) makes a nuanced analysis of this duality, concluding that the poem does not exhibit a confusion between pagan and Christian elements, but rather "a fusion that has occurred *at a given point* of contact between old and new." He also believes that the monsters' central position in the narrative is the key to our understanding of it, asserting that their prominent role in *Beowulf* is due to the influence of Norse mythology, in which the gods, apart from being titans, are mortal and exposed to constant danger (in fact, most of them will die in Ragnarök).[40] The fusion expressed by the poem would then be a result of the protagonism of the pagan monsters, whose threatening presence undermines the heroes' faith in a Christian God.

---

38 In Alexander's (1973:30) view, "the main subject is the human challenge to death and the glorious and tragic potentialities of that challenge." This is one of the most prominent themes of the Classical epic poetry, as we have seen.
39 Schlauch (1967:43) claims that the Christian moral shines through, however feebly, in the warnings about excessive pride and vengefulness, while Alexander (1973:14) considers that Beowulf's main motivation is "[t]he desire for 'a name that shall never die beneath the heavens'" – a violent contrast to the Christian conception of humility as a condition for posthumous access to the heavenly kingdom.
40 For a clear and detailed study of the Norse gods, see Davidson (1964).

Apart from this, the poem features most of the characteristics that we have outlined as proper to the epic narrative tradition. In the first place, the action takes place in a remote past – in this case, in the 5th and 6th centuries C.E. – that blends historical events with legends and myth.[41] The poem also exposes, celebrates and explores the implications of the feats of a central hero with supernatural powers; furthermore, the hero is a man who represents his community favourably. The presentation of the heroic world is expanded with digressions and similes (the most important of which deal with the fight at the Finnsburg, and the wars between Gautland and Sweden). The traditions and customs of the aristocratic society are transmitted almost encyclopaedically to the reader,[42] and the main themes of the poem are of universal importance, such as the cyclical reality of life (the beginning and end of people, cultures and epochs) or Man's relationship with his destiny and his community. Last but not least, the style is marked by an elevated language and a solemn tone, and the length of the narrative corpus is considerable.

While the text does not allude explicitly to previous epic works, Tolkien (1997: 23) affirms that the poet was a man "learned in old tales who was struggling, as it were, to get a general view of them all," which would indicate a purpose not far from the consciously effected encyclopaedic compilation of literary traditions of the past which is present in both the *Argonautica* and in the *Aeneid*, as we have seen.

As for the possible influences from the Classic epic tradition, Virgil seems to have been at least in the back of the mind of the *Beowulf* poet. Alexander (1973:39) highlights the pious character of the protagonist, saying that Beowulf embodies "the modification of ideal hero from adventurer (Sigemund) to a relatively pious man," and that he is "a more God-fearing, responsible and civilized hero," while Schlauch (1967:44) takes the argument further, claiming that the poem bears the mark of the Latin epic tradition in the conventions of language, alluding to certain linguistic features that can only be explained

---

41 While some characters and episodes are purely fictional, like Beowulf himself, some of its actions are supposedly historical. For example, the death of King Hygelac during a raid by the Franks in the year 521 is described in Gregory of Tour's *Historia Francorum*.
42 Alexander (1973:24) believes that the presentation of traditions in the narrative "[is] crystallized into generic scenes: voyage, welcome, feast, boast, arming, fight, reward."

by the presence of Latinisms, which in turn would be the result of a possible translation. She also mentions the parallels between the report of the Trojan War that Aeneas offers Dido, on the one hand, and Beowulf's account of his deeds in Denmark presented to Hygelac on the other, adding that the latter is not vital for the reader's understanding of those events (which have already been mentioned in the text), whereby the reiteration would seem to be a result of a conscious imitation, if not a feature common to 'oral' poetry.

These arguments based on analogues may of course be interesting, but I do not deem them particularly relevant to a deeper understanding of the narrative. Tolkien (1997:24) considers that "the smaller points in which imitation or reminiscence [of the *Aeneid* in *Beowulf*] might be perceived are inconclusive, while the real likeness is deeper and due to certain qualities in the authors independent of the question whether the Anglo-Saxon had read Virgil or not." What is important for our purpose, as Tolkien seems to point out, is not to outline the influence of particular aspects of previous works, but rather to contextualize the general narrative plan. Both authors have written epic works, so they inevitably share many narrative strategies and devices. Among them is the meta-literary discourse, which may inspire speculation about the sources employed by the poet, but a comparative analysis based on such particular phenomena as events or names will not reveal the 'deeper likeness' that Tolkien speaks of.

For now, it is enough to say that *Beowulf*'s great contribution to the epic narrative tradition is the combination of pagan elements, with an ethos taken from Norse mythology, and a general Christian worldview, superficially implanted on a portrait of a world under constant threat, in which no great hope of heavenly salvation is offered. This curious and dramatic blend will have a profound impact on Tolkien's imagination, 1200 years later.

2.2. Romance

As we move on to the Middle Ages, literature begins to acquire a different hue, though not completely foreign to the epic tradition. Romance, in its literary sense, is a somewhat elusive, very much impermeable genre and not an easy one to define with just a few words. The general idea that appears in most definitions is that romance refers to romantic novels or stories of chivalry, love, adventure or mystery. It can also be a medieval literary form or a poetic composition written in a Romance language; that is, a language derived from Latin.[43]

However, none of these definitions, or even a combination of them all, seems to me very satisfying. We have already seen how some scholars referred to certain passages in the works of Homer and Appolonius using the English concept of 'romance', as a result of their amorous and fantastic themes and elements. The definition of literary romance that we will be using from now on refers to the narratives about chivalry, love, adventure and mystery that were first written towards the end of the 12th century in France, but then transformed over the years, adopting different literary forms, until they emerged as the gothic novel of the eighteenth and nineteenth centuries, the fantastic novel of the nineteenth century, and the fantasy novel of the twentieth century. In this context, a narrative of the romance-type may be of the sentimental kind, but it can also be fantastic, pseudomedieval or utopian, or a combination of all these aspects.

In the end, more than by the mere presence of a number of formal characteristics, a literary work may feature romance traits by exhibiting a particular fluctuating attitude towards reality, a special ambience or spirit which, in one way or another, expresses the previously mentioned themes and traits. In this way, the term may be applied to Homer, Appolonius, Chrétien de Troyes, Malory, Ariosto, Horace Walpole, Hawthorne, William Morris and Tolkien, as we shall see.

2.2.1. Romance from the Middle Ages to the 19th century

Medieval romance

In France, the rediscovery of the works of Classical Antiquity during the 12th century inspired poets to compose a series of *romans* based on themes from the great epic narratives of the Classical period, as well as from famous biographies and mythological tales. *Roman de Troye*, written by Benoît de Sainte-Maure,

---

43 The *Encyclopaedia Britannica* defines romance as a medieval story about chivalric adventure including themes of love and religious allegory.

was the first of the works that offered 'medievalized' renderings of the legends of Antiquity. The versatility of the new genre was manifest from the very beginning, and the classical themes were soon complemented with stories taken from the corpus of Arthurian legends, recorded in writing first by Geoffrey of Monmouth in the first half of the twelfth century. Chrétien de Troyes, a French poet of the second half of the twelfth century, was among the first to invest the stories and episodes referring to the adventures of the knights of the Round Table with a romance flavour, while Chaucer perpetuated the medieval vision of the classical legends in *Troilus and Criseyde* two centuries later.

Several factors may explain the change in narrative standards that took place with the introduction of romance tales. On the one hand, the new medieval vision of the individual in search of self-perfection was already established among the aristocracy, whereby the literary themes were brought closer to the personal and subjective level.[44] On the other hand, in an age totally dominated by the Christian credo, there was a need to express ideals more in line with contemporary views, stories that proposed alternatives to the biblical tales and the purely religious values (Stevens 1973:227).

Hence, while romance literature shouldered the old epic purpose of providing the audience with ideal models and idealizations of the aristocracy, the focus changed due to the growing interest in the individual and the personal quest. Furthermore, it is the *essence* of the experience that is important, not the political consequences. The experiences of the romance heroes are obviously intimately related to the particular concerns of each age, as indicated by the genre's variation in thematic and formal emphasis over the centuries. This is a consequence of the extraordinary flexibility – or even a certain 'parasitical' quality – inherent in romance narratives, which enables them to adapt their standards and infiltrate different literary forms, such as the epic and the novel. As was the case with the epic narratives, the contemporary themes are often expressed through stories that date back to a remote past, and with clearly fantastic tinges.

In romance literature, we are often faced with a pseudo-reality, consciously designed to convey the most interesting themes of the moment. Jewers (2000:4),

---

[44] According to Vinaver (1984:2), "the change [from heroic legend to romance] was due to a shift from communal exercise to a view of life as […] the spiritual growth of the individual."

discussing medieval romance, describes this reality as a symbolic backdrop that eludes verisimilitude. This, of course, makes it very susceptible to allegorical interpretations. Beer (1977:9) feels that the reality expressed by medieval romance narratives is "multiple and interwoven," containing "mythic levels of suggestion." The term *suggestion* is important for the treatment of mythical themes in romance literature. The gods, now turned into the Christian God, frequently intervene by means of mysterious manifestations in nature, or by other signs that only the knight-errant is able to perceive due to his special sensitivity and spiritual insight. Hence, the exhibitionist character of the divinities in the Classical epic works is substantially moderated. There is also a combination of pagan and Christian motifs – as in, for example, *Sir Gawain and the Green Knight* – that, because of its subtle expression, enhances the secularity of the tales without offending the dominant Christian dogma.

The literary world of medieval romance is so saturated with marvels[45] and mysteries that the physical space becomes eroded, and the landscape in which the knights move is often indistinct, without clear perspectives or measurable distances. To complete the vagueness of the descriptions, the events often occur gratuitously and a great number of prosaic, quotidian details mingle with symbolic elements without any clear sense of balance.[46] In such an unstable and fluctuating setting it is naturally difficult to express themes that require coherence and amplitude. The world of medieval romance lends itself more readily to subjective and internal questions that do not require a palpable reality but can be favourably explored in settings of this elusive and symbolic kind.

Courtly love and its consequences, the most recurrent theme in medieval romance, has left a deep mark on the evolution of the Western narrative tradition, and its influence has not ceased operating on present day literature, judging by the enormous amount of bestsellers that still exploit it with considerable commercial success. But medieval romance was not only about love. Jewers (2000:4) mentions

---

45 Stevens (1973:4) classifies the fantastic elements of medieval romance in four categories: the exotic or remote; the mysterious and inexplicable; the strictly magic (the fantastic controlled by man), and the miraculous (the fantastic controlled by God).
46 While Vinaver's (1984:5) view, that "romance dispenses with temporal and rational links and transitions," is perhaps too categorical, it is true that medieval romance literature is marked by a dreamlike conception of reality.

the Bildungsroman; the hero tormented by existential doubt; the sentimental education; the quest, and a special sense of adventure, as other prominent thematic features of the genre.

The adventure is the knight-errant's favourite activity, and also what formally puts him in touch with the exterior world. At the same time it provides him with a thread – however loose, fragmented or incoherently related to other adventures – for the treatment of the amorous and educational themes. As opposed to the central action of the epic narratives, the hero of medieval romance is constantly involved in adventures of different kinds, that seem to arise out of nowhere as soon as he leaves his castle, when returning from a previous one or while engaged in another. The essence of medieval romance is a melting pot of different adventures that follow each other in a breathless chase. The reasons to engage in one, apart from defending the honour of a lady, are diverse. García Gual (1974:49-50) says that

> the essence of the knight consists in manifesting, through his actions, a lifestyle, with its peculiar spiritual virtues (fighting ardour and skill, a taste for heroic deeds and adventures, generosity and courtesy for the ladies, protection of the weak). On the other hand, the most important thing is the family, the lineage and the blood.[47]

We can also mention the isolation of the hero, whose adventures are not public in the epic sense, and the fact that he is not perfect – in spite of being an idealized character who embodies many virtues – but *searching* for perfection, which is also something that will place him outside the orbit of the epic hero's characterization.

Chrétien de Troyes, one of the first and perhaps the most interesting of the poets composing medieval romances, made extensive use of the image as a rhetorical figure which enabled him to organize and make sense of the hero's adventures. In one of the most famous scenes of *Perceval, the Story of the Grail* – the last work written by Chrétien – Perceval witnesses how a goose is attacked by a falcon and leaves three drops of blood in the snow. The knight, when contemplating the blood, is reminded of the face of his lady and spends the rest of the morning absorbed in reflection on this matter, until he is interrupted

---

47 My translation.

by another knight who wants him to engage in a joust. Alvar, commenting on the scene, claims that

> The passing from reality to remembrance, the motif of white and red as ideals of beauty, and the ephemeral quality of the vision, as the snow will soon melt, make the image an example of Chrétien's art. The theme [...] constitutes the last stage in Perceval's education, related to his moral perfection.[48]

The scene clearly shows how Chrétien concentrates on certain aspects of the hero's experience at the expense of others (as, for example, the cold he must feel while standing motionless in the snow for hours). At the core of the image-making is not external action or external agents as such, but the effects they have on the subject. The image is used as a poetic tool that confers a particular meaning to the experience.[49]

In the same way, the space surrounding the knight could not exist without the knight crossing it. The whole world seems to emerge from and take shape around the knight, and not the other way around. Stevens (1973:149), alluding to the scene with the blood in the snow mentioned above, believes that the objects, creatures and places, often with names directly related to the knight's spiritual adventure, are invested with meaning through the experience: "It snows only for there to be a background to the three drops of blood." This is, naturally, a consequence of the narrative's generally symbolic character.

As opposed to epic poetry, medieval romance tends to develop many themes and adventures simultaneously, instead of placing them in subordinate digressions, deviating from the central action. The effect is that the reader does not perceive one single reality expressed in the text, but many, and not only this, but these realities also intermingle. This contributes to the unstable and incoherent vision of the world[50] and adds power to the enlightening visual image.

In the tradition of medieval romance, apart from Chrétien de Troyes, whose works include *Erec and Enide, Yvain, the Knight of the Lion*, and *Lancelot, the*

---

48 *El Cuento del Grial* (edited and translated by Carlos Alvar 1999:149, note 138). My translation.
49 Stevens (1973:147), discussing the imagery of medieval romance, claims that "central to the experience conveyed by the text is not an idea, an attitude, a feeling or responses of a character, but an emphatically realized visual object pointing beyond itself, there to crystallize the meaning of the scene."
50 In Vinaver's (1984:76) view, the authors of the Arthurian cycle, (among others Chrétien) "wanted to create a feeling that there is no single beginning or end [...] until the reader loses every sense of limitation in time or space."

Knight of the Cart, all devoted to Arthurian themes, we may also mention Robert de Boron[51] and Wolfram von Eschenbach, whose work *Parzival* will later be of much interest among the German romantics. *Sir Gawain and the Green Knight* is another famous poem in the same tradition, written by an anonymous English poet at the end of the fourteenth century. As the title suggests, it tells of Gawain's adventure with a mysterious green knight, and it displays many of the features of romance literature that we have discussed in this chapter.

Medieval romance is the first unabashed manifestation of the romantic spirit that began taking hold of the poetic imagination in the Middle Ages. However, in the centuries to come, we find many other literary expressions of the genre. Beer (1977:4) highlights three fundamental types: medieval, Elizabethan of the sixteenth-century, and the romance novels of the nineteenth century. We will now take a look at the way in which the vestiges of epic poetry, in the shape of *chanson de geste* narratives, began converging with romance, mainly in the works of English and Italian poets who created hybrid works.

Romance and Epic blended:
chanson de geste – narratives and Renaissance epics

As we have seen, the combinations between romance and epic can be very varied. Beginning with the *Odyssey*, the two traditions tend to go hand in hand to a greater or lesser extent, which not only indicates that one does not necessarily exclude the other, but also that they can even come to depend upon each other up to a certain point. A peculiar medieval descendant of the classical epic is the *chanson de geste*, that began taking shape in France at the end of the 11th century. The three most well known representatives of the genre are the French *Chanson de Roland* (1080-1090), the Spanish *Cantar del Mío Cid* (around 1140) and the German *Nibelungenlied* (around 1200).

The *chanson de geste* is, essentially, a long poem that celebrates the exploits of a hero. It shares many features with the classical epic, such as the traits of the

---

51 One of de Boron's most important contributions to the treatment of the Arthurian theme is that he turns the Grail, which in Chrétien's version was a magical golden dish, into the vessel used by Joseph of Arimathea to gather Jesus's last drops of blood.

protagonist, who is a grandiose, larger-than-life hero, sometimes with supernatural powers and objects at his disposal, who acts like a representative of his community and whose feats are of utmost importance for that community. Moreover, the action normally takes place in a more or less remote past (with the exception of the *Cantar del Mío Cid*), the society presented in the narrative is aristocratic and the diction elevated.

However, the *chanson de geste* lacks the epic amplitude in almost all senses. The digressions, when existing, are brief, and they do not contribute very much to create temporal or spatial depth in the world evoked. The themes are usually related to the central heroic action, such as the social code of the warrior, the implications of honour and the importance of making one's name immortal through impressive deeds. In other words, we might say that the *chanson de geste* is a simplified epic,[52] though there are exceptions: the *Nibelungenlied* is not far from the previous epic tradition as regards themes, characterization of the heroes and presentation of the past.

The *chanson de geste* was contemporary to medieval romance, but in spite of this, at a first glance the differences seem enormous. García Gual (1974:55-65) contrasts the public character of the former with the spiritual adventure of the latter, claiming that while the *chanson de geste* focused on historical events and was expressed in a rigid style, medieval romance centered on contemporary concerns and presented a greater narrative fluency.[53] To this we may add the presentation of reality – sharp, coherent and concrete in the *chanson de geste*, diffuse and mysterious in the romance – and the austerity of the epic hero as compared to the almost sportif stance of the romance knight, who is always looking for new adventures, battles and jousts, and constantly surrounded by marvellous elements.

Of the two, romance achieved greater acceptance among the medieval audience, while the *chanson de geste*, little by little, became relegated to the periphery. However, the epic strain in literary composition was not entirely forgotten. At

---

52 See Auerbach (1979:110).
53 Beer (1977:24) considers that while the *chanson de geste* concentrates on bellicose motifs and deals almost entirely with males, in romance greater importance is given to contemplation, amorous themes and women.

the beginning of the fourteenth century, Dante composed the *Divine Comedy* (1307-1320), which in its scope comes close to epic amplitude (though it also presents important differences),[54] and the French works about Raoul de Cambrai, Garin le Loherain and Guillaume d'Orange perpetuated, in their own way, the *chanson de geste* – tradition.

One of the first writers to develop a formula for the union of romance and epic standards was Sir Thomas Malory. With *Le Mort D'Arthur* (1485), he created the greatest compilation of the Arthurian legendarium up to date. In order to combine both traditions, Malory engaged in the difficult task of investing the romance elements with a greater coherence, while preserving its underlying essence. The different stories were now put on a subordinate level compared to the axis, which rested on the figure of King Arthur.

Lawlor (1969:xiii-xvi), summarizing Malory's treatment of the Arthurian cycle, highlights the author's determination to reduce the number of marvellous events and to decrease the importance of the amorous themes while at the same time emphasising the idea of an inevitable destiny. Furthermore, he introduced a greater blend of genres, retaining the respective styles of the different sources, and separated the different stories – happily mixed and intertwined without apparent connection in previous literary renderings of the legends – from each other. All these measures contributed to bringing the romance legendarium closer to epic standards.[55]

In Italy, at the same time, another poet was involved in a similar literary project. Boiardo, whose work *Orlando Innamorato*, composed between 1476 and 1492, established the main features of a genre known as romance epic, later consolidated by Ariosto (*Orlando Furioso*, 1516-1532) and Tasso (*Gerusalemme Liberata*, 1579). These three narratives were much longer than the typical medieval romances, but they exhibit the same chaos of interlaced adventures, as well as

---

54 Frye (1971:57) mentions the *Divina Commedia* as the work of this age that comes closest to the epic's encyclopaedic incorporation of traditional knowledge. Greene (1963:17), for his part, maintains that "Commedia Divina is not an epic in the sense that the protagonist only acquires power over himself, not over the world," alluding to the fact that all power in this narrative belongs to God.

55 It is also interesting to notice that Malory shares the project of synthezising a corpus of literary expressions of a previous tradition with Appolonius and Virgil, though the latter winked, more or less explicitly, at the works of a whole era, while Malory focussed on the works on the Arthurian legend only.

a great abundance of marvellous elements. The tone is often parodic, and this tends to trivialize the hero and his project, and to lessen the seriousness of his religious devotion (Greene 1963:138-140).

In spite of this, there are other aspects of these works that separate them from medieval romance narratives. The adventures take place in a more or less historical setting, the narrative is sometimes interrupted by elaborate catalogues describing the participants in battles, and so forth. Furthermore, the marvellous elements are almost always placed in a reality which is much more palpable than the dreamlike setting of romance.[56] In this way, though at a first glance epic romance may seem nothing more than an extended romance narrative, these works reveal their epic inheritance in characteristics like spatial and temporal depth, encyclopaedically transmitted information of the past, and the blend of genres. As for the literary sources of inspiration, Hainsworth (1991:144) argues that "Renaissance neo-classical epic is doubly sentimental, recreating Virgil as Virgil had recreated Homer," while Greene (1963:136) offers the somewhat curious view that book VI of the *Aeneid* (the episode relating the meeting with the Sibyl of Cumae and the descent to the Subterranean World) was the model for the Renaissance epics.[57] The particular source, however, is less interesting for our purpose than the disclosure of a new meta-literary narrative strategy that combines epic and romance in a different way compared to Malory's method.

Of the three authors mentioned, Tasso is the one who takes the blend of the two traditions the furthest. In Ariosto's writings he had appreciated the particular treatment of the marvellous elements and, even if the classical epic models provided him with the seriousness he aimed at,[58] he believed that the

---

56 Lewis (1988:309) argues that the Italian epic – he refers mainly to Boiardo and Ariosto – presents three different levels of reality. In the foreground we find the knightly adventure, which takes place in a fantastic world, the next level is the quotidian world, which is there to enhance the credibility, and the backdrop is made up of what Lewis terms "venerable legend with a core of momentous historical truth."
57 In Segre's (2002:10) opinion, the influence of Virgil on Ariosto is most clearly shown in the imitation of episodes – Ruggiero seduced by Alcina in a sequence that recalls Aeneas's sojourn at Dido's court, for example – and in the fact that the story's *raison d'être* is the establishment of a famous lineage.
58 Tasso wrote in the context of the Counter-Reformation, a movement which encouraged the expression of Catholic creeds and ideas with a higher zeal and seriousness compared to the epoch in which Boiardo and Ariosto composed their works.

poet could only get through to his readers if he was able to amaze them with the inclusion of fantastic elements (Hainsworth 1991:143).

In the sixteenth century, epic narratives were considered to be related to concepts such as didacticism, verisimilitude, coherence and rigidity of style, while romance narratives were thought to be more bent on entertainment, fantasy and diversity, and expressed with a flexible style (Greene 1963:203). Tasso wanted his poem to be read as a mirror of Creation in miniature, whereby he needed a formula capable of combining the unity of the epic (a single creation) with the variety found in romance (the diversity within this creation). As Greene (1963:206) says,

> Tasso fused the single movement of antique epic with the diversity of romance. He [...] adapts the magic of romance to the celestial machinery of classical epic and adjusts both to Christianity [...] The solution was the 'maraviglioso verosímile'.

The poet justifies his formula with reference to the Christian doctrine, attributing the fantastic elements to divine intervention. However, Tasso did not always find it easy to blend the two traditions and they often remain separated, shaping clearly differentiated sets of epsiodes. Quint (1985:179), when attempting to show how the movement, within a single narrative, from a story of epic characteristics towards one of the romance type usually marks the beginning of a digression that breaks with the central action, refers to an episode taken from *Gerusalemme Liberata* in which Rinaldo, the main hero, lets himself be led astray from his historical (epic) mission by embarking on a romance adventure. As he does so, "time is broken down into unrelated moments isolated from one another and from any larger historical or narrative plan." When Rinaldo returns to the course of the main action, the epic presents him with a clear objective that organizes the events in a coherent narrative (Quint 1985:182).[59]

The English poet Spenser (*The Faerie Queene*, 1590-96) is one of the most important followers of the Italian tradition of romance-epics, but this does not prevent him from adding several new traits to his version of the genre. With

---

59 Something similar happens in the *Odyssey*, where the fantastic adventures in the enchanted archipelago are separated from the main action and correspond to a series of episodes that lead Ulysses astray from his true purpose.

reference to this, C.S. Lewis (1988:306) states that while Spenser follows the Italians formally and thematically, the action is slower and his imagination is less brilliant.[60]

On the other hand, Spenser applies Christian allegory, which was present in Boiardo, Ariosto and Tasso, to a greater extent than the Italians did, and for this reason he does not need to place the fantastic elements in a firm and tangible reality. As a consequence, the narrative world is again imbued with a distinct romance flavour, though the narrative retains certain epic features, such as the amplitude of purpose and action. It is difficult to distinguish a predominant tradition or tendency in Spenser's work. Is it an epic, a romance, or an epic romance? No one seems to be very sure about where to place *The Faerie Queene* on the generic map,[61] perhaps because its 'sceptical' attitude towards previous tradition makes it markedly different from the earlier hybrids, proposing, instead, a third route. While Malory modifies the romance towards epic stances (however inconsciously), and the writers of the Italian epic romances use the previous epic tradition as a starting point for the fusion, Spenser chooses a sort of spontaneous mélange, the general direction of which is less easy to define.

The generic blend, and the half-parodic element present in at least part of the Italian school's literary production, helps setting the scene for a new paradigm-shift in the evolution of the Western narrative tradition. Only a few years after Spenser's *Fairie Queene* was hailed as the masterpiece of English Renaissance literature, something entirely different emerged on the European literary scene, shaped like a knight-errant but flanked by a radically more prosaic figure. With *Don Quijote de la Mancha*, two world visions crashed into each other. On the following pages, we will discuss how romance blended into the novel, initiating a new and – at least after some time – immensely popular literary expression.

---

60 Personally I do not believe it less 'brilliant', but rather less frivolous and carefree, as Lewis seems to hint at when he later compares the works of Ariosto and Boiardo with the adventures of Baron von Munchausen, while Spenser's tone is described as "gravely imaginative" (Lewis 1988: 307).
61 Greene's (1963:312) opinion is that "Spenser hesitated between a fanciful imitation of Ariosto and a severer Virgilian poem," and that he moved at will between genres, selecting the one that best suited his purposes for each episode. (Greene 1963:334). Hainsworth's (1991:144) comment is similarly vague: "*The Fairie Queene* is edifying and patriotic, but more of a medieval allegory than a descendant of *The Odyssey*."

Epic romance and the novel

Traditionally, the tendency in literary criticism has been to overlook previous genres as the roots of the modern novel,[62] but in more recent years, the later romance narratives have come to be regarded as a possible (and possibly decisive) influence on the new genre. We have seen how romance was able to change over the centuries, as the writers of such narratives appropriated elements of the epic and the *chanson de geste* and created new standards. This phenomenon is not exclusive to the Middle Ages and the Renaissance. At the beginning of the seventeenth century, the bourgeoisie was consolidated as an important social class in most European countries, and it was rapidly gaining power due to a general increase both in domestic mercantile enterprises and international trade ventures. The corresponding increase in independence – though limited in its social scope to the most powerful representatives of the bourgeoisie – from the Church and the aristocracy made many artists interested in portraying a society ruled by the forces of a market economy, featuring more mundane themes. In literature, the epic, traditionally addressing aristocratic lifestyles and affairs, was too rigid in its structure to be able to adapt itself to the new situation, even if blended with romance. Quint (1985:191), in his discussion of *Orlando Innamorato*, *Orlando Furioso* and *Gerusalemme Liberata*, says that the romance adventures in these works acquire a frivolous character because of their relationship to mercantile enterprises – and, if we read between the lines, due to the 'grander' epic backdrop – because "epic goals correspond to ethical goals, by which a martial aristocracy claims to distinguish itself from lower classes." [63]

The structure of romance, on the other hand, was flexible enough to meet the new demands. Jewers (2000:7) mentions the peculiar narrative *Tirant lo Blanc*, written in Valence in the midst of the fifteenth century by Joan Martorell, as an early experimental blend between romance and more realistic fiction that poked fun at previous literary tradition, concluding that "Romance reacted to its own revolving narrative and shaped its literary fortune as it de-regulated itself into the novel [...] through parody."

---

[62] An example of this is Watt's canonical study *The Rise of the Novel* (first published 1957).
[63] See also Bakhtin (1989:449-486).

The most sublime parody of romance of the age is, of course, *Don Quijote de la Mancha* (1605) by Miguel de Cervantes. In this narrative, the transition from romance to the novel is clearly appreciated in the friction between the two protagonists: on the one hand, Don Quijote, immersed in a dreamlike romance reality that only he perceives; on the other, his prosaic squire Sancho Panza, who is constantly (and painfully) aware of the crude reality that surrounds them. *Don Quijote* introduces in narrative fiction the novelty of a realistically described world, whose marvellous elements only exist in Quijote's imagination. However, as Jewers points out, the narrative does not break completely with the previous romance tradition – it becomes a version of it, adapted to a contemporary outlook upon life[64] – because Cervantes necessarily has to use the romance formula to be able to parody it. At the same time, *Don Quijote* represents the end of the medieval and Renaissance versions of the genre. From this moment on, romance needed to get rid of the epic stylistic encumbrance and adapt itself to contemporary times in order to survive. As Quint (1985:197) says: "The bourgeois reading public grew and romance changed while epic died. The future of romance lay with the new world of money and materiality – and with the novel."

The seventeenth century still saw some expressions of the previous traditions, such as *Le Grand Cyrus*, a prose romance that combined *chanson de geste*-themes with medieval romance much in the fashion of Ariosto and Tasso, and, at the end of the century, some works of a curious subgenre usually called 'criminal romance', that merged romance and novel standards. But romance would have to wait until the appearance of the modern novel before it could realize its full potential as a complement to the new genre.

---

[64] Jewers (2000:175), referring to Chrétien, Martorell and Cervantes, claims that "they illustrate a playful familiarity and comic contempt for what has gone on before." The difference between *Quijote* and the works by Boiardo, Ariosto, Tasso and Spenser in this respect is that Cervantes introduces the novelty of the open confrontation between the 'real' (realistically described) world, represented by Sancho Panza, and the romance perspective of Don Quijote. Beer's (1977:43) view that "Sancho and Don Quixote are necessary to each other: they interpret the world for each other, illustrating the interdependence of the impulse to imitate and the impulse to idealize," underscores the importance of generic blend in this narrative.

2.3. The modern novel

In 1719, Daniel Defoe published his famous novel *Robinson Crusoe*, initiating a new narrative tendency which would later, in the nineteenth century, be called realism. Three years later appeared *Moll Flanders*, by the same author, and in 1740, Samuel Richardson continued in the same style with the publication of *Pamela*. From this moment on, the modern novel was soon established as the most popular literary genre.

Watt, in his influential study *The Rise of the Novel* (first published 1957), mentions educational, technological and economic factors as the main contributors to the early development of the novel. According to Watt, the growing rates of literacy among many workers of the middle class increased the interest in reading books of all sorts. The new masses of readers also constituted a solid economic basis for the commercialization of books, and the recent technological improvements in printing facilitated their production on a large scale. Books were beginning to be considered a commodity among others, accessible to everyone.

Watt claims that the novel adopted realism due to the influence of the preceding philosophical tradition of the Enlightenment,[65] arguing that both the literary and philosophical novelties were a result of the general transformation of Western society, from the unitary vision of the Middle Ages to an increasingly fragmented reality "which presents us with a developing but unplanned aggregate of particular individuals having particular experiences at particular times and places" (Watt 1983:34).

Particular individuals having particular experiences at particular times and places – this is the reality that the modern novel transmits to its readers, though we might add the adjective 'credible' to the notion of particularity. As a consequence, the new novelists reject the traditionally bombastic and/or fantastic plots in favour of quotidian themes and events. Furthermore, their characters are of the common kind, usually members of the low or middle classes and

---

[65] Watt highlights Descartes's *Discourse on Method* (1637), that describes a rational method for truth-seeking based on individual experience and a systematization of the principles of science.

by no means idealized,[66] and they are placed in a detailed, easily recognizable world in which they act motivated by psychologically plausible impulses. In short, the biased idealism of previous narrative traditions disappears, making room for a 'disenchanted' reality.

One of the greatest advantages of the novel compared to romance narratives was that while the latter sometimes became entangled in overly subtle or even inaccessible allegories, the former spoke directly to contemporary readers about more or less contemporary characters and events close to ordinary experience. However, the absolutist regime of the realist novel would soon be threatened by a new literary tendency. Romance, that seemed destined to die, disguised itself yet again in order to survive, and the gothic novel entered the scene.

The gothic novel and supernatural fiction

In 1764, Horace Walpole published *The Castle of Otranto*, a short narrative that laid the foundations for what would later be known as the gothic novel. In the eighteenth century, the term 'gothic' had certain connotations of primitivism, as regards both architecture and people, but with the attribution of the adjective to Walpole's work, the word acquired a complementary meaning. Beginning with *Otranto*, it was also used to describe a new kind of literature which, in the words of Clery (1998:xii), was "a 'blend' of the 'imagination and improbability' found in ancient romance, and the accurate imitation of nature that is the hallmark of the modern novel."

Walpole was conscious of the fictional demands of his time, and *The Castle of Otranto*, a narrative full of ghosts, giants and miracles, had to be presented as the translation of a supposedly authentic manuscript to prevent it from being rejected both by publishers and the reading audience.[67] However, the tradition of

---

66 Frye (1971:44) characterizes the novel-hero of this epoch as "a hero ordinary in virtues but socially attractive." Samuel Johnson, the famous contemporary critic who exerted a significant influence on the British writers of the age, believed that the novel should show virtues but not hesitate to describe vice. See Beer (1977:51).

67 The first edition was presented as a translation of an Italian manuscript from 1529, which in turn told of mysterious events that had taken place in the twelvth or thirteenth centuries. When in the second edition Walpole, inspired by the book's success among the general readers and critics alike, confessed his authorship, he apologetically justified his purpose of writing it by stating that "diffidence of his own abilities, and the novelty of the attempt, were his sole inducements to assume that disguise" (Walpole 1998:9).

gothic literature was perpetuated without the need to resort to such justifications by writers such as Clara Reeve, Matthew Gregory Lewis and Ann Radcliffe, each with a different rendering of the genre. Clara Reeve decides to adapt the gothic material to make it compatible with the standards of the realist novel. Clery (1995:86), describes Reeve's most famous novel, *The Old English Baron* (1777), as a re-writing of *Otranto* in the fashion of Richardson's *Pamela*,

> in fancy dress with the spice of the paranormal, an illustrative conduct book for the proper correlation of wealth and virtue [which] redirected the modern romance from novelty status to the professional mainstream [...] making romance publishing and romance writing look like a viable business.

In the preface to the novel, the author explains that her formula is based on the need to exploit marvellous incidents in order to excite the reader's attention, to use realist descriptions for the verisimilitude, and to include a certain dose of pathos to move the reader.[68] *The Old English Baron* set off the gothic novel commercially, and this, by now, seemed to be an indispensable condition for the continuity of a literary genre.

Radcliffe, for her part, took Reeve's strategy one step further, bringing it even closer to the realm of the realist novel by offering rational explanations for the supernatural events in works like *The Mysteries of Udolpho* and *The Italian*, while Lewis chose the opposite direction – *The Monk* (1794) explores a world full of squalor, secret vice, black magic, ghosts and supernatural horror.

In spite of the apparent diversity, these works share a number of traits that may be said to define the gothic genre. In the first place, the action usually takes place in some Mediterranean location in medieval or late medieval times. Secondly, gothic stories frequently feature old, dark, oppressive spaces, such as castles, ruins, catacombs and tombs. These places acquire so great a protagonism that they almost seem to have a proper personality, being the guardians of secrets and ghosts.[69] In the third place, the gothic novel often tells the story of a young, virtuous woman whose innocence is threatened by the sexual desires of some old, or at least older man. Fourth, transgressions

---

68 See Reeve (1778), *Preface to the Second Edition of The Old English Baron*, in Reeve (1967:4).
69 To transfer part of the protagonism to the physical space as such is a novelty compared to previous traditions. This is a trait that would be further exploited by writers of the Romantic literary movement.

always play a fundamental role, whether merely insinuated, as in the novels of Reeve, or exposed in all their scandalous details, as in *The Monk*. Finally, supernatural elements are present in one way or another, producing hysterical reactions in the protagonists.

Later on, these conventions would be affectionately satirized by Jane Austen in *Northanger Abbey* (1818), and used by Walter Scott for his romantic re-elaboration of the Middle Ages. Rabkin (1976:187-188) describes the evolution of the genre in the following way:

> From the roots of Shakespeare and the Oriental tale, together with the rise of antiquarian interest and sentiment, English literature begat mainstream Gothicism [*Otranto, The Old English Baron*]; by becoming more fantastic [*The Monk*] begat naturalized Gothicism [*Mysteries of Udolpho*], these two genres [...] begat satirized Gothicism [*Northanger Abbey*] and these three genres, by yet another fantastic reversal, begat romanticized Gothicism [Scott's *Quentin Durwood*].

The gothic novels of the eighteenth century would also be a source of inspiration for the Romantic literary movement, above all due to the implications of the subconscious powers that inform them,[70] but also because of their particular vision of the Middle Ages.

In this way, the gothic novel re-introduces romance on the European literary scene, but this time through the medium of the novel, the influence of which can be seen in the character-drawing, the temporal relationships and in the descriptions of places and situations. The geography is usually quite exact, and even if the coincidences on which the plot often rests are totally improbable, at least they conform to the internal coherence of the story, making the genre lean closer to the realist novel than to the traditional romance narratives. The use of a physical space which is described more or less realistically – and with internal coherence – as the setting for supernatural and mysterious events, had a notable influence on the nineteenth-century writers of prose romances and fantastic novels that yet again adapted the novel standards towards a more imaginative realm.

---

70 According to Manlove (Schlobin 1982:21-22), in the gothic novel "the supernatural expresses the revolt of a purely human subconscious against reason, figured in organized religion and social civility", the purpose of which would be "to stimulate the reader's unconscious terrors." See also Beer (1977: 57-58).

The romantic imagination and the novel: the legend in broad daylight

The Romantic emphasis on emotions and the individual's interior world brought a radical change to artistic creation. In literature, the gothic novels helped setting the scene for this shift of focus, with its medieval scenery and flirts with the supernatural elements, which often, as in the novels of Radcliffe, turned out to be a result of the protagonist's own imagination. The Romantics, for their part, centered on the emotional reality, looking for inspiration in sources as varied as classical mythology, old ballads, fairy tales and medieval legends, in their search for an adequate formula to express how the mind's internal processes relate to the exterior world.

Naturally, imagination was a fundamental tool to achieve that purpose, especially for the creation of fantastic (albeit emotionally true) spaces, in which the poets could locate their visions without having to yield terrain to the strictly empiric and external credibility of realist narratives. The Romantic poet was seen as a creator of private poetic universes, with a proper internal logic.

Nature also played an important role, whether as an expression of divine forces beyond man's control, or as a counterbalance to society, which was perceived as an artificial construction that separated the individual from emotional and spiritual reality.[71]

A new kind of novel, that perpetuated certain aspects of the gothic novel and reflected the outlook of the Romantic philosophy, began taking shape, represented by works like Mary Shelley's *Frankenstein* (1818) and Charles Maturin's *Melmoth the Wanderer* (1820). As a response to the new interest in the Middle Ages, Walter Scott invented the historical novel in an attempt to recover – and make room for – the romance spirit within the framework of a nineteenth-century sensitivity.[72]

As for the literary treatment of romance in this age, Frye (1971:306) argues that it can be found in a neutral space between the world of the novel, that

---

[71] According to Day (1996:40) the main Romantic idea was that true contact with God could only be found in Nature, and that to study Nature would bring both pleasure and higher moral standards.
[72] In Beer's (1977:65) opinion, "[Scott] wanted to find some permanent ground between the remote picturesqueness of romance and the ephemerality of the present day."

deals with men, and the world of myth, that deals with gods, and offers the view that the prose romances appear as a late extension of classical mythology. However, the prose romances of the nineteenth century are not entirely separated from, or integrated in, either of the two, sharing features both with the realist novel and with the mythological tales.

One of the most illuminating examples of this blend in the nineteenth century is found in the works of the American novelist Nathaniel Hawthorne. In his preface to *The House of the Seven Gables* (1851), the author gives us a valuable first-hand opinion regarding the character of prose romances. Hawthorne (1986: 1) says that as opposed to the novel (the implicit reference is to the realist novel), that sets out to portray possible, probable and ordinary experiences with exact fidelity, the writer of prose romances may take the liberty of manipulating or even inventing reality in his fiction: "[...] he may so manage his atmospherical medium as to bring out or mellow the lights and deepen and enrich the shadows of the picture."

Regarding his own literary production, and this time with explicit reference to *The House of the Seven Gables*, Hawthorne (1986:2) claims that

> The point of view in which this Tale comes under the Romantic definition, lies in the attempt to connect a by-gone time with the very Present that is flitting away from us. It is a Legend, prolonging itself, from an epoch now gray in the distance, down into our broad daylight, and bringing along with it some of its legendary mist.

The quotation brings us straight to one of the most conspicuous consequences of the blend between the realist novel and the romance, namely the particular presentation of the world, which does not belong completely to any of the two traditions. In this type of novel, there is almost always a conscious tendency to guide the reader towards allegorical and, by extension, archetypal interpretations. The narrative seems designed to convey some sort of message, hidden behind a set of symbols, and the environment – the characters, the settings, the sequence of events – complements the message in a coherent and suggestive way that takes the narrative far beyond a mere realistic representation of the quotidian world. The result is that the characters acquire archetypal traits and functions, representing different roles, in order to provide the narrative with some sort of mythic or legendary mystery.

However, the allegorical aspects are not as developed as in mythological and classic romance tales. The world is an easily recognizable place, with distances in miles, in which the hero will be hungry if he does not eat, or fall asleep if he is tired. Frye (1971:137) says that

> Romance is the tendency to displace myth in a human direction and yet, in contrast to realism, to conventionalize content in an idealized direction [...] In a myth we can have a sun-god, in romance a person significantly associated with the sun [...] In more realistic modes, the association becomes less significant and more incidental as imagery.

Hawthorne's novels do feature persons and settings significantly associated with myths – by which standard it would be a romance, according to Frye's definition. This definition is, however, rather too blunt for the present purpose. In Hawthorne's prose romances, the archetypal and the natural worlds come together, creating an effect similar to the epic presentation of reality, but with far greater generic interaction and flexibility of style.

New worlds, old traditions:
the fantasy novels of MacDonald and Morris

As we have seen, the dominant literary tendency of the eighteenth and nineteenth centuries, realism, was sporadically challenged by literary undercurrents that questioned its authoritarian world-vision, mainly derived from standards of the Enlightenment. Naturally, most of these subversive narratives had a more or less fantastic character which was expressed with romance and romantic outlooks upon life. However, the fantastic literature of the nineteenth century has many faces. Apart from the echoes of the prose romances and the gothic novels, which could be appreciated in the works by authors like Mary Shelley, Maturin, Poe, Stevenson, Haggard, Stoker and Buchan, there were also the 'original' fairy tales.

At the beginning of the century, fairy tales were an important source of inspiration for many writers, especially for the German Romantics, such as Novalis, E.T.A. Hoffmann and others, who saw in them clear manifestations of Man's essential desires and concerns. The interest in using fairy tales as a medium for the expression of subconscious impulses did not cease with the progressive decadence of Romantic values, but was rather prolongated into the Victorian era, and this generated a favourable intellectual climate for the creation of *original* fairy tales.

Other factors also made the genre appealing. Manlove (1983:2-3) believes that the popularity of the fairy tales in the nineteenth century was at least partially due to a general European interest in finding the vestiges of a national identity, which gave rise to compilations of folk-tales such as the collections of the Grimm brothers, or of national myths, like those of the Finnish *Kalevala*, gathered by Elias Lönnroth. Manlove claims that the main part of the new fantastic fiction written in England in the nineteenth century took the shape of original fairy tales, written for children.[73] Manlove (1983:11-12) further divides this literature into two main fields: *comic* and *imaginative fantasy*. In his view, the first category corresponds to works of authors like Nesbit or Thackeray, aiming merely at entertaining their readers. In the second category we would find the narratives of MacDonald, Kingsley and Morris, conveying a totalizing vision of a fantastic world that appears as real as our own.[74]

George MacDonald and William Morris were two of the most successful imaginative writers of the nineteenth century. Morris began publishing fantastic tales in 1856 (*The Hollow Land*), while MacDonald's novel *Phantastes*, the story of a man whose chamber is turned into a great forest that swallows him, appeared in 1858.[75] In spite of the fact that the two writers had very different personalities and interests – MacDonald was a theologian, whereas Morris was a convinced socialist[76] – they are commonly regarded as the fathers of the genre known today as fantasy literature. Mathews (2002:16) claims that

---

[73] Manlove mentions Thackeray's *The Rose and the Ring*; Kingsley's *The Water Babies*; Lewis's *Alice's Adventures in Wonderland*; MacDonald's stories (except *Phantastes*), and Lang's *Prince Prigio* as the most prominent examples of the new genre.

[74] According to Manlove (1983:258), this type of fantasy, as opposed to previous fantastic literature, was based on a separation between the real world and the invented narrative universe. This would be derived from the Romantic idea of the heterocosm – "the belief that the artist created a truth-system of his own which needed have no empirical connection with our own."

[75] MacDonald was best known for his books for children and adolescents, such as *The Princess and the Goblin* and *The Princess and Curdie*, though these stories were also highly popular among adult readers.

[76] Apart from his political activities, Morris had an incredible number of interests and talents. Among other things, he painted, wrote poetry, translated Homer and the Icelandic Sagas, designed furniture and tapestries, and edited books.

in their novels, MacDonald and Morris established an antirealistic mode of writing, recovering syntax, vocabulary and archetypal schemes from different literary traditions of the past, and presented

> interesting philosophical alternatives in the early-fantasy genre through a marked contrast of values that emerged in their writing: radical, secular, idealist values (Marxist values) in the work of Morris; traditional, religious, spiritual values (Christian values) in the work of MacDonald. This polarity of divergent values [...] set a thematic course for the genre, since fantasy was from the outset a more purely philosophical mode of writing than was realism [...] It was less concerned with real, individual characters and situations than with embodying philosophical, intellectual, moral, and social discourse.

MacDonald and Morris are the first writers to design, describe and develop invented worlds with an internal coherence as a complete spatial framework for their stories. They had several reasons to do so. Landow (1982:132) suggests that Morris's novels *The Well at the World's End* and *The Water of the Wondrous Isles* are the result of a creation of worlds in which the writer could dramatize the spiritual problems of contemporary society with greater poignancy. Zanger (1982:179), for his part, believes that both Morris and MacDonald "turned to fantasy as an alternative to the utilitarian world of hard fact and Victorian bourgeois commodity culture [proposing] an ordered society instead of the social disorders created by the Industrial Revolution."

In his utopian novels, *A Dream of John Ball* and *News From Nowhere*, Morris also criticized the materialistic society and the blind faith in progress, but it was with *The House of the Wolfings* (1888) and *The Roots of the Mountains* (1889) that he turned back to the pseudomedieval themes he had pursued thirty years earlier, using mythical structures in his attempt to propose alternative social modes of life. Of *The House of the Wolfings*, Mathews (2002:43) highlights the communal values and the symbolic representation of a female identity through Mother Earth and the Sun, while arguing that *The Roots of the Mountains* establishes the use of "imagined landscape as an important symbolic and creative element of fantasy that places even greater importance on geography and on elemental symbols – water, wood, mountain, plain."

Both novels, together with *The Story of the Glittering Plain or the Land of Living Men*, (1891) and *The Wood Beyond the World* (1894), pointed towards Morris's most accomplished work, *The Well at the World's End* (1896), in which the author manages to crystallize his vision and purpose in one single, if extensive, book. Here, Morris uses a great variety of popular legends, fairy tales, and heroic myths,[77] placing the combination of these elements in an invented, pseudomedieval world and using heroic action as the main thread of the story. This narrative system would later, in the twentieth century, be used by many other writers, initiating a subgenre of fantastic literature called 'high fantasy', or 'heroic fantasy', by the main part of the critics, including works by writers such as Dunsany, Eddison, Tolkien, Moorcock and Le Guin.[78]

Zanger, in his article 'Heroic Fantasy and Social Reality' (1982:226-236), summarizes what he perceives as the most common traits of this genre, mentioning an essentially pagan, pseudo-medieval setting that combines fairy tale schemes with knightly tales and which is given coherence by the adventures of a central hero. Other prominent elements would include an aristocratic society threatened by chaotic forces; a story that tells of the struggle to eliminate the threat and restore peace to the world by means of individual heroic action; and evil creatures that are most effectively destroyed by examples of moral virtue, rather than by the use of magic weapons or sorcery.[79]

Evidently, judging by what we know of other genres, what Zanger describes seems to be a melting pot of Western narrative traditions. Myth, epic, romance and novel coincide in fantasy literature, making it a catalyst for the different stages and tendencies in previous narrative traditions. In Beer's (1977:67) opinion, the relationship between romance and realism in Morris's works is grounded on the portrayal of a world which is of a spiritual complexity while at the same time addressing contemporary issues. We might add that the simultaneous influence of the epic and the realist novel on a work like *The Well at the World's End* lies in the particular inner coherence of the narrative universe: in spite of its fantastic character, the setting is very concrete, with particular characters whose actions are, within the context, 'realistic', depending as they do on previous events and exerting influence over later action – in other words, narrative coherence does not depend strictly on a credible

---

77 See Attebery (1980:8).
78 Personally, I do not agree with this label when applied to Tolkien's work. For a fuller discussion of Tolkien's place in twentieth-century literature, see chapter 3 of the present study.
79 See also Mathews (2002:229-231).

appliaction of the laws of the real world but on a sort of epic *alêtheia*.[80] The fact that the world is not our own increases the demands of narrative cohesion, since an invented physical space requires a stricter attention to the relationship between its invented components in order to ensure credibility.

For this reason we might say that *The Well at the World's End* forges a new link in the great and heterogeneous chain that has taken us from Homer's Greece through the Roman Empire and European feudal societies, picking up Renaissance and Enlightenment beliefs and thoughts before hastening on to collect the elements from the Industrial Revolution and the Romantic mindset until finally reaching the end of the nineteenth century, where the four major tendencies – myth, epic, romance and novel – are suggestively combined, now transferred to an invented world due to the particular intellectual climate of the age. It is the invented, pseudomedieval world that enables these writers to recover the heroic myth as a suitable and legitimate vehicle for the main action,[81] to express it with romance and epic syntax and style, to exhibit an attention to detail and internal coherence proper both to the realist novel and the epic, and to use the blend to address contemporary concerns. Mathews (2002:52) speaks of the literary legacy of *The Well at the World's End* in the following terms:

> By creating a fully coherent fantasy reality, [Morris] in effect provides a parallel world, a world of correspondences in a medieval sense but one where potential and possibility are unleashed – a world no longer constrained by the actual, where imagination can shape alternative ideals. Other significant and enduring contributions include his invented language, syntax, and style; his semimedieval settings; his liberation of the feminine, or anima; his validation of both male and female as equally strong and heroic; and his shaping of a romantic heroic model.

In other words, Morris looks back at the literary past of the Western world and tries to integrate many of its tendencies in a coherent whole, much in the vein of the encyclopaedic ambitions of epic poetry.[82] However, the paradox of his time – the world made smaller by scientific progress and literature made

---

80 See pp. 24-25 of the present study.
81 An interesting alternative is presented by Haggard who, instead of using an invented world, sets the heroic action of novels such as *King Solomon's Mines* and *She* in remote and unexplored regions of Africa.
82 Frye (1976:4) highlights Morris's "encyclopedic approach to romance, his ambition to collect every major story in literature and retell or translate it."

larger by an increased generic diversity – brought him the possibility, and the need, to place the action in an invented world in order to find a space ample enough to host the dialogue between the different traditions, styles and narrative strategies of the past with sufficient fluency. I would say that this meta-literary, highly imaginative encyclopaedic approach to literature is one of the strongest influences on Tolkien, who later used a similar – though much more sophisticated – strategy to create the narrative universe of *The Lord of the Rings*.

2.4. Myth and the Western narrative traditions

One thing which is common to Western literature since Homer is the integration – albeit to different degrees – of mythic patterns in its evolving narrative expressions. As opposed to the greater part of these traditions, the action described in myths does not take place in historical time, but in a primordial reality. The stories set in the primordial world seem necessary to provide us with answers to such metaphysical or religious questions that reason and science cannot explain satisfactorily – at least not on their own. The contact between the two realities – the reintegration of the two temporal rhythms – is of fundamental importance for a myth to make sense (Eliade 2000:27). But what is this sense?

Campbell (1997:218) claims that the aim of myth is to reconcile the consciousness of the individual with the universal will. The mythological world would then become a complementary world, whose elements and stories, because they are presented as true, provide the individual with a model in order to understand the meaning of his or her existence. For this reason, any mythology must feature an ample range of characters, gods, enemies, places and circumstances to ensure the possibility of a personal relationship, for all the members of the community, to the primordial world.

Formally, a mythology is an extensive *corpus* of tales that collectively and encyclopaedically gather the habits and social codes considered ideal by the community. Mythic tales speak of the desires and concerns of mankind as it was before the civilization that we have designed for ourselves twisted our attention towards more mundane matters. They reflect a primitive culture that runs the risk of falling into oblivion but which is still very much valid.[83] Because of the displacement in time and space, and because of the doctrinal character of its action, the mythic tale acquires a symbolic significance that appeals to both imagination and faith for an acceptance of the primordial reality it describes.

Cupitt (1997:5) outlines five basic features of all myths, stating that its protagonists are antropomorphic supernatural beings with supernatural powers; that the action takes place outside of historical time or in a supernatural world; that they may tell of irruptions between the supernatural world and historical time; that the stories are not realistically described but show the fragmented logic of a dream; and, finally, that myths explain and legitimate the action they describe.

Each community needs a person who can help them get into contact with the primordial reality. This mediating function is embodied by the reciter of myths, who independently of his or her shape or designation – shaman, witch, bard, preacher, poet, etc. – is usually a person with an excellent memory, powerful imagination and literary talent, who transmits transcendental experiences by the use of fantastic and impressive settings (Eliade 2000:128-129).

The role of the reciter of myths was partially shouldered by poetically gifted writers as orality slowly turned into literacy. Because a written text could be copied and read to large audiences by any literate person, the social impact and potential of the written epic narratives could be enormous. The written versions of the tales attributed to Homer, and Virgil's original *Aeneid*, were decisive for the establishment of a national identity based on the community's relationship to its divine origins.

It is noteworthy that the power of the mythical elements in these narratives has been strong enough to survive the allegorization of their 'irrational' character on behalf of the authorities of reason, as in the case of the continued appreciation for Homer in the age of ionic rationalism,[84] or by the Catholic Church – as

---

83 See García Gual (1987:21). Nietzsche labels 'mythic' a tale which evokes dimensions of the past that cannot be found in the present, and that reveals the true essence of a culture (Gadamer 1997:46).
84 For an outline of the evolution of the status of myths in Greek culture, see chapter 3 in García Gual (1987). See also Eliade (2000:135).

shown by the persistent idolatry of Virgil during the Renaissance.[85] We have also seen that even in Christian times, pagan myth was still considered adequate as a narrative vehicle for the transmission of more recent epic tales, as in *Beowulf*, where the 'proto-Christian' hero is unable to shake off his pagan inheritance. The epic tradition shows a progressive decadence of myths that gave rise to more mundane characters and settings, an evolution that reaches its final stage in the *chanson de geste* narratives of the Middle Ages. However, the pretension of telling the truth remains intact.

Literary romance also moves away from primordial reality. As we have seen, romance narratives are much more oriented towards adventure, entertainment and the spiritual education of the protagonists. However, the mythic backdrop still adds meaning to the adventures. The quest myth, the heroic activity *par excellence* in medieval romance, is born out of the combination of the fertility myth and the hero myth.[86] While in many tales of medieval romance the quest myth is recurrent, in the Renaissance, classical myths became popular again but had to be modified towards allegorical interpretation to fit into the dominant religious context. These allegories were written for the broad reading public, whereas the pure myths in the classical works were considered bearers of a "mysterious significance apt only for perfect spirits" (García Gual 1987:70).[87]

Coupe (1997:104) claims that allegorical versions of myths will inevitably make them seem 'domesticated'. We have previously seen how writers of medieval romance tended to concentrate on certain aspects of reality, using a potent central image that clarified the message. In this, both medieval and Renaissance romance come close to the Bible in their expression of a reality imbued with

---

85 In García Gual's (1987:64) view, the medieval artists "turned to the aesthetics of Antiquity because of the poverty and sadness of Christian iconography" in order to express a new conception of the world by means of allegory (my translation).
86 Briefly summarized, the quest myth is about a hero, whose conceptual image is intimately associated to spring, youth, fertility and order, who travels to a strange and perilous land, fights a crucial battle against an enemy related to concepts such as winter, old age, sterility and chaos, and triumphs, thereby revitalizing his community. See Frye (1971:187-189). Other definitions include that of Campbell (1997), who in his exhaustive survey of the hero's general characteristics in universal myths and literature, produces a single scheme of action and significance that he calls the monomyth.
87 My translation.

mythic significance.[88] On the other hand, as opposed to the Old Testament and other myths, in romance the representatives of the supernatural world rarely intervene personally in human affairs – while it is true that a great number of monsters and other fantastic creatures appear in the romance narratives, they have been naturalized as inherent parts of the human world. In this sense, it is true that myth in romance becomes decidedly domesticated.

Compared to the epic, which explores and explains the present by applying myths to human history, in romance narratives the myths are often present for more frivolous reasons, partly as a result of literary and cultural fashion. The quest myth was an adequate complement to the stories because of its particular capacity to suggest attractive secular mysteries that stimulated the audience's imagination, and it was partially used to spice up the more serious affairs related to the social code of the aristocracy with magic encounters and tales.

The modern novel, on the other hand, emerged in the context of the Enlightenment's cult of reason, whereby realism and credibility gain in importance. However, avoiding mythical paradigms at all costs was not the only road taken by novel-writers. In an age that seemed to have forgotten the pleasures of imagination, the exotic was an attractive alternative, as certified by the success of Defoe's *Robinson Crusoe* in the first half of the eighteenth century. While the plot of Defoe's novel was goverened by rules of probability and science, Walpole, some thirty-five years later, decided to dispense with such constraints. The link between nostalgia for a bygone age, exotic settings and imaginative fiction is often very strong and intuitive, and Walpole managed to combine the three 'weaknesses' with a certain dose of realism, presenting his tale as a translation of a supposedly authentic manuscript, thus making his work attractive to the readers of his age.

Modern negative criticism of Walpole's work tends to concentrate on the poor characterization and the lack of internal coherence, but *The Castle of Otranto* is interesting enough as an early example of how mythical structures were made available to the novelist in the context of realism. Beginning with the gothic

---

88 Auerbach (1979:29) writes that the Old Testament is characterized by a general lack of connection, the need for interpretation, the highlighting of some parts at the expense of others, among other things.

novel, archetypal schemes will be consciously applied to plot and characters by the authors of prose romances.

However, the setting could also be re-elaborated in the framework of the novel. Writers like MacDonald and Morris exploited this possibility to a full extent, creating complete imagined worlds in which the old myths could reappear without having to conceal themselves behind 'significant associations', and blending many different literary traditions and mythic motifs. The new fantastic setting, neither entirely primordial nor belonging completely to historical time, is created with such scrupulous attention to the details that it acquires levels of internal verisimilitude similar to that of realist fiction. As we have seen, these fantastic novels became immensely popular, in spite of their invented setting. One explanation may be that, as Frye (1971:305) says, "[p]opular demand in fiction is always a mixed form: a romantic novel just romantic enough for the reader to project his libido on the hero and his anima on the heroine, and just novel enough to keep these projections in a familiar world."

It is interesting to notice that the "familiar world" Frye refers to can be a fantastic world, if designed by using certain realist criteria.

Some twenty years after the publication of *The Well at the World's End*, J.R.R. Tolkien began working on another mythical vision, that would eventually branch out in different directions, one of them taking the formal shape of the novel – the narrative we today know as *The Lord of the Rings*. The difference in focus between Tolkien and the above-mentioned writers of fantasy literature is highly revealing of the changing ideological, political and cultural panorama of the new century. At the same time, Tolkien's work offers a far more sophisticated dialogue between the literary traditions.

In the next chapter we will take a look at how Tolkien's particular strategy differs from that of other contemporary writers that aimed largely at the same thing.

Chapter 3

The Lord of the Rings and Ironic Myth

Over the years, there have been many proposals concerning the literary genre of *The Lord of the Rings*. Of the most recent ones, we may mention Shippey (2002:xix), who claims that Tolkien invented a new genre, that he calls *heroic fantasy*. Lobdell (2004:14-19), for his part, considers that the dominant generic vehicle in the work is the Edwardian adventure novel, while Segura (2004:109) offers the view that *The Lord of the Rings* is an elegiac epic, a milestone in the development of modern epic narratives. This diversity of opinion is not only an indication of the work's narrative wealth, it also reveals the difficulties of analysing genre in Tolkien's literary narratives. In other words, there seems to be a lack of adequate critical methodologies to contextualize his work. I believe that a general tendency to consider Tolkien's work as an anomaly, an extravagance or a simple romantic evasion with no particular ties to the literary context of the period between the two World Wars, has been mainly responsible for this.[89]

While it is true that Tolkienian literature breaks with the predominant literary fashion of the age, we must also bear in mind that Tolkien was intimately connected to the great political and cultural events of his times, as Flieger (1997: 2) points out. Like poets and writers such as Rupert Brooke, Edward Thomas, Siegfried Sassoon, Wilfred Owen and Robert Graves, among others, he fought in the First World War. Professionally, he was a distinguished scholar at Oxford University, at one of the most prestigious colleges for humanist studies in the world. It would have been very difficult for him to stay immune to the literary outcome of the age, as Garth (2003:288)[90] claims, and not to be at least conscious of the dominant literary expressions of the times, such as that of the war

---

[89] Spacks (2004:67), writing in 1959, voiced one of the first statements on Tolkien and genre, saying that *The Lord of the Rings* is "far outside the central modes of 20th century fiction." This has, ever since, been the stance of most criticism, positive as well as negative, regarding the literary context of Tolkien's best known work.

[90] Garth says that "two new and enormously influential literary movements emerged: firstly, a style of war writing that has attained 'classic' status; secondly, modernism. But the impact of these on Tolkien were negligible."

poets or the modernist experimentation of T.S. Eliot and Ezra Pound, among others, even if he did not find their aesthetic principles appealing.

Over the last thirty or forty years, a great number of studies pretending to disclose the narrative sources of *The Lord of the Rings*, and many others that show its analogies to the historical events of the twentieth century, have been published.[91] Some of these studies are very perspicacious, but they usually fail to offer any hints about the particular narrative dynamics of the work in strictly literary terms. The vast majority of the critical works devoted to *The Lord of the Rings* have ignored its relationship to the contemporary literary context, and only in recent years more serious attempts at such a contextualization have appeared. Flieger (1997), for instance, links Tolkien's treatment of time to a perception proper to the twentieth century; Shippey (2002) puts Tolkien among the most representative British writers of the postwar period; Rosebury (2003:134-157) dedicates a chapter to analysing the connection between Tolkien's work and Modernism; Brennan Croft (2004) compares Tolkien's fiction to that of the war poets, while Mortimer (2005) explores the relationship between Tolkien and Modernism from the point of view of 'Art for Art's sake'.

There is, on the one hand, an important connection between *The Lord of the Rings* and the First World War;[92] a connection that is further extended to the works of the war poets and to certain manifestations of modernist literature. On the other hand, I believe that the reason for the great abundance of studies devoted to the literary sources in Tolkien's work lies well beyond a mere collector's desire for accumulation of samples. Evidently, Tolkien, in his own way, incorporates a great part of the Western literary canon in *The Lord of the Rings*. As we shall see, this is symptomatic of several works considered paradigmatic of modernist literature, such as *Ulysses*, *The Cantos*, and *The Waste Land*.

---

91 Some examples include Carter, *A Look Behind The Lord of the Rings* (1969), Day, *Tolkien's Ring* (1994), Clark and Timmons (eds.), *J.R.R. Tolkien and his Literary Resonances* (2000), and Chance (ed.), *Tolkien and the Invention of Myth* (2004). As for the connections between *The Lord of the Rings* and the twentieth century, see Veldman, *Fantasy, the Bomb and the Greening of Britain* (1994), Curry, *Defending Middle-earth* (1997), and Weinreich and Honegger (eds.), *Tolkien and Modernity 1 & 2* (2006).
92 C.S. Lewis (1955) was one of the first to acknowledge the presence of imagery and themes of the First World War in the War of the Ring (Isaacs and Zimbardo 2004:13). Garth (2003) offers the most exhaustive study of the impact of the First World War on Tolkien. See also Brennan Croft (2004).

Northrop Frye (1971) includes this type of literature in the literary mode of 'ironic myth', which becomes fashionable after the First World War. This literature is characterized by exhibiting a cyclic perception of time that involves an almost epic compilation of different literary traditions on a simultaneous level, and a generalized return towards mythic structures and themes that are given an ironic treament.

The Lord of the Rings shares most of these features, except the irony, though Tolkien offers a different approach to the mode of 'ironic myth'. By transferring the action to an invented but fully coherent pre-modern world, he manages to liberate it from certain factors that hamper a flexible and dynamic interaction between the different narrative traditions in the modernist works. In *The Lord of the Rings*, Tolkien creates a self-referential narrative universe which is able to sustain the relationships between cultural, narrative and poetic traditions in a coherent, non-elitistic way, and this implies a constant mediation that turns the narrative into a very suggestive exploration of the intertraditional dialogue's limits.

In this chapter I wish to propose a new approach to the position of *The Lord of the Rings* on the map of English twentieth-century literature. To do so, I will begin by taking a look at the effects of the Great War on the literary imagination of the so-called war poets. We will then look at some manifestations of modernist literature, and see how both 'schools' relate to the concept of 'ironic myth' in general, and to *The Lord of the Rings* in particular.

3.1. The Great War

Nostalgically looking back at the age immediately preceding the Great War, literary memory centers not only on the ostentatious dinner parties, hunting expeditions and luxurious holidays,[93] but also on a simple, rural, domestic life marked by a sense of community, innocence and idealism. Both things were

---

93 While P.G. Woodehouse resorted to satire and humor in his portrayal of the carefree Edwardian spirit in the immensely popular series of novels about Psmith (a style later perpetuated in his works about Jeeves and Wooster, written largely in the same spirit), Robert Graves, in *Good-bye to All That* (1929), provides us with a more objective and sombre overview of the lifestyle of a well-to-do English family in the years prior to the Great War.

justified by the ideas of the influential philosopher Moore, who considered that the most important thing in life was artistic experience and personal relationships, and everything else should be looked upon as means to achieve these ends (Lloyd 1993:28). With this philosophy, Moore paved the way for a paradoxical combination of hedonism and puritanism that became immensely popular among a great part of the English population in the first decade of the twentieth century, giving rise both to the literary vanguard of the Bloomsbury group, in which writers like Virginia Woolf and Lytton Strachey took part, and the more traditional school of Georgian poetry, perhaps best represented by the poet Rupert Brooke (Lloyd 1993:29).[94]

The War Poets

The First World War dealt a brutal blow to this mentality, a blow from which the innocent pre-war England never quite recovered. Two critics on the literary production during and after the First World War, Paul Fussell (1975) and Modris Eksteins (1990), attempt to explain the fracture with reference to the particular conditions of trench warfare. The former dedicates the main body of his study, *The Great War and Modern Memory*, mostly to the effects of life in the trenches on the production of the so called 'war-poets', such as Wilfred Owen, Siegfried Sassoon, Edward Thomas, Ivor Gurney, and Robert Graves, among others. Fussell argues that war-time routines that were connected to natural events, such as stand-to at sunrise and sunset, or a contemplation of the sky from the 'grave-perspective' of the trenches, frequently provided poets with motifs in their conscious attempt to find some sort of traditional meaning in the war which would help them in making sense of it.

Julian Grenfell's poem 'Into Battle, Flanders, April 1915', shows this tendency as the poet appeals to the forces of Nature for strength and protection with almost religious undertones: "The fighting man shall from the sun / Take warmth, and life from the glowing earth; / Speed with the light-foot winds to run / And with the trees to newer birth." Even in the moments of profound anguish, the natural cycles may give the soldier solace: "The thundering line of battle stands, / And in the air Death moans and sings; / But Day shall clasp

---

[94] On Georgian poetry as a school, see Reeves (1968).

him with strong hands, / And Night shall fold him in soft wings." (Driver 1996:63-64)

Furthermore, the idea of the enemy as a constant presence, a threatening element ready to attack at any moment, would, in Fussell's view, condition a strongly dichotomized world view reflected in what he calls the 'versus habit'. The simplifying oppositions good/bad, friend/adversary, day/night, etc., found in much of the WW I poetry, would be a consequence of this. Fussell also considers other effects of the war, such as nostalgia for the Edwardian age as a result of the soldiers conceiving time in terms of 'before' and 'after' the war. In addition, the inability to communicate the terrible and bewildering experiences in the trenches would lead to an extensive use of the pastoral, as an antithesis of the infernal sceneries, supported in turn by a strong English tradition in pastoral poetry.

In Ivor Gurney's poem 'De Profundis', first published in 1919, we find several of the previously mentioned traits, such as the pastoral treatment, the elegiac tone, the break with the past and nostalgic references to rural England. The poem begins with the poet's complaint about not being able to evoke the comforting visions of home:

> If only this fear would leave me I could dream of Crickley Hill
>   And a hundred thousand thoughts of home would visit my Heart in sleep;
> But here the peace is shattered all day by the devil's will,
>   And the guns bark night-long to spoil the velvet silence deep.
>
> O who could think that once we drank in quiet inns and cool
>   And saw brown oxen trooping the dry sands to slake
> Their thirst at the river flowing, or plunged in a silver pool
>   To shake the sleepy drowse off before well awake?

The war has annihilated that pure and innocent world of the past:

> We are stale here, we are covered body and soul and mind
>   With mire of the trenches, close clinging and foul,
> We have left our old inheritance, our Paradise behind,
>   And clarity is lost to us and cleanness of soul.
> (Featherstone 1995:120)

Given the extensive reading and literary learning of most soldier poets, they would be referring to the literary canon in order to establish an intelligible ground for their poetry, by way of ironic allusion. In this context, the literary quest romance, notably the versions presented in the form of the Victorian pseudo-medieval romances of William Morris – Fussell (1976:135) mentions *The Well at the World's End* as one of the most frequent sources of imagery for the soldiers – and in Bunyan's Christian allegory *The Pilgrim's Progress*, were particularly appealing. Likewise, military secrets, rumors and the general apocalyptic atmosphere in the trenches gave rise to a whole series of legends and superstitions that flourished during the war.

In general terms, the break with the 'innocent' past and the following experience in the trenches is, according to Fussell (1976:82), accompanied by "the passage of modern writing from one mode to another" (in terms of Northrop Frye's well-known theory of modes), given that the writings of the war-poets describe a sense of transition, pointing both backward, towards the low mimetic mode, and forward, towards the ironic mode's return to myth.

Wilfred Owen's poem 'Strange Meeting' features both sceneries and themes easily associated with myth. It begins with the poet descending from the battlefield to hell, where he meets an enemy that he has killed a day earlier. The dead soldier complains about the lost years, and then he goes on to prophesy about mankind's destiny:

> Now men will go content with what we spoiled,
> Or, discontent, boil bloody, and be spilled.
> They will be swift with swiftness of the tigress.
> None will break ranks, though nations trek from progress
> Courage was mine, and I had mystery,
> Wisdom was mine, and I had mastery:
> To miss the march of this retreating world
> Into vain citadels that are not walled.
> Then, when much blood had clogged their chariot-wheels,
> I would go up and wash them from sweet wells,
> Even with truths that lie too deep for taint.
> I would have poured my spirit without stint
> But not through wounds; not on the cess of war.
> Foreheads of men have bled where no wounds were.
> (Hayward 1993:422)

Owen taps clearly into different traditions of the past in his almost sacramental language ("I would go up and wash them from sweet wells, / Even with truths that lie too deep for taint. / I would have poured my spirit without stint"); a prophetic tone ("None will break ranks, though nations trek from progress"); and images of the past ("vain citadels", "chariot wheels", "sweet wells", etc.). The motif of the descent into the underworld is also a clear echo of epic poetry, such as that of Homer, Virgil and Dante, offering a return to mythic sceneries, not strictly real, in order to communicate the experience of war in intelligible terms.

High Modernism: T.S. Eliot, Pound and Joyce

Modris Eksteins, while writing largely about the same subject, provides us with a different focus in the more recent *Rites of Spring: The Great War and the Birth of Modern Age*, in which he discusses the influence of the war on the modernist movement. Eksteins acknowledges a general British pull towards the preservation of the social values of the Edwardian age – respectability, civility, dignity, controlled progress, etc. – as opposed to the German drift towards a questioning of the nineteenth-century values and an urge to build a new civilization from the ashes of the previous. The disillusion among the fighting men during the war would in Eksteins' view lead to a break with the past and to a new conception of the soldier, representing a creative force in the process of destruction and renewal. Eksteins (1990:214) further argues that "the horror had [...] little interpretative potential except in very personal terms," and that the "signs and sounds of war are connected with an art in which the rules of composition were abandoned and provocation became the goal." Quite in contrast with Fussell, Eksteins claims that an abandonment of conventional forms was seen as the most adequate aesthetic response to the experience. Another effect of the war, according to Eksteins (1990:214), is that language as such lost its social meaning and became a more personal vehicle for the poets, and that irony was adopted as the natural mode for poetic expression.

By comparing the writings of Pound, Eliot and Joyce with the poetry of the war poets in the light of these thoughts on the literary influence of the Great War, we are presented with two distinctively different aesthetic responses to the conflict – one represented by those who fought in it, and another by those who witnessed it from the homefront. While the use of irony and myth is shared by both 'currents', it is commonly acknowledged that the so called 'high modernism', to which Pound, Eliot and Joyce belong, is anti-historicist, that it rejects sequential time and absolute polarities, that it is elitist and exhibits a sense of cultural despair. Furthermore, moral relativism is a prominent feature, as is the attention to the cultural consequences of a technological society and the fascination with chaos and irrationalism – characteristics which have led some historians and literary critics to claim that the intellectual mood it created helped setting the scene for the rise of fascism in the decades following the war. High modernism was extremely technical – I would say almost *clinical* – in its use of language and emphasis on the precise word; it strove to create self-referential narrative universes, and usually exhibited a vast literary erudition which was exploited partly in order to give coherence to the works by using the so called 'mythical method'.[95]

Broadly speaking, the authors mentioned looked upon history as being simultaneous with the present, and considered their age a time of transition – perhaps a perpetual transition.[96] Nevertheless, or perhaps just because of this, modern man grows very conscious of the cultural heritage of the past. Modernist writers tried to make sense of the present by incorporating a good deal of the literary canon into their respective works, juxtaposing the allusions and imitations with examples from modern life to create an ironic effect by means of a kind of bricolage technique that fitted well their perception of modernity as a fragmented and heterogeneous state of affairs.

Frye (1957:62), discussing the narrative mode of ironic myth (alluding to Yeats and Joyce, among others) mentions that cyclical theories of history helped rationalize the idea of the return to myth. As we have mentioned before, the consciousness of being immersed in an age of transition was widespread among the modernists. The resulting mode, ironic myth, would seem to imply an encyclopaedic incorporation of the total literary heritage of the past, ironically contrasted with the present. Myth as such, however, was often applied merely as a prop, to provide a structure that would keep the apparently chaotic mixture of images together.

---

95 Two good introductory studies on modernist literature and modernism as a cultural response to the conditions of the twentieth century are offered by Bradbury (ed.) (1976) and N.F. Cantor (1988).
96 See Kermode (1966) on the literary effects of contemplating time as a perpetual transition.

Joyce, in *Ulysses*, invented the method by using Homer's *Odyssey* as a constant reference for structure, episodes, places and characters, as a means of compensating for the weakening of narrative structure and unity. Joyce pays careful attention to words and to the power of language, in an attempt to illustrate just to what extent the world we live in is a linguistic product, trying to "stress the need to get rid of the enslaving structures that language imposes on us." (Gross 1974:9) As a result, the reader is overwhelmed by references to all kinds of literary traditions. There is also a tendency in Joyce to use his own previous writings as significant references, having, among others, the protagonist of *A Portrait of the Artist as a Young Man*, Stephen Dedalus, reappear in Dublin after his stay in Paris, which means that we need to be familiar with the previous work in order to grasp the full meaning of the new.

Pound's approach to narrative tradition is largely the same: the whole canon should be seen as a simultaneous order, which new works of art may modify as they are incorporated. One of Pound's aims was to display the interrelations between the great works of art, judging them from a simultaneous standpoint. According to Witemeyer (1981:10-11), Pound's theory of the 'Luminous Detail' postulates that some details can reveal the essential characteristics of a whole epoch, and he tried in his poetry to disclose these instances of revelation and put them in a meaningful relationship with each other largely by the use of allusion (to provide ironic contrasts), imitation (to write in the 'spirit' of some author) – and by using persons and characters from history and literature as spokesmen. Inspired by Joyce's 'mythical method', the structure of the *Cantos* is likewise based on Homer's *Odyssey*. The technique of self-referentiality is in Pound extended to the idea that every single part of his writings should be read in the context of the whole body of his work, criticism and poetry alike.

T.S. Eliot shared the idea of the simultaneous order with Pound, and it is perhaps in his poetry where literary reference is most conspicuous – "a literature of literature" as Aiken (1968:93) calls it. His symbols are drawn from myth, legend, literature and history, and once again used to provide ironic contrast. Brooks (1968:157) claims, however, that the surface parallelisms that, in Eliot, establish ironical contrasts, are matched by the surface contrasts that create parallelisms, and that the combination gives the effect of chaotic experience ordered into a new whole. This dichotomy is a tool that Eliot uses to renew and vitalize old symbols turned to clichés and thus emptied of meaning by excessive familiarity.

The main arguments against the effectivity of these works are based on their elitist character. Some parts of *Ulysses* only make sense if one is familiar with the corresponding autobiographical event, and the reader is often perplexed by the complexities, the seemingly irreconcilable contradictions and the sometimes arbitrary use of symbols. In the case of Pound, the reader must necessarily be aware of the poet's opinion of the sources referred to – and share them – for the Luminous Detail to work. As for Eliot, we need to be equally familiar with a large corpus of texts, references, languages and their implications in order for the poems to make sense, a task certainly not made easier by the abstract presentations. In response to these complexities, Craig (1969:212) claims that the limited public response to *The Waste Land* is an indication that it is *not* the representative work of the present age. The same could be said of *The Cantos* and *Ulysses*.

3.2. Ironic Myth

By means of some examples from modernist and war poetry, we have seen the two different ways of instrumentalising literary tradition in order to portray contemporary reality. Undoubtedly, the different personal experiences of the writers – war experienced directly, on the one hand, and indirectly, on the other – conditioned the literary response to some extent. The war poets resorted to literary tradition in order to develop forms and techniques to communicate their external experiences of the war in an intelligible way, while several modernists juxtaposed images from the present with brief glimpses of the past, radically breaking the norms of narrative linearity and incorporating a great number of references to different traditions which, for a proper understanding, often required a considerable erudition on behalf of the readers.

However, apart from the many differences, there are also similarities. Both groups offer literary expressions in which the approach to mythic structures and themes, through the rhetorics of irony, is central. The First World War is probably one of the main reasons for such a treatment. The break with the past that took place with the onset of the conflict implied a new conception of time – we have already mentioned the idea of 'time before' and 'time after" – and a new distrust in linear progress (concerning both the welfare state and time). During and after the war there seemed to have been a generalized feeling that one cycle had concluded and another epoch was being initiated, the characteristics of which were still very unclear, even chaotic. We have previously mentioned that the war poets recreated pastoral settings in their poetry, in order to soften the destructive aesthetic effects of the battles on the landscape. That tendency would disappear after the war, when the modernists tried to delve deeper into contemporary reality, centering instead on the sordid and unpleasant aspects of the modern world.[97]

The particular conditions of the First World War, with its massive destruction, contributed to the anxiety, generating a general mistrust in modernity's capacity of finding a stable route towards the future. These doubts marked a great part of modernist literature, which often denies the possibility of finding something similar to happiness in the modern world. At the same time, the idea of being immersed in a process of destruction and renewal must have been inspiring to the literary imagination, offering, as it did, what looked like a fresh perspective: because of the complete break with the past it seemed possible, for the first time, to achieve a global vision of the cycle that was coming to an end,[98] and to put fragments taken from the chaotic birth of the new era next to images of the past in order to show the sundering effects on the collective imagination, or perhaps as a desperate attempt to connect the fragmented present with a more stable past. This, among other things, was what Joyce, Pound and Eliot tried to do in works such as *Ulysses*, *The Cantos* and *The Waste Land*, as we have seen.

---

[97] Eksteins (1990:237) claims that modernism, "which in its prewar form was a culture of hope, a vision of synthesis, would turn into a culture of nightmare and denial [...] The Great War was the axis on which the modern world turned." See also Garth (2003:303).

[98] Auerbach's classical study *Mímesis*, first published in 1944, is emblematic of this assumption, offering a survey of how the world has been portrayed in different literary traditions, from Homer up to the twentieth century. According to Kermode (1968:94), Auerbach was convinced that European civilization was on the verge of being replaced by another era, and that the historical moment taking place after the First World War offered a unique opportunity to achieve a global vision of the true character of Europe. Oswald Spengler's *The Decline of the West*, first published in 1918, is another example of this approach to contemporary history.

Frye (1971:33-34), in his theory of modes, concludes that the Western literary tradition has been marked by five major tendencies: *myth*, in which the heroes are superior to men and to their environment (as, for example, the figure of Thor in Sturlusson's *Edda*); *romance*, where the protagonists are superior *in degree* to other men and their environment (some heroes of the homeric epics, such as Achilles); *high mimesis*, featuring heroes superior in degree to other men but not to their environment (like Roland of the *Chanson de Roland*); *low mimesis*, dealing with heroes that are neither superior to other men nor to their environment (Moll Flanders of Defoe's eponymous novel); and the *ironic* mode, whose protagonists are inferior to other men and to their environment (for instance Svejk, in Hasek's *The Good Soldier Svejk*).[99]

Frye (1971:42) considers that all modes may coincide to a greater or lesser extent in a single literary work, and that the mimetic modes (romance, high mimesis, and low mimesis) are examples of 'displaced myth' that move progressively towards the opposite pole compared to mythic standards of verisimilitude, which is the starting point, until they begin to lean back towards myth in the ironic mode:

> Irony descends from the low mimetic: it begins in realism and dispassionate observation. But as it does so, it moves steadily towards myth, and dim outlines of sacrificial rituals and dying gods begin to reappear in it. Our five modes evidently go around in a circle. This reappearance of myth in the ironic is particularly clear in Kafka and in Joyce [...] However, ironic myth is frequent enough elsewhere, and many features of ironic literature are unintelligible without it.

This return to myth, Frye argues, alluding to Yeats's ideas about the conclusion of the Western cycle, and to Joyce's vision of modernity as a frustrated apocalypse, is reinforced by cyclical theories of time, "the appearance of such theories being a typical phenomenon of the ironic mode." (Frye 1971:62) However, as we have already said, it was not easy to discern a general direction of the new age. Critics such as Kermode (1966) and Eksteins (1992) believe that the concept of 'time after' was seen as a transitional phenomenon: a new cycle had not begun, but Western civilization had rather reached some sort of limbo between two cycles.[100]

---

99 The examples are mine.
100 See Eksteins (1992:256-259) and Kermode (1968:98).

After the apocalypse, symbolized by the Great War, there were no clear sights or open views of the new future. It is only natural that the ensuing frustration should lead to a feeling of transition and the use of irony to reflect the bitterness, but the reasons for another, more creative response, aiming to recover what could still be saved of the past cycle, are not difficult to imagine either. In Kermode's (1968:112) view, T.S. Eliot pretended to "reunite the history of all that interested him in order to have past and present conform [...] He saw his age as a long transition through which the elect must live, redeeming the time [...]."

In other words, the need to recover traditions from past ages becomes particularly important in times of transition, and the tendency to incorporate significant fragments — see Pound's Luminous Detail — from those traditions in newly-written poetry may be a consequence of this. Because, as Ricoeur (1987:33-34) concludes when discussing modernist attitudes towards plot-making, without reference to accumulated tradition it would be impossible to see how the new style differed from the old.

The phenomenon of encyclopaedic literature as such was far from new, as we have seen, but the main difference between its twentieth-century expressions and those of previous times was that the former had taken place in the context of what was perceived as a much more radical break with the past, on the one hand, and a sense of a transitional errantry through a modern, fragmented landscape of chaos and uncertainty, on the other.[101]

The works of the war poets are formally less experimental and more focussed on external, palpable experiences. At the same time, they offer as clear a version of ironic myth as the modernists did. The tendency to look to nature for universal significance; the use of the narrative traditions of the past to convey experiences foreign to 'normal' life; the soldier's identification with the questing knight; the consciousness of a break with the past; the uncertain boundaries between death and life; the superstitions and alleged miracles; the use of an ironic language due to the difficulties of expressing the otherwise inexpressible

---

101 Moretti (1996:5) claims that this is the reason why the modern epics are "flawed masterpieces: revealing an antagonism between noun and adjective; a discrepancy between the totalizing will of the epic and the subdivided reality of the modern world."

and unbelievable events... All of this is reflected in their poetry and is intimately connected to ironic myth.

Fussell (1975:131) interprets the poetry of the war poets in Frye's terms, stating that its general movement "was towards myth, towards a revival of the cultic, the mystical, the sacrificial, the prophetic, the sacramental, and the universally significant," and sees in the war memoirs, like those of Graves, Sassoon and Blunden, a clearly transitional trait:

> [...] for all the blunt violence they depict, they seem so delicately transitional, pointing at once in two opposite directions – back to the low mimetic, forward to the ironic and – most interestingly – to that richest kind of irony proposing [...] a renewed body of rituals and myths. (Fussell 1975:82)

Ironic myth may not have been a direct consequence of the Great War only, but, if we consider it a latent condition in the development of modernity, it was at least accelerated by it.

Another salient characteristic of the works of ironic myth is that they are not always easily accessible to the critics and to the general reading audience. Fussell (1975:82) feels that the strong dichotomies present in the war poetry deprive it of artistic credibility, while the arguments against modernist poetry usually centre on their elitistic character – not only do they take for granted an elevated erudition on behalf of the reader, they also assume that (s)he is familiar with the author's personal taste or opinions.[102] For this reason, the intended meaning of the juxtaposition of images does not always transcend. These works, in spite of their self-referential pretensions, do not depend on themselves only, since they do not combine the past with the present *in their own terms* in order to efficiently transmit a vision of the present state of Western civilization and its particular characteristics.

On the other hand, not everybody agreed with the modernists' vision of reality. Craig (1968:205), for example, says that *The Waste Land* shows "an impos-

---

102 See Witemeyer (1981:11) on Pound: "[...] the mere presentation of a fact, a name, or an allusion is meant to convey a highly complex evaluation but often fails to do so because the reader is not privy to Pound's personal ratiocinations [...] When Pound says '*Turned from the eau-forte/Par Jacquemart*', not only do we need to know that he is referring to the frontispiece of the 1884 edition of Gautier's *Emaux et Camées*, we also need to know what he thought of Gautier's achievement in that book, if we are to evaluate Hugh Selwyn Mauberley's allegiances. The dangers of this method are obvious." See also Gross (1974:21) on Joyce.

sibly partial outlook on culture," because it presents the past as more desirable than the present. Craig adds: "History, reality, are being manipulated to fit an escapist kind of prejudice."

Leaving aside the questions generated by such an argument – what reality is being manipulated? – Craig's response recalls much negative criticism accusing *The Lord of the Rings* of exhibiting an intolerable escapism.[103] We will soon see how Tolkien defended himself against such accusations, but before doing so, we will take a look at two poetical works written at the time Tolkien worked on *The Lord of the Rings*, namely T.S. Eliot's *Four Quartets* (1935-1943) and David Jones's *In Parenthesis* (1937). These two works show a substantial modification of the modernists' initial literary response to post-war modernity, and they might help us shed some light on Tolkien's particular version of ironic myth.

The cases of *In Parenthesis* and *Four Quartets*

Just like Robert Graves and Siegfried Sassoon, David Jones served in the *Royal Welsh Fusiliers* during the Great War, and the experiences in the battle of the Somme provide the subject matter for his long poem *In Parenthesis*, published more than twenty years later. This work shows far greater affinities with modernist technique than with the works of the war poets, as Jones mixes images of the present with fragments of the past and incorporates many allusions to literature from previous cultural traditions. The style is half-way between prose and poetry, as in T.S. Eliot's poetry or in Joyce's prose.

Jones argues that the experiences in the Great War were fundamentally "mysterious", and that they triggered a consciousness of the past in the imagination of the soldiers. In his introduction to *In Parenthesis*, Jones says:

> [...] I think the day by day in the Waste Land, the sudden violences and the long stillnesses, the sharp contours and unformed voids of that mysterious existence, profoundly affected the imagination of those who suffered it. It was a place of enchantment. [...] I suppose at no time did one so much live with a consciousness of the past, the very remote, and the more immediate and trivial past, both superficially and more subtly. (Featherstone 1995:240)

---

103 For a summary of the critical reactions to Tolkien's work, see Hammond (1996).

Jones also perceived a particularly British spirit among the soldiers of his unit, in which Londoners and Welshmen mingled – "These came from London. Those from Wales. Together they bore in their bodies the genuine tradition of the Island of Britain" (Featherstone 1995:240) – which will have a profound impact on his poetic vision.[104]

In *In Parenthesis*, Jones shows this peculiar 'Britishness' by means of allusions to the history and mythology of different Northern European communities. However, the way in which he incorporates the images from the past is very different from the technique used in other modernist poetry, like Eliot's *The Waste Land*, or Pound's *Hugh Selwyn Mauberley*. The simultaneity in this poem does not arise from an ironic juxtaposition of images, but through a profound sense of how the soldiers *themselves* embody and internalize the different traditions. The sequence showing the soldiers at rest in a grove ("as undiademed / princes turn their gracious profiles in a hidden seal, so did / these appear, under the changing light") and receiving presents from "The Queen of Woods", reveals the simultaneous combination of past and present features that Jones perceived in his comrades-in-arms:

> Some she gives white berries
> Some she gives brown
> Emil has a curious crown it's made of golden saxifrage.
> Fatty wears sweet-briar, he will reign with her for a thousand years.
> For Balder she reaches high to fetch his.
> Ulrich smiles for his myrtle wand.
>   That swine Lillywhite has daisies to his chain – you'd hardly credit it.
>   She plaits torques of equal splendour for Mr. Jenkins and Billy Crower.
>   Hansel and Gronwy share dog-violets for a palm, where
>   They lie in serious embrace beneath the twisted tripod.
> (Featherstone 1995:159-160)

The atemporal community is exposed to the modern conditions of the Great War, firmly situated in twentieth-century history, but it does not lose its status as a catalyst for British traditions – rather are these traits reinforced by the conditions of the war. In Jones's vision, the traditions are not reduced to

---

[104] In Featherstone's (1995:37) view, "[Jones] finds in the trenches an essential Britishness, which had been displaced in England itself by industrialism, imperialism and a debased public rhetoric. Unlike other English nationalists, Jones recognizes such a culture as a present reality rather than a historical remnant, and his poetry creates a discourse through which to express its complexity."

the strictly autochthonous: the names in the quotation – Emil, Fatty, Balder, Ulrich, Lillywhite, Jenkins, Crower, Hansel, Gronwy – show their different origins,[105] though all represent traditions belonging to Northern Europe that, in Jones's opinion, have been part of the development of the present British identity.

According to Featherstone (1995:35), in *In Parenthesis*, as opposed to the dominant nationalist attitude, derived to a great extent from imperialist thinking, "Englishness becomes no longer a dominant ideology which marginalizes other cultures, but an acknowledgement of cultural and historical plurality." In this way, the ruralism present in the works of earlier poets such as Rupert Brooke, Thomas Hardy, Ivor Gurney and Edward Thomas, among others, which was part of a discourse foreign to imperialist values, is in Jones's poetry extended to a realm beyond England, embracing and evoking a wider set of interrelated traditions. In his imagination, the strictly modern scenery of the Great War is transformed into an atemporal setting where the present is so firmly rooted in the past that the soldiers acquire, simultaneously, features of a vast historical and cultural legacy:[106]

> Tunicled functionaries signify and clear-voiced heralds cry
> and leg it to a safe distance
>   leave fairway for the Paladins, and Roland throws a kiss –
>   they've nabbed his batty for the moppers-up
>   and Mr. Jenkins takes them over
> and don't bunch on the left
> for Christ's sake. (Featherstone 1995:157)

The absence of ironic effects is worth noticing; the blend of colloquial and classical terminology is not presented as a grotesque contrast between a glorious past and a sordid, trivial present, but rather as something natural.

Jones also makes consistent use of nature as a force that protects the soldiers and yields coherence to the atemporality of his vision. In the first quota-

---

105 Balder is a god from Norse mythology (not in vain, the Queen of Woods must reach far to get his plant – the mistletoe, which in the myth was used by Loki to kill him); Hansel belongs to German folklore; Ulrich is a Germanic name; Lillywhite, Jenkins etc. are English and Gronwy is Welsh.
106 In Bergonzi's (1993:183) words, Jones "was fascinated by myth, though by native rather than classical mythology. [He was interested in] literature, history, mythology, theology and archaeology, and in his consciousness these subjects were interpreted in terms of, or used to interpret, his wartime memories, which he turned into a personal mythology."

tion from the poem, we saw how the soldiers acquire the shape of princes as they sit under the trees, and in another scene, while they are preparing an attack, the birds offer a soothing contrast to the machinery of war: "In regions of air above the trajectory zone, the birds / chattering heard for all the drum-fire / counter the malice of the engines" (Featherstone 1995:151). In *In Parenthesis*, as in the traditional war poetry, nature helps the soldier to find a meaning in a destructive present, but it also rationalizes its own atemporal simultaneity.

T.S. Eliot uses a similar approach to the simultaneity of tradition in *Four Quartets*, a cycle of long poems, which shows the evolution of his poetry since *The Waste Land*. In *Four Quartets*, Eliot has softened the incorporation of allusions and images considerably, so that his vision of the atemporality/ simultaneity, in which the juxtapositions no longer produce ironic effects, becomes much more harmonious.[107] This is, to some extent, a result of the narrator's voice, more unitarian than the fragmented babbling of the *The Waste Land*. In *Four Quartets*, the poet speaks with one voice that assimilates previous traditions instead of reproducing, like a chaotic medium, apparently disconnected voices. The difference can be seen by looking at examples from the two works, the first of which is taken from *The Waste Land*:

>A crowd flowed over London Bridge, so many,
>I had not thought death had undone so many
>[...]
>There I saw one I knew, and stopped him, crying:
>   'Stetson!
>'You who were with me in the ships at Mylae!
>'That corpse you planted last year in your garden,
>'Has it begun to sprout? Will it bloom this year?
>   'Or has the sudden frost disturbed its bed?
>   'Oh keep the dog far hence, that's a friend to men,
>   'Or with his nails he'll dig it up again!
>   'You! Hypocrite lecteur! – mon semblamble – mon frère!'
>   (Eliot 1999:25)[108]

---

[107] Traversi (1976:89) believes that the references in *Four Quartets* "no longer stand out or need to be identified by appending notes to elucidate the poetry. They have been, as it were, assimilated into the body of a continuing meditative discourse [...] The sense of the poetry as proceeding from a single voice reflecting a continuous but expanding point of view is central to Eliot's conception in the *Quartets*."

[108] 'The Burial of the Dead', lines 62-76.

The quotidian image of the traffic on London Bridge is radically juxtaposed with a quotation from Dante's *Inferno*, as Eliot explains in a note. Immediately after this, the poet meets a contemporary English man, Stetson, but on the next line we are informed that this man was with the poet at a historical moment of Classical Antiquity. The notes – inherent to the poem – tell us that the next reference is an allusion to Webster's *White Devil*, and that the final exclamation belongs to the preface to Baudelaire's *Fleurs du Mal*.

Compared to the overwhelming amount of references, allusions and ironic juxtapositions that voice frustration and fracture, in 'East Coker', the second poem of *Four Quartets*, Eliot presents the atemporality/simultaneity of a rural village with a much smoother approach to the transitions:

>   [...] Now the light falls
> Across the open field, leaving the deep lane
> Shuttered with branches, dark in the afternoon,
> Where you can lean against a bank while a van passes,
> And the deep lane insists on the direction
> Into the village, in the electric heat
> Hypnotised. In a warm haze the sultry light
> Is absorbed, not refracted, by grey stone.
> The dahlias sleep in the empty silence.
> Wait for the early owl.
>
>   In that open field
> If you do not come too close, if you do not come too close,
> On a summer midnight, you can hear the music
> Of the weak pipe and the little drum
> And see them dancing around the bonfire
> The association of man and woman
> In daunsinge, signifying matrimonie –
>   A dignified and commodious sacrament.
>   Two and two, necessarye coniunction,
>   Holding eche other by the hand or the arm
>   Whiche betokeneth concorde. [...] (Eliot 1970:177-178)

Like Jones, Eliot uses nature as a backdrop which generates simultaneity. The road on which the van travels leads on to the village, where the old grey stones *absorb* the light instead of refracting it. This is the key: Eliot does not pretend to offer fragmented (refracted) images, but a natural *assimilation* of tradition. In this way, the transition itself becomes natural.

After showing us the picture of a contemporary village, the poet goes on to describe the nature associated with it: the sleeping flowers, the imminent call of the owl. Then, there is a blank line, after which follows a curious statement: if we remain at a certain distance from the field, we may be able to witness a dance around a bonfire, where men and women move in "daunsinge, signifying matrimonie." The Middle English ortography and choice of words is preceded by a smooth transition, made possible by a description of nature based on tangible visual images that give coherence and direction to the scene. For this reason, the voice of the poet does not seem fragmented to us; we perceive it rather as one voice capable of hosting and expressing many others.[109]

The central theme of 'The Dry Salvages', the third poem of the sequence, is, in Traversi's (1976:152) words, "man's journey in time: that of the individual engaged in recovering the instinctive, half-conscious memories of the human past." We might conclude that this is the predominant theme of the whole cycle. In the first poem, 'Burnt Norton', the poet says: "Footfalls echo in the memory / Down the passage which we did not take," and, a little later, "Other echoes / Inhabit the garden. Shall we follow?" And in 'Little Gidding', the last of the poems, the poet claims that "We shall not cease from exploration / And the end of all our exploring / Will be to arrive where we started / And know the place for the first time."[110]

In spite of the fact that the theme is recurrent in Eliot's poetry, there are important differences between the Eliot of 1922 and the Eliot who composed *Four Quartets*. In general, these late works of Jones and Eliot show an approach to ironic myth which is slightly modified compared to the initial modernist stance, describing a movement towards a coherent and harmonious simultaneity, in which the description of nature as an atemporal element contributes to the shaping of the identity of a civilization that, though most people do not see it, is significantly imbued with the accumulated traditions of the past.

---

[109] Of the different voices in the poem, Murray (1994:237) highlights "the confident voice of the Christian ascetic, and the calm voice of human reason [but] we hear also the trembling, questioning voice of 'the wayfarer' and the sceptical voice of the urbane modern philosopher, and the voice of the confused and frightened human individual."

[110] In Traversi's (1976:213) opinion, this sequence shows that "[l]ife in time [...] is to be regarded in terms of a voyage of discovery: a voyage, however, the end of which is to bring us back to the initial moment [...] which we now see in the light of the intervening development as having a new, a more universal significance."

As Eliot says in 'Little Gidding':

> [...] A people without history
> Is not redeemed from time, for history is a pattern
> Of timeless moments. So, while the light fails
> On a winter's afternoon, in a secluded chapel
> History is now and England. (Eliot 1970:197)

Twentieth-century England is, thus, the sum of its traditions, and these, as the late poetry of Jones and Eliot shows, may be portrayed without the need to juxtapose fragmented images from the past and the present.

In *The Lord of the Rings*, the different traditions that have moulded the present-day English character and culture are also presented on a simultaneous level. However, the presentation, and the interaction between the traditions, is very different. We will now try and put Tolkien's work in the context of the Great War and the literary manifestations of ironic myth.

3.3. Tolkien, Modernity and *Ironic Myth*

It is common knowledge that Tolkien began working on his mythology while recovering from trench fever, as early as 1916.[111] In the years that followed he became a distinguished scholar at Oxford University, and he kept up an extensive correspondence with his sons when they fought in the Second World War. Those who accuse Tolkien of escapism tend to overlook the fact that such a curriculum vitae would make it virtually impossible for him to remain ignorant of the events that changed the world and the literature in the first half of the twentieth century and not in some way to reflect in his own literature.

The Lord of the Rings and the Great War

In spite of the dislike Tolkien felt for allegory,[112] I consider that one of the most important connections between the First World War and *The Lord of*

---

111 Garth (2003) offers a complete account of Tolkien's experiences in the First World War, and their relationship to the genesis of his legendarium. For a summary, see Carpenter (2000:80-94).
112 See Tolkien's preface (first published in 1966) to the revised edition of *The Lord of the Rings* (Tolkien 1993), in which he underscores the lack of allegorical intentions in the work, with reference to the *applicability* of the story, which gives rise to different possible interpretations.

the Rings[113] rests on the plot itself, given that its structure generates a literary expression similar to that of the First World War narrative, as expressed in the works of the war poets.

As for the formal similarities, the story begins in the Shire, a rural region of limited dimensions, isolated from the rest of the world. The Shire is a synthesis of an idealized image of rural England in late Victorian and Edwardian times (Flieger 1997:7), shared by many during the years prior to the war.[114] The idyll is threatened by a dark power that aims to destroy the world with the use of technology and military force, and to build a new civilization from the ashes of the previous. The old civilization is forced to an armed response to the threat. The hobbits of the Fellowship, who can be seen as representatives of the people of the Shire (and, by analogy, the fundamental values of the idealized rural England) become involved in a conflict marked by a destruction of people and lands by technological means – a conflict so massive that the hobbits hardly give credit to what they see, experiencing a strong nostalgia for their home and the past. The forces of Mordor are portrayed as a brute, repugnant and dark force, a threatening mass of monsters with an identity that does not reach beyond the concept of the 'Enemy'.[115]

Apart from this, the general feeling that a cycle, the Third Age, is coming to an end with the War of the Ring, and that a new age of unknown characteristics will begin after the apocalypse, permeates the whole narrative, giving it a marked sense of transition. The stormy passage from one era to another is reflected by Frodo's mission, which in many ways is similar to the quest

---

113 For an exhaustive study of Tolkien's work in the context of the impact of the Great War on the literary imagination as outlined by Fussell (1975), see Croft (2004).
114 Featherstone (1995:25-29) claims that there were two basic types of discourse about English identity in the times prior to the Great War: 'militarist patriotism', related to imperialist ideas, and 'ruralism'. In Featherstone's opinion, the image that best showed the second attitude, which was made popular by Hardy in *The Dynasts*, is that of a small rural community that represents the nation in the face of a foreign threat. See also Hopkins (2003:171-178). The great popularity of Kenneth Grahame's *The Wind in The Willows* (1908), that shows idealized sceneries and rural communities struggling to preserve the order, is indicative of the power and attraction of such themes and imagery in the years immediately preceding the war.
115 While the forces of Mordor are thus portrayed, there are also many nuanced portraits of 'enemies' in Tolkien's work, like Saruman, Gollum, Gríma and Denethor. Such portraits prevent a simple dichotomy between 'Good' and 'Bad' from dominating the characterization.

romance. He and his helpers, just like the Enemy, all play a creative part in the process of destruction and renewal. However, as opposed to prose romances like *The Well at the World's End*, Frodo in the end completes his mission almost in spite of himself, and once the Ring is destroyed he is unable to enjoy the glories of victory, forever marked as he is by the transitory 'limbo' between the two ages, symbolized by the War of the Ring.

One example of the change of mentality and perception that takes place in periods of transition is the narrator's use of hobbit poetry, tracing a movement from innocence and carefree stability to uncertainty and frustration. This makes it similar to the development of Georgian poetry, a poetic school showing certain affinities to the Romantic movement of the previous century,[116] that appeared shortly before the war. We will look at two examples. The first is taken from a poem by Rupert Brooke, representative of the jocose and trivial attitude usually associated with the literature of Edwardian times, titled 'The Little Dog's Day'. The poem is about a dog that makes a pact with the gods Odin and Thor saying that it may do whatever it pleases during one day, on the condition that it will die at the end of the day. Said and done, the dog provokes a terrible brawl, disturbing the whole village:

> He took sinewy lumps from the shins of old frumps
> And mangled the errand-boys – when he could get 'em
> He shammed furious rabies, and bit all the babies,
> And followed the cats up the tree, and then ate 'em!
> (Driver 1996:30)

Finally, the day ends and the dog dies, and that is the end of the poem too. It is a humorous sort of verse with a rural theme, expressed in a simple, quotidian and jovial language, which creates a folk-tale atmosphere with a direct and unpolished humor, based on burlesque scenes and situations.

---

116 Reeves (1968:xv) says about Georgian poetry that it had a markedly popular character, expressed rural sentiments and discussed typically English matters: "The celebration of England, whether at peace or at war, became a principal aim of Georgian poetry. The English countryside, English crafts, and English sports offered suitable subject-matter. Poems about country cottages, old furniture, moss-covered barns, rose-scented lanes, apple and cherry orchards, village inns, and village cricket expressed the nostalgia of the soldier on active service and the threat to country life which educated readers feared from the growth of urbanism." Reeves's anthology features poetry by Rupert Brooke, Walter De la Mare, John Masefield, Ivor Gurney, Edward Thomas, Robert Graves, Siegfried Sassoon and Wilfred Owen, among others.

We find something quite close to this in Bilbo's song 'The Merry Old Inn', that Frodo sings at The Prancing Pony. 'The Merry Old Inn' is about a rural inn that is visited one night by the Man in the Moon, who wants to try the famous local beer. At the inn there is a cat that plays the violin, a dog that laughs at jokes, and a dancing cow. The Man in the Moon takes a slug of the beer and falls asleep under the table, endangering the arrival of the new day. The animals, inspired by the inn-keeper, try to wake him up:

> Now quicker the fiddle went deedle dum-diddle;
>   the dog began to roar
> The cow and the horses stood on their heads;
> The guests all bounded from their beds
>   and danced upon the floor.
>
> With a ping and a pong the fiddle-strings broke!
>   the cow jumped over the Moon,
> And the little dog laughed to see such fun,
> And the Saturday dish went off at a run
>   with the silver Sunday spoon. (Tolkien 1993:176)[117]

The song ends with the Man in the Moon back on the Moon where he belongs and the sun coming up.

The burlesque situations, the jocose tone, the popular language, the exclamations and the use of natural cycles as a temporal framework make the similarities with Brooke's poem obvious. It is also significant that both poems were composed before the start of the conflict that changed the world – the Great War and the War of the Ring, respectively – i.e. at a time when when it still made sense to write such poetry. The narrator of *The Lord of the Rings* even states, as an introduction to the song, that "Only a few words of it are now, as a rule, remembered". (*LotR*, 174)

The contrast with the poem 'Roads' by Edward Thomas, another poet writing about matters of the English countryside and who also participated – and died – in the Great War, is notable. This poem is marked by a pastoral and elegiac tone and it ponders the places to which roads may lead us, and their permanence beyond the brief scope of time that man spends on Earth:

---

117 Henceforth, I will refer to this edition as *LotR*.

> Roads go on
> While we forget, and are
> Forgotten like a star
> That shoots and is gone
>
> The next turn may reveal
> Heaven: upon the crest
> The close pine clump, at rest
> And black, may Hell conceal
>
> Often footsore, never
> Yet of the road I weary
> Though long and steep and dreary
> As it winds on forever

The poet then compares the roads of different mythologies, contrasting them with the present ones, which lead to France and the war: "Now all roads lead to France / And heavy is the tread / Of the living; but the dead / Returning lightly dance; // Whatever the road bring / To me or take from me / They keep me company / With their pattering." (Driver 1996:48-49)

The ambiguity of this poem, written after the beginning of the war, brings about an elegiac tone which takes it far from the attitude expressed in poems such as 'The Little Dog's Day'. In this, and in many other aspects, it recalls 'The Road Goes Ever On', another song that Frodo sings as the hobbits approach the borders of the Shire.

> The Road goes ever on and on
>   Down from the door where it began,
> Now far ahead the Road has gone,
>   And I must follow, if I can,
>
> Pursuing it with weary feet
>   Until it joins some larger way
> Where many paths and errands meet.
>   And whither then? I cannot say. (*LotR*, 86-87)

Just like Thomas's poem, the song shows a very different attitude compared to the jolliness of Bilbo's inn-song, or the bathing song that the hobbits sing at Crickhollow. This song also features a melancholy, almost elegiac tone: the hobbits will have to follow the road, leading them where it may. Frodo, who at this moment believes he will be travelling east alone, suspects that he will leave his beloved Shire never to come back, and that the world, from this moment on, will not be the same. This is indeed what happens. Frodo does come back, but he is not the same as he used to be: the world has changed, and he has changed with it. Having been intimately associated with the Ring, and the Third Age, he disappears little by little from the narration when his mission is accomplished, and the Fourth Age begins.

In a sense, Frodo as a character reflects the disillusionment among many people after the Great War, an attitude which questions a basic cornerstone of spiritual well-being – is this world worth fighting for? Frodo seems to be affected by the same kind of melancholy, already before he knows that he will be going West with the elves. Frodo's looking down the road in doubt is premonitory of later events: when the hobbits return home after having participated in a bloody war that marks the end of an era and the beginning of another, the Shire has turned into a sad dystopia under the hand of Saruman (or 'Sharky' as he is called after his debacle at Isengard). Saruman has brought modernity to the region, establishing a regime of oppression and exploitation that inspires only sadness and defeatism among the people. However, Tolkien subverts the classic pessimistic stance of the war poets and the modernists. The hobbits returning from war rebel against the general disillusionment,[118] bring down Saruman's dictatorship and reinstate the old order.

Is this an escapist or simplistic vision of reality? Not necessarily. In the first place, it is a challenge to the apathy concerning the negative aspects of modernity that Tolkien perceived in the writers of his times; a protest that he considered necessary at a time when the world was seriously threatened by what he perceived as the ugliest faces of modernity, such as fascism, nazism, and stalinism, as well as the first signs of exhaustion of the natural resources. It is also a response with several nuances. Frodo – whom I perceive as the most interesting character in this context, embodying and expressing the traditions of the whole cycle which is coming to an end – does not share his friends' enthusiasm for the redemption of the lost paradise, and the Elves remind him that nothing will last forever, not even the Shire. This, among other things, is a clear example of the transitory spirit that informs the literature of ironic myth.

---

118 In Cantor's (1993:212-213) view, Tolkien and C.S. Lewis showed "a more positive response to these conditions and events than the postimperial stoicism, cultural despair, and resigned Christian pessimism that were the common response of their British contemporaries [...] Out of the medieval Norse, Celtic, and Grail legends they conjured fantasies of revenge and recovery, an ethos of return and triumph." See also Veldman (1994).

Apart from the narrative of the Great War, Tolkien also occasionally takes recourse to a traditional language in order to express the experiences of Frodo (the principal narrator of the story), and he refrains from exposing the narrative to excessive formal experimentations that otherwise would have made it more difficult for many readers to read and understand. However, the language (we should really speak of the langua*ges*) used by Tolkien is much more versatile and dynamic than that of the war poets. There is a continuous and persistent mediation between different traditions that, in my opinion, lays the foundation for the dialogues, the descriptions, the different narrative rhythms and the character-drawing, among other things. This simultaneity of narrative and cultural traditions of Northern Europe comes closer to certain modernist strategies.

The Lord of the Rings and Modernism

At a first glance, the differences between Tolkien's work and that of the modernists we have studied may seem irreconcilable. The formal experimentation of the modernists, with the inclusion of rhetorical resources such as the stream of consciousness, the juxtaposition of poetic images, the deliberately chaotic perception and description of reality, the elitistic selection of allusions and references, together with the absence of any firm moral standards, the fascination for the effects of modernity on the human mind, such as irrationalism, fragmentation and frustration, are all aspects of modernism that Tolkien implicitly questions and attacks in *The Lord of the Rings*.

At the same time, the similarities to other characteristics of modernism are also conspicuous.[119] Tolkien shares with Joyce an obsession with the creative potentiality of words and the opinion that language makes up the foundation for all civilizations. In fact, Tolkien goes much further than Joyce in this, not necessarily because of a superior erudition or more refined linguistic skills – though his widely recognized prominence as a scholar rested on both qualities – but as a result of his particular narrative strategy, which centered on drawing an entire mythological world out of the fertile soil of invented

---

119 For a comparison between the modernists' concept of Art for Art's sake and Tolkien's, see Mortimer (2005).

words and languages, instead of the other way around.[120] In other words, the geography, the characters, the history, the mythology and – as a logical extension of these – even the general design of the plot in *The Lord of the Rings*, all emerge from the obsession with creating a credible context for the invented languages.[121]

In order to achieve internal coherence, the invented world needed to be self-referential. In the works of Joyce, Eliot and Pound we see how the allusions and quotations are selected so as to give shape to a closed entity which is not supposed to depend on any external references. Here, too, Tolkien proposes a different solution. While the former built on myths and concrete works of different traditions, Tolkien 'invented'[122] the whole mythological, cultural and narrative context for his own references, though these almost always present important similarities to real traditions from the Western world. Traversi (1976: 182-183) says that T.S Eliot had to invent his own symbolical structures, "rather as though Milton had needed to invent the story of the Fall before writing *Paradise Lost* or Dante to work out the details of his cosmic scheme before writing his poem." To be sure, this is exactly what Tolkien does, but on a far vaster and more elaborate scale than Eliot. Tolkien uses *The Silmarillion*, a work that collects parts of the mythology of Middle-earth, and other stories set in the same world, such as *The Hobbit*, as *meta-texts* (Segura 2004:27-42); but, as opposed to the modernist works we have studied, *The Lord of the Rings* does not depend on a knowledge of the sources in order to be properly understood (though it is true that such knowledge *enriches* the narrative). When in *The Waste Land* or *Ulysses* we come across a quotation, the poet may or may not declare where it comes from, but in any case, the reader needs to be familiar with the work, the artist or the character referred to if the allusion is to be invested with meaning.

---

120 Segura (2004:33-34) offers a concise account of this process.
121 For scholarly studies of Tolkien's invented languages, see Noel (1980), González (1999), and Salo (2004).
122 Tolkien always claimed that he did not invent anything, but "discovered" what was already there. In Carpenter's (2000:102) words, "As the years went by, he came more and more to regard his own invented languages and stories as 'real' languages and historical chronicles that needed to be elucidated. In other words, when in this mood he did not say of an apparent contradiction in the narrative or an unsatisfactory name: 'This is not as I wish it to be; I must change it.' Instead he would approach the problem with the attitude: 'What does this mean? I must discover it.'" See also *Letters*, 145.

In *The Lord of the Rings*, the treatment is different.[123] The references to previous traditions are in most cases integrated in a harmonious and natural way. The allusions to the literature or to historical events of Middle-earth are revealed to us through songs, poems or tales, well contextualized, and contribute to the coherence and depth of the world, instead of shaping a world-vision with emphasis on fragmentation, absurdity and chaos by means of ironic juxtapositions. An example of how Tolkien integrates traditions in his narrative is when Sam, after hearing Aragorn mention the name Gil-galad in relation to Weathertop, which they are approaching, recites part of a song about this historical-mythological character. Aragorn then explains that it was not Bilbo who wrote the song, as Sam thinks, but that it is part of the lay called *The Fall of Gil-galad*, composed in an ancient tongue (only a few pages later, Aragorn also sings the tale of Tinúviel, and when he has finished he gives a full account of the story's context).

This contextualization of references and allusions is, together with the absence of intentional irony, a fundamental feature of Tolkien's work that makes it very different from the creations of writers and poets like Joyce and Eliot. It is a consequence of the voluntary invention of the secondary world, of which no reader can have previous notions.

Eliot's *Four Quartets*, and Jones's *In Parenthesis* come closer to Tolkien's vision, mainly because of their apparent lack of ironically imbued contrasts and their use of natural images to integrate the simultaneity of traditions within characters and places. *Middle-earth* is also a natural setting that is able to accommodate the different traditions on a simultaneous level. Furthermore, Jones portrays in *In Parenthesis* an open-minded nationalism that admits a variety of traditions from Northern Europe as inherent to the British essence,[124] while Eliot considers it fundamental to renew our perception of the world by enhancing our consciousness of the preceding traditions.

---

123 For a thorough explanation of Tolkien's mythical method, see Honegger (2006).
124 Tolkien shared with Jones the purpose of revitalizing the perception of the world and the multicultural vision of the English essence (*Letters*, 144-145). Shippey (2003), in his Appendix 'A' ('Tolkien's Sources: the True Tradition', pp. 343-352), offers a survey of the works that in his opinion inspired Tolkien most, mentioning *Beowulf*, *Voluspá* of the *Elder or Poetic Edda*, Sturluson's *Prose Edda*, and the *Tales* of the Grimm brothers, among others.

The literary, encyclopaedic strain of ironic myth is as evident in *The Lord of the Rings* as it is in the modernists' work, and here too, we find a 'return' to mythical structures and themes. As for the irony, Tolkien, in linking his work to modernity and its problems through the story's *applicability* – which I believe is achieved to a great extent by the particular intertraditional dialogue in the narrative – ensures effects that are similar to the ironic juxtapositions of the images of Eliot, Pound and Joyce, with the important difference that the irony is not intended, nor an internal part of the narrative, but *external* to it. References to our own world are not explicit, and we perceive the possible irony (an interpretation which in any case depends on the reader, not on the author's conscious attempt at conveying ironic contrasts) only when comparing Middle-earth with our own world and its present conditions. In this sense, in Tolkien's work (as in Eliot's) we may also speak of contrasts that really are parellelisms, and parallelisms that are turned into contrasts.

The Secondary World in context

Because of these technical procedures, structure and themes, I deem it safe to say that *The Lord of the Rings* can be read as yet another example of ironic myth. However, Tolkien's particular approach to this literary mode often obscures the similarities. Apart from the obvious influence of his academic and personal interests, one of the factors that distanced Tolkien from modernist ways of expression was that he never accepted their view of the post-war human condition as a state marked by frustration, desolation, uncertainty or hopelessness, as the only possible stance to confront and portray the conditions of modernity in literature. The modernists, on the other hand, tended to *accept* the chaotic state of affairs, and this attitude conditioned even the late poetic expressions of Eliot and Jones, in which the simultaneity of traditions does not reach the same degree of autonomy, flexibility and self-exploration as in *The Lord of the Rings*.

In Tolkien's perhaps most famous essay, *On Fairy-Stories*, there is a particularly illuminating passage that shows the author's attitude towards literature and modernity:

> We may indeed be older now, in so far as we are heirs in enjoyment or in practice of many generations of ancestors in the arts. In this inheritance of

> wealth there may be a danger of boredom or of anxiety to be original, and that may lead to a distaste for fine drawing, delicate pattern, and 'pretty' colours, or else to mere manipulation and over-elaboration of old material, clever and heartless. But the true road of escape from such weariness is not to be found in the wilfully awkward, clumsy, or misshapen, not in making all things dark or unremittingly violent; nor in the mixing of colours on through subtlety to drabness, and the fantastical complication of shapes to the point of silliness and on towards delirium. Before we reach such states we need recovery. We should look at green again, and be startled anew (but not blinded) by blue and yellow and red [...] This recovery fairy-stories help us to make. [...] (Tolkien 1966:76-77)

Tolkien seems to say that some modern literature is unable to recover a fresh perception of reality due to its excessive formal experimentation and the attention to the negative details of modernity. He speaks of the need to avoid this apathetic attitude towards tradition and modernity, stating that fairy tales, as he understands the term, may help us renew our perception of the world and see new possibilities.

In the same essay we find Tolkien's response to the accusations of escapism in his work,[125] in which he relates the concept of escape to a prisoner who is trying to flee. According to Tolkien (1966:79), those who criticize the attitude of the prisoner who "thinks and talks of other topics than jailers and prison-walls [...] confound the escape of the prisoner with the flight of the deserter." He adds: "To such thinking you have only to say 'the land you love is doomed' to excuse any treachery, indeed to glorify it." (Tolkien 1966:79-80)

Tolkien wanted to make clear that fairy tales, for him, were a tool to avoid the defeatism that he saw as the trademark of contemporary literature and literary criticism. He did not accept the course that the modern world had taken and wished to recover a vision of the world that had disappeared.

---

125 The question of escapism has been at the centre of most of the polemic debates regarding the literary value of *The Lord of the Rings*. Negative criticism, tending to view Tolkien's work as little more than juvenile and escapist entertainment, reaches back to the 1950s and belongs mostly to representatives or inheritors of the school of New Criticism that arose with modernism (see, for example, the articles by Edmund Wilson, in *The Nation*, April 4, 1956, and Philip Toynbee, in *The Observer*, August 6, 1961), whose influence is also present in the criticism of Manlove (1978) and Jackson (1981). On the other hand, C. S. Lewis's early reviews and, more recently, the works of Curry (1997), Flieger (1997), Pearce (1998), Shippey (2002), and Segura (2004), among others, prove that the accusation of escapism in Tolkien's work is the result of a narrow critical outlook that wilfully excludes the applicability of the tales to modern times. For a summary of the different critical reactions to *The Lord of the Rings*, see Hammond (1996).

Campbell (1997:227) perceives the problem from a psychoanalytical perspective, referring to the need to look to the inspired past in order to illuminate lost areas of iconography, as long as the modern age is reflected in such images. This solution was adopted by Joyce, Pound and Eliot, as we have seen. T.S. Eliot was conscious of the need to reinvigorate the old truths in the face of spiritual unease, and to create a proper system of symbols based on references to the 'inspired past' in order to communicate his message to modernity. We have also seen the disadvantages of this method.

Tolkien looked for a different way of reintegrating the forgotten iconography in his literary works which would avoid the fatal combination of "over-elaboration of old material" and defeatism. As a Christian specialist in Norse mythology and Old English literature, his ideological allegiance may have been divided (Burns 2006:178), but independently of its content, like T.S. Eliot he was conscious that he could not propose a new evangelium completely in the 'old style' if he wished modern readers to relate to it. He felt that he must avoid all explicit reference to Christian dogma and propose a new myth, deeply rooted in the traditions of Northern Europe. The secular myths that emerged in the decades following the war – Soviet marxism, fascism, nazism or neoliberal capitalism (Mardones 2000:141-142) – all seemed to him more or less abominable.[126]

Tolkien did not feel the need to portray modern Western civilization as it was in order to make people see its dangers, perhaps because it was already there, day and night, speaking for itself. The time had come to propose a radically different vision. His alternative was a self-referential 'secondary world'[127] with a proper mythology, in which the different traditions were able to co-exist simultaneously and the past could interact with the present with a certain amount of fluency, in order to renew our vision of the world (Curry 1997:23). This decision is crucial to our understanding of the particularity of Tolkien's vision within the contemporary literary context.

---

[126] For Tolkien's personal opinions on these aspects of modernity, see *Letters* (letters nos. 30, 45, 52, 77, 81, 83, and 100).

[127] Tolkien (1966:60) distinguishes between "Primary World" and "Secondary World", explaining the difference in the following terms: "[...] the story maker [...] makes a Secondary World which your mind can enter. Inside it, what he relates is 'true': it accords with the laws of that world. You therefore believe it, while you are, as it were, inside. The moment disbelief arises, the spell is broken; the magic, or rather art, has failed. You are then out in the Primary World again, looking at the little abortive Secondary World from outside."

Hence, the fact that *Middle-earth* is, formally, a pre-modern world does not mean that it is completely cut off from the twentieth century. In fact, the mere wish to transcend the limits of the modern world is a reflection of modernity.[128] Beriain (2000:152) does not mention Tolkien, but as he outlines what he perceives as the five necessary steps for a 're-enchantment' of the world in modern times, his vision comes very close to some of the central themes expressed in *The Lord of the Rings*. The first step, according to Beriain, is "the reorientation of the world towards nature as habitat-dwelling and not as an object of exploitation"; the second "to reject the unpersonal action of the market and the bureaucracy"; the third to show an "open-minded attitude towards religious and mythological experiences and practices [...] beyond the ecclesiastic institutions that in the Western world have a markedly monotheistic character"; the fourth a "rediscovery of 'meaning' in art and a new aesthetic of quotidian life"; and the fifth "a rediscovery of historical consciousness: from inevitable progress to possible progress".[129] In other words, respect for the natural world, rejection of depersonalized capitalism, admittance of multiple mythologies, aesthetic appreciation for simple things, and sustainable development. It is interesting to notice that *The Lord of the Rings* expresses these impulses[130] more clearly than many of the other contemporary literary works with ambitions of reinvigorating traditions of the past in the present, such as *Four Quartets* or *In Parenthesis*.

The Lord of the Rings is, of course, not the only literary work to reveal and express such attitudes, or, for that matter, the first one to take place in a secondary world. We have already discussed the works of MacDonald and Morris in the nineteenth century, and as for writers of the twentieth century, we may mention authors and works such as David Lindsay (*A Voyage to Arcturus*, 1920), E.R.R. Eddison *(The Worm Ouroboros,* 1922), Lord Dunsany (*The Prince of Elfland's Daughter,* 1924), and Robert E. Howard *(Hour of the Dragon,* 1935).

---

128 Flieger (1997:2) writes that the hobbits are in themselves a response to modernism's response to Victorian ideals, and concludes that Tolkien's treatment of time is emblematic of his age: "[...] his world of Faërie, clothed though it was in the magic of Other Time, reflected the dissociation, dislocation, and psychological ravagement of modern life quite as much as did that of the more obviously mainstream authors who were his contemporaries."
129 My translation.
130 The hobbits are to a great extent catalysts for these 'strategies'. Carretero González (1997) analyses Tolkien's utopian vision of the Shire, highlighting the hobbits' communion with the land they inhabit, their simple cares and pretensions, and their anarchistic (etymologically) and anticapitalist political system, etc. See also Curry (1997).

These works, together with later narratives such as Tolkien's *The Lord of the Rings*, C.S. Lewis's *The Chronicles of Narnia*, Ursula K. LeGuin's *The Earthsea Trilogy*, and Lloyd Alexander's *The Prydain Chronicles*, are usually grouped together as 'high fantasy' or 'heroic fantasy'.

However, apart from the formal aspects, these works are really very different from one another in style and tone, and none of the attempts at generic definition[131] seems to me very satisfying. To place *The Lord of the Rings* in this context is especially unsatisfactory, unless we deliberately choose to see only the fantastic elements as disconnected from contemporary culture, and consciously close our eyes to other features, such as its links to the literature of ironic myth and the re-elaboration of incomplete fragments from different narrative traditions of the past (Tolley 1992) that substantially enrich the narrative. Zanger (1982: 229) is perhaps the one who comes closest when he says that in heroic fantasy, "the value structure of each age is revealed in the characterizations, imagery and metaphors, giving evidence of the social situation that the fantasy retains and transforms".

This is exactly what Tolkien does in *The Lord of the Rings*, but he also does many other things – so many that the work eludes any attempt at a more specific generic classification. Placing his work in the context of ironic myth would account for the presence of features such as the insistent intertraditional dialogue and the self-referential symbolic structure, as well as the work's relevance within the context of twentieth-century culture and literature.

A different dialogue

The quality that makes his vision so particular and different from the other manifestations of ironic myth, on the one hand, and from the works of heroic fantasy, on the other, is the ease and fluency with which the different traditions interact, and the constant exploration of its constraints.

Let us look at an example from the text, taken from the scene describing the meeting of Merry and Pippin with Gandalf, Gimli and Legolas, in the pres-

---

131 See Attebery (1980:12-14), Zanger (1982:226-236), Manlove (1978:1-12), Swinfen (1984:121), and Mathews (2002:2).

ence of King Théoden. After a few formal words of introduction, which we perceive as ironically pompous ("Meriadoc, son of Saradoc, is my name; and my companion, who, alas! is overcome with weariness [...]"), Gimli and Legolas, having risked their lives to save the hobbits, reproach them for their carefree attitude and ask them where they have found the pipe-weed[132] and the wine they are enjoying.

> 'One thing you have not found in your hunting, and that's brighter wits,' said Pippin, opening an eye. 'Here you find us sitting on a field of victory, amid the plunder of armies, and you wonder how we came by a few well-earned comforts!'
>
> 'Well-earned?' said Gimli. 'I cannot believe that!'
>
> The Riders laughed. 'It cannot be doubted that we witness the meeting of dear friends,' said Théoden. 'So these are the lost ones of your company, Gandalf? The days are fated to be filled with marvels. Already I have seen many since I left my house; and now here before my eyes stand yet another of the folk of legend. Are not these the halflings, that some among us call the Holbytlan?'
>
> 'Hobbits, if you please, lord,' said Pippin. (*LotR*, 581)

The conception of the hobbits and the Shire is fundamentally based on the English nineteenth-century novel[133] and culture. They often use irony to express their perception of reality, though they try to modify their language as much as they can when in the presence of characters that hardly comprehend their discourse because of their stubborn allegiance to other traditions. In this case, Gimli and Legolas, characters with certain characteristics of romance, are able to understand the pragmatics of the hobbits and to adopt a language apt for the interaction with them, partly because they have grown used to the hobbits' ways over many hundred pages, partly because romance is a very flexible tradition (see section 2.2, page 42). Théoden, a character with markedly epic traits, while realizing that the insolence of Merry and Pippin is feigned, must express such an insight explicitly (as opposed to Gimli, who plays along) – otherwise the

---

132 Shippey (2003:69) explains that Tolkien avoided the word 'tobacco' for etymological reasons: its roots do not fit in well with the essential Englishness that the words associated with hobbits should have: "'Pipeweed' shows Tolkien's wish to accept a common feature of English modernity, which he knew could not exist in the ancient world of elves or trolls, and whose anachronism would be easily betrayed by a word with the foreign feel of 'tobacco'."
133 For a more thorough discussion of the narrative zone of the Shire, see section 4.1, of the present study (p. 119ff).

reader cannot take for granted that the irony really gets through to the king. Furthermore, Théoden expresses this pragmatic tautology using a relatively elevated diction; that is, without altering his habitual style of speech.

As we can see, the different traditions do not interact with monolithic rigidity, clashing with each other, but are to a great extent flexible (though some more than others), and the dialogue constantly tests the limits of the particular combinations. An example of this exploration is when Merry turns to Théoden to explain the history of smoking in the Shire. The hobbit begins in a quite formal language that soon deteriorates into a very unsuitable colloquial tone:

> '[...] it is an art that we have not practised for more than a few generations. It was Tobold Hornblower, of Longbottom in the Southfarthing, who first grew the true pipe-weed in his gardens, about the year 1070 according to our reckoning. *How old Toby came by the plant...*' (*LotR*, 581)[134]

Gandalf, experienced in Middle-earth pragmatics, takes on the role of mediator and interrupts the intolerably provincial Merry as soon as he notices the hobbit's choice of theme and tone, which he considers very unappropriate for the occasion. Gandalf's comment reveals a discourse capable of addressing, simultaneously, both Merry and Théoden (in other words, the ironic novelistic tradition, represented by the first string of my italicized words in the quotation below, and the solemn epic, expressed by the second):

> 'You do not know your danger, Théoden,' interrupted Gandalf. 'These hobbits will sit on the edge of ruin and discuss the pleasures of the table, or the small doings of their fathers, grandfathers, and great-grandfathers, and remoter cousins *to the ninth degree*, if you *encourage them with undue patience*. Some other time would be more fitting for the history of smoking.' (*LotR*, 581-582)

Gandalf, as opposed to Théoden, does not use a unified discourse, but adapts it to the narrative circumstances of the intertraditional dialogue. Some of the hobbits, like Frodo, will learn to do the same at a later stage of their journey through Middle-earth, while the characters of romance, such as Legolas and Gimli, use an all-round language, half-way between novel and epic, that they do not need to modify much when in contact with other traditions. However, the characters with fundamentally epic traits, and those who are more stub-

---

134 My italics.

bornly and prosaically novelistic in conception, will find it rather difficult to adapt their discourse to other traditions:

> The king was already there, and as soon as he entered he called for Merry and had a seat prepared for him at his side. 'It is not as I would have it,' said Théoden; 'for this is little like my fair house in Edoras. [...] But it may be long ere we sit, you and I, at the high table in Meduseld; there will be no time for feasting when I return thither. But come now! Eat and drink, and let us speak together while we may. And then you shall ride with me.'
>
> 'May I?' said Merry, surprised and delighted. 'That would be splendid! [...] I am afraid I am only in everybody's way', he stammered; 'but I should like to do anything I could, you know'.
>
> 'I doubt it not,' said the king. 'I have had a good hill-pony made ready for you. [...] You shall be my esquire, if you will. Is there gear of war in this place, Éomer, that my sword-thain could use?' (*LotR*, 808)

The solemn diction, expressing the ethical code of hospitality and the austerity of duty in the face of war is very much present in Théoden's speech, far removed from the informal dialogue that Merry seems to ask for with his carefree response. Théoden will stick to his epic discourse in his later conversations with Merry, while the latter will modify his speech in order to make it more compatible with the King's.

We have been, and will be, using the concepts of epic, romance and novel according to the standards outlined in the first chapter of this study. However, this does not mean that *The Lord of the Rings* lacks any formal relationship with Frye's theory of modes. Shippey (2003:210-211) correctly points out that *The Lord of the Rings* shows Frye's five modes in simultaneous interaction,[135] and says that "[t]his resonance of passages which can be read with different levels of suggestion at once, with 'myth' and 'low mimesis' and 'irony' all embedded deeply in 'romance', is perhaps the major and least considered cause for the appeal of *The Lord of the Rings*". (Shippey 2003:219)

Taking into account its central role, it is indeed strange that this interaction between modes – i.e. the intertraditional dialogue, which is not exclusive to

---

135 He identifies Sam and Gollum as representatives of the ironic mode, associates the rest of the hobbits with low mimesis, Éomer and Boromir with high mimesis, Aragorn, Legolas and Gimli with romance, and Gandalf, Tom Bombadil and Sauron with myth.

the proper dialogues, but operates on several levels of the narrative – should not have been studied in greater depth.

I have mentioned previously that the possibilities of flexibility offered by the invention of a secondary world are crucial to our understanding of the particularity of Tolkien's vision within the context of ironic myth, and before we move on to study the dynamics of Tolkien's intertraditional dialogue in greater detail, we will stop to take a brief look at Mikhail Bakhtin's theories about novelistic narrative universes, to see if they may shed some light on the peculiar characteristics of Middle-earth.

Bakhtin (1989:237-238) defines the literary chronotope as the artistically portrayed symbiotic relationship between space and time in literature, in which the temporal elements transcend through space, and vice versa. From his point of view, literary genres are composed of particular chronotopes, that determine the work's artistic unity within the framework of its projected reality and organize the plot (Bakhtin 1989:393).

In order to demonstrate the validity of his theory, Bakhtin surveys a series of Western narrative traditions, beginning with the so-called "Greek novel", moving on to the medieval quest novels and the picaresque novels, and then on to more modern genres. Thus Bakhtin, for example, argues that the chronotope that governs the Greek novel's overall artistic unity is the idea of the foreign and strange world that exists as long as the adventure lasts. This chronotope would be new compared to previous traditions, because the elements of different genres take on a new shape and specific functions, which would make this type of narrative different from other genres (Bakhtin 1989:242).

Hence, Bakhtin believes that each genre features one major controlling chronotope that organizes a theoretically unlimited number of minor chronotopes. The interaction between the chronotopes is essentially dialogic (Bakhtin 1989: 402-403), and this, according to Bakhtin, is a distinctive characteristic proper to the novel. In his opinion, the novel attracts other genres into its orbit, and because it was not created as a mirror of an absolute past but as a medium for what he terms an "imperfect present", it is able to liberate these genres from their rigid bounds (Bakhtin 1989:483-484).

The ideas about the chronotope and the dialogic character of the novel are significant to our study of Tolkien's work in the context of other contemporary literary narratives. It is possible to see Middle-earth, at least as it is portrayed in *The Lord of the Rings*, as the artistic construction of a new chronotope. As such it differs from others in so far as the Western narrative traditions interact in a previously unknown world[136] that, because of the particular cohesion required by such a chronotope, exhibits a clear contextualization of references to the previous, metatextual traditions and does not need to resort to irony or parody – two literary devices Bakhtin (1989:451) considers fundamental in order to liberate the "dead" genres of the past.

This, I believe, is the main formal reason why the work shows such a dynamic intertraditional dialogue, in which the different traditions explore and interrogate each other in a new way compared to contemporary works written in the same mode.

---

136 In spite of its invented space, history and mythology, Middle-earth is, of course, not completely foreign to the modern reader. In Curry's (1997:24) opinion, *The Lord of the Rings* shows "exactly the world that is under severe threat from those who worship pure power, and are its slaves: the technological and instrumental power embodied in Sauron [...] and the epitome of modernism gone mad. We thus find ourselves reading a story about ourselves, about our own world."

Chapter 4

The Exploration of the Limits of the Intertraditional Dialogue in *The Lord of the Rings*

In a narrative that constantly puts narrative traditions in dialogue, like *The Lord of the Rings*, it becomes peremptory for any critic who aims at analysing the presence of different literary genres in this work, to take into account the particular *dynamics* of the intertraditional dialogue. Quite obviously, given that *The Lord of the Rings* is not *exclusively* a novel, it would be misleading and absurd to read and judge it exclusively from a novel perspective, as it would be to complain about the limited psychological evolution of Ulysses in the *Odyssey*, the impossibility of Atlas being turned into a mountain in Ovid's *Metamorphoses*, the excessive emphasis on heroic feats in *Chanson de Roland*, or the lack of verisimilitude in the descriptions of physical space in *Le Mort D'Arthur*, to mention four examples from different narrative traditions.

The challenge of analysing literary genre in Tolkien's work is further increased by the fact that the character-drawing, the descriptions of action and the treatment of different themes are not coherent from the point of view of any fixed, genre-based conventions, but seem to acquire coherence from the *dialogue* between traditions. Depending on the particular narrative characteristics of each situation, the traditions may merge or clash, adding or aborting the influence of others. This process defines a great deal of the narrative treatment of characters, physical space and action, and an important part of the narrative is dedicated to exploring the constraints of the literary traditions in dialogue.

One of the many striking features of *The Lord of the Rings* is the flexibility with which the main characters move between different narrative traditions. I think mainly of Frodo, who ends up assimilating all of these traditions to a greater or lesser extent, but also of Gandalf and Aragorn. Lobdell (2004:36) says that "Tolkien's use of different style for different stages of the action may not be entirely successful [...] but it is important to see that this is what he is trying to do", and he adds: "Throughout *The Lord of the Rings*, the diction matches, or is intended to match, the action". (Lobdell 2004:37)

The question is whether the diction is only intended to match the action, or whether there are other factors that may be able to alter it. When contemplating the flexibility of the above-mentioned characters, a great number of questions inevitably come to my mind. For example, is Aragorn, an essentially epic character, influenced by the hobbits toward novel standards in Bree, or is it the other way around? If he *is* influenced, is it due to the characters, the physical space or to the action? And why is Sam hardly mentioned in the episode taking place at Tom Bombadil's house? Could it be that the setting, events and characters of the sequence are more related to romance and myth than to the predominant narrative tradition of the Shire, and Sam, being more informed as a character by the nineteenth-century novel than the others, is unable to relate to them?

This leads me to the more general question of whether all of the apparent contradictions and inconsistencies regarding character-drawing, style, choice of focalization, etc., may be explained by the particular dynamics of the intertraditional dialogue. However, the most interesting question is perhaps the following: to what extent does the totality of the work depend on the narrative demands of this dialogue?

In order to carry out the analysis as such, I will take into account three different narrative levels. The first one is the *generic* level, which is composed of what I perceive as the four fundamental Western narrative traditions – myth, epic, romance and novel. Within each of these traditions there are a number of sub-genres and possible combinations, such as the *chanson de geste*, the medieval romance, the adventure novel, etc., which will be considered parts of the basic paradigms mentioned above.

The second narrative level is the *situational* one. This level is made up of five main influences that, depending on the circumstances, *may* be capable of altering the general direction of the intertraditional dialogue: the physical space, the characters, the theme, the action, and the focalization. Because of their potential as decisive conductors of the dialogue, we can also call them 'dialoguemes'. I will call any particular combination of these five influences a 'narrative zone' (which in Bakhtin's terminology would correspond to a minor chronotope).

With the *physical space*, I will refer to any given location of variable extension, such as the Shire, Rivendell, Minas Tirith or Mordor. It can also be a particular building, for example the *Prancing Pony* and the tower of Cirith Ungol, or a natural environment, like the fields of Cormallen or the Old Forest.

When talking about the *characters*, I will refer to the dominating narrative tradition associated to a particular character, or set of characters, in a given narrative zone. There are characters, like Gandalf, Aragorn and Frodo, that show different degrees of adherence to different traditions depending on the narrative zone, while others, like Éomer, Legolas and Sam, are less flexible.

The main activity carried out by the protagonists of each narrative zone will be considered as the *action*. The action may be both internal (thoughts, dreams) and external (warfare, conversation, travelling, etc.).

The *theme* is the basis for the action, whereby the presence of different characters may add different themes to a given situation. As with the chronotopes, there are major and minor themes. For example, we might say that the two great themes in *The Lord of the Rings* are the moral corruption brought by power and the implications of the passing of time for mortals and immortals. Within this global thematic context, there are a number of lesser themes, associated to different characters and places, such as the price and rewards of loyalty in the case of Sam Gamgee, Aragorn's renewal of the kingdom, the defeatism of Denethor, etc. Each narrative zone may also yield even lesser themes, such as Éowyn's unrequited love for Aragorn, Boromir's heroic redemption, the courage of Merry on the fields of the Pelennor, etc.

The *focalization* is another resource that the narrator may use in order to manipulate the presentation of the fictional reality. In *The Lord of the Rings*, Frodo is the narrator of the greater part of the story, but he is not always the focalizer. As narrator, he may choose to transfer the focalization to another character, usually when he has not been there himself to bear witness of the events, but sometimes also when he *has* been present (as in the episode that takes place in front of the Black Gate), due to the demands of the intertraditional dialogue.[137]

The third narrative level which is part of our analysis is the *transitional*; that is, the way in which the narrative moves from one tradition to another in a given narrative zone. There are seven basic types of transitions, divided in two groups. The first group is made up of *prepared transitions*. Within this group, there are five different types: the *accepted invitation*, that takes the narrative quickly, and without hardly any dialogue, from one tradition to another due to a powerful presence of one or more elements of the situational level; the *rejected invitation*, that blocks the transition due to an inhibiting presence of elements of the situational level; the *dialogue*, which combines two or more traditions for some time and ends up with the predominance of one of them; the *mélange*, that combines different traditions without any clear direction; and the *meta-dialogue*, that involves an explicit reference, on behalf of the narrator or the characters, of the presence of a narrative transition.

The second group is made up of *unprepared transitions*; that is, transitions that are not preceded by a growing presence of new narrative elements from other traditions. These may have two results: either they manage to efficiently introduce a new tradition into the narrative (from the point of view of narrative fluency), in which case we would speak of an *intruder*, or else they don't, which would be called *arrested intruder*.

The present analysis is not an attempt at disclosing *all* the aspects of the interaction between traditions in *The Lord of the Rings* – this would be impossible in a work of this limited extension – but rather to offer an introduction to its dynamics that might explain the general movements, which in turn condition both the writing and the reading of Tolkien's masterpiece. For this

---

137 As Segura (2004:122-129) explains, Frodo compiles all the information needed for his chronicle from the different members of the Fellowship. After that he turns the information into a narratively efficient sequence, which implies, among other things, a careful selection of what we may call secondary narrators and focalizers. Sometimes, Frodo the narrator yields his focalization to other characters, for instance to Aragorn in the chapter 'The Breaking of the Fellowship', or to an omniscient eye, as in the battle on the Fields of the Pelennor.

reason, I will concentrate on certain situations and characters that show how the presence of different narrative paradigms are integrated in the dialogue, and how the combination becomes a self-exploratory process that lays the foundation for a great part of the plot-making and character-drawing in this work.

Finally, my aim is not to offer a definitive explanation of the creative process that gave rise to *The Lord of the Rings*, to which no one but Tolkien himself – and perhaps not even he, as he implies in one of his letters (*Letters*, 145) – ever had access, but to interpret the interaction between narrative traditions using the text as the only point of departure. If this approach should yield plausible evidence for how the creative process may have worked, it should be looked upon as an addition to (rather than an attempt at annihilation of) other critical interpretations.

I am also conscious that Tolkien would probably not agree with many of the interpretations that will be presented in this chapter. However, if the text itself should offer the possibility of such interpretations, I will not refrain from presenting them just because the author categorically denies, for example, that the theme of courtly love should be among his favourite subjects in medieval romance. Whether the author wants it or not, it is perfectly possible that such a theme might sneak into the narrative at one point or another. At the same time, the author's opinion is as interesting as that of any other qualified critic of his work, therefore I will not deny him the right to speak whenever he should have something to say about the situation that is being analysed, whether supporting or denying the hypothesis.

As a consequence, the autobiographical data or opinions of the author will never constitute a decisive argument for or against the presence of any narrative tradition in the text, but there will be room for them in the analysis. Likewise, the explicit mentioning of possible literary sources for places, characters, actions and themes will only be used as support for the argument, not as a validation. In the first place, I will always detect the presence or absence of narrative paradigms with reference to the conclusions of the second chapter of this study, which will be further complemented with opinions taken from other studies on the characteristics of particular literary genres.

We will begin by looking at four exemplary passages from *The Lord of the Rings* that show its generic diversity. The first piece takes place at Bag End:

> Gandalf crept to one side of the window. Then with a dart he sprang to the sill, and thrust a long arm out and downwards. There was a squawk, and up came Sam Gamgee's curly head hauled by one ear.
>
> 'Well, well, bless my beard!' said Gandalf. 'Sam Gamgee is it? Now what may you be doing?
>
> 'Lor bless you, Mr. Gandalf, sir!' said Sam. 'Nothing! Leastways I was just trimming the grass-border under the window, if you follow me.' (*LotR*, 77)

The second example comes from Amon Hen:

> He heard himself crying out: *Never, never!* Or was it: *Verily I come, I come to you?* He could not tell. Then as a flash from some other point of power there came to his mind another thought: *Take it off! Take it off! Fool, take it off! Take off the Ring!*
>
> The two powers strove in him. For a moment, perfectly balanced between their piercing points, he writhed, tormented. Frodo, neither the Voice nor the Eye: free to choose, and with one remaining instant in which to do so. He took the Ring off his finger. (*LotR*, 421)

Our third passage is taken from the Battle of the Pelennor Fields:

> Then Théoden was aware of him, and would not wait for his onset, but crying to Snowmane he charged headlong to greet him. Great was the clash of their meeting. But the white fury of the Northmen burned the hotter, and more skilled was their knighthood and bitter. Fewer were they but they clove through the Southrons like a fire-bolt in a forest. Right through the press drove Théoden Thengel's son, and his spear was shivered as he threw down their chieftain. Out swept his sword, and he spurred to the standard, hewed staff and bearer; and the black serpent foundered. (*LotR*, 872-873)

The final example is from the fields of Cormallen:

> And all the host laughed and wept, and in the midst of their merriment and tears the clear voice of the minstrel rose like silver and gold, and all men were hushed. And he sang to them, now in Elven tongue, now in the speech of the West, until their hearts, wounded with sweet words, overflowed, and their joy was like swords, and they passed in thought out to regions where pain and delight flow together and tears are the very wine of blessedness. (*LotR*, 990)

Put next to each other in this way, out of context, it is hard to imagine that the narrator of these passages is one and the same, the stylistic and thematic differences being so great. However, while almost all readers of *The Lord of the Rings* are aware of the varied diction, they do not usually seem to consider the variations incongruent and the work fragmented. In this chapter, I will try to explain why this is so.

4.1. Leaving the Shire

In *The Lord of the Rings*, the narrative treatment of the Shire entails a series of problems related to the question of how to integrate it in the larger universe of Middle-earth. These difficulties are to a great extent derived from the creative labours of the author, who did not know how or where the story would end when he first wrote this part of the narrative.[138] The tale starts off almost casually in the Shire, the land of the hobbits, where Tolkien had left Bilbo at the end of *The Hobbit* several years earlier, but the story soon becomes more complicated than that of its predecessor, and the first chapters of *The Lord of the Rings* clearly show the problems that arose when Tolkien subsequently realised that he needed to take the hobbits and the reader from one narrative universe (that of *The Hobbit*) to another (Middle-earth as presented in the greater part of *The Lord of the Rings*). This first part of the journey, from Hobbiton to Crickhollow, becomes an exploration of the strategies that Tolkien had to develop in order to bring the two worlds closer to each other.

The outcome of this process shows the Shire as an idealised reconstruction of a rural England, prior to the Great War,[139] and the literary traditions that Tolkien uses to portray this world belong fundamentally to the realm of the novel,[140] especially the Victorian novel. As an example, we can clearly see the influence of Dickens's *The Pickwick Papers* in Bilbo's birthday speech. Two examples from the texts will make our point clearer. The first one is taken from Bilbo's

---

138 The best book to understand the creative process behind the writing of this part of the story is, naturally, *The Return of the Shadow* (Tolkien 2000). Christopher Tolkien's annotated transcription of the original manuscript (together with the successive revisions) reveal that the author of *The Lord of the Rings* did not know from the start what would happen to his main characters, nor where they were headed. See also *Letters* (letter 163).
139 See Shippey (2003:102-103), and *Letters* (letters 181, 183).
140 See Forster (1963:29-31) on the relationship of the novel with "life in time". To a certain extent, the Shire is also similar to the "chronotope of the provincial town", as defined by Bakthin (1989:398). See also Bobes Naves (1993:179–180).

birthday speech, together with the responses from his audience, which Tolkien describes in the following way: *"I hope you are all enjoying yourselves as much as I am*. Deafening cheers. Cries of *Yes* (and *No*). [...] The noise subsided. *I shall not keep you long*, he cried. Cheers from all the assembly." (*LotR*, 41-42). Dickens portrays Pickwick's inaugural discourse in a similar way:

> He (Mr Pickwick) would not deny, that he was influenced by human passions, and human feelings, (cheers) – possibly by human weaknesses – (loud cries of "No"); but this he would say, that if ever the fire of self-importance broke out in his bosom the desire to benefit the human race in preference, effectually quenched it. (Dickens 2003:17)

One of the big differences in these two works is the somewhat distanced and ironic presentation of Pickwick on behalf of the narrator, whereas the narrator of *The Lord of the Rings* shows a much more respectful attitude towards Bilbo (even if it is not wholly deprived of irony). We find another similarity between the two works in the character of Sam Gamgee, who shares several features with his namesake Sam Weller (Pickwick's servant), such as his role as quick-tongued and good-natured servant, his craftiness, his prejudices and a general pragmatic attitude towards life. There are of course many other examples of this type of servant in Victorian literature, such as in the works of Geroge Eliot or Elizabeth Gaskell, among others, but the analogue with Sam Weller is perhaps most conspicuous since it is further enhanced in the episode taking place at *The Prancing Pony*, which is very similar to chapter 16 of *The Pickwick Papers*.[141] At the same time, it should be noted that Tolkien was not very fond of this work (*Letters*, 349).

Sam as a character can also be identified with one of the prototypes of the hero's friends in the British imperial adventure novel of the Victorian and Edwardian eras (Toda Iglesia 2002:27), like those of Rider Haggard (especially Job, from *She*). This could also be said of Gandalf, who initially takes on the role of the particular "helper-initiator" inherent in this genre, defined by Toda Iglesia (2002: 27-28) as "the wise and powerful with fantastic and supernatural connections."[142] The kind of relationship that exists between Frodo and Sam is also present in other emblematic representatives of the novel tradition, such as Don Quijote

---

141 For further similarities between the works of Dickens and Tolkien, see Nelson (2005:145-149).
142 The translation is mine.

and Sancho Panza in Cervantes's famous novel, or Tom Jones and Partridge in Fielding's, but the couple made up by Frodo and Sam is closer to the treatment of these 'types' in the Victorian and Edwardian adventure novels.[143]

We also perceive touches of the narrative universe of Victorian novelists such as Thomas Hardy, George Eliot, Elizabeth Gaskell and George Moore, particularly in the portraits of English nineteenth-century rural life in general, in the parallels to the gossipy tone of the rustic villagers found in the dialogues that take place at *The Ivy Bush* and *The Green Dragon* in Hobbiton. The tone, setting and atmosphere of the episode that tells of the dinner at Farmer Maggot's house clearly recall several scenes from *Far From the Madding Crowd*.[144]

In addition, we notice an occasional humoristic strain, similar to the tradition of elegant wit based on paradox and usually centered on the revelation of a cynical human nature, which was the trademark of Oscar Wilde:

> 'You don't belong here; you're no Baggins –you – you're a Brandybuck!'
>
> 'Did you hear that, Merry? That was an insult, if you like,' said Frodo as he shut the door on her.
>
> 'It was a compliment,' said Merry Brandybuck, 'and so, of course, not true.' (*LotR*, 52)

While the hobbits travel through the Shire during *daytime*, their leisurely behaviour is not far from that of the jolly group of travelling friends in *The Pickwick Papers*, but it is also close to Jerome K. Jerome's *Three Men in a Boat*, another novel belonging to a similar tradition, if more straightforwardly expressed than in the pedantic diction of Dickens's narrator. The irreverent joking of the members of the excursion is a constant feature of this part of the narrative, and the travelling as such is more like a walking holiday in the countryside than a dangerous expedition:

---

143 Regarding *LotR* as "an adventure story in the Edwardian mode," see Lobdell (2004:1-24).
144 For example, the episode that relates Gabriel Oak's arrival at the village where the woman he loves keeps her farm, and his conversation with the locals at the inn (Hardy 2000:46-63). Allen's (1971: 244) opinion about Hardy's novels is also interesting in that it shows the similarities with Tolkien's attitude towards past and present: "[P]erhaps it is on the word story telling that the emphasis should fall. Of current theories of realism he was highly critical [...] [Hardy] turned to the primitive oral tale. [...] Acutely, painfully aware of the modern world as he was, he looked back to the past and summed up in his fiction a life that was dying when he was a child, a life cut off from the main stream of national life, more primitive, more pagan [...]."

'All right!' said Pippin. 'I will follow you into every bog and ditch. But it is hard! I had counted on passing the *Golden Perch* at Stock before sundown. The best beer in the Eastfarthing, or used to be: it is a long time since I tasted it.' (*LotR*, 101)

Part of the explanation for this lack of 'seriousness' lies in the fact that the Shire is already known to us from a previous narrative – that of *The Hobbit* – which is much closer to the carefree and humoristic tradition found in the novels mentioned before, on the one hand, and that of the fairy-tale, on the other. This blend was a formula used by several well-known British writers in the nineteenth century, such as Thackeray (in, for example, *The Rose and the Ring*), Lewis Carroll (*Alice in Wonderland*), George MacDonald (*The Princess and the Goblin*), Andrew Lang (*Prince Prigio*), Oscar Wilde (*The Selfish Giant*), or Dickens (*The Magic Fishbone*), but it can also be detected in some writings belonging to the first category; stories which avoided the fairy-tale on the surface level, but kept its spirit as an underlying essence. Allen (1971:162), says that the world that Dickens evokes in *The Pickwick Papers* is "a world as innocent as Beatrix Potter's [...] the world of fairy tale, with the bad fairies not monstrous but absurd."

The statement brings us straight to the core of the problem which Tolkien had to face when he wanted to move the hobbits out of the Shire and place them in the far bigger and immensely more complex narrative universe of Middle-earth. The setting that Tolkien first presented to the readers in *The Hobbit*, and which he later used as the starting point for *The Lord of the Rings*, shares many features with the blend between the nineteenth-century novel and the fairy tale;[145] it is a cosy narrative microcosm in which the truly bad monsters, as well as the other deadly serious and ominous elements of the grand, epic scenarios of the greater world beyond its limits, simply do not make any sense. The absurdity of the monsters in the Shire is revealed in the inflexible response to Sam Gamgee's somewhat dreamy reflections on dragons and walking trees at *The Green Dragon* in Bywater:

---

[145] Segura (2003) provides a useful introduction to the narrative strategies Tolkien employs in order to carry out the transition from the fairy-tale world (of the Shire) to the more majestic, epic sceneries of the outside world.. See also Segura (2004:129-130). For a more detailed and precise explanation of the term 'fairy-tale', or 'fairy-story', as Tolkien saw the genre, see 'On Fairy-Stories' (Tolkien 1966).

'No thank 'ee,' said Ted, 'I won't [talk about dragons]. I heard tell of them when I was a youngster, but there's no call to believe in them now. There's only one dragon in Bywater, and that's Green,' he said, getting a general laugh. (*LotR*, 57)

The defensive tone in the reply seems, at the same time, to acknowledge that there is a real threat implied in Sam's mentioning of these strange phenomena. The effect of this is that the reader perceives the Shire as a momentarily safe but fragile utopia, into which more mundane and darker elements may penetrate in a not too distant future. In effect, the plot will soon demand that darker elements enter this idyllic microcosm. Frodo, Sam and Pippin will have to flee from nothing less than the Ringwraiths, Sauron's most powerful servants, who have come to find the One Ring and will stop at nothing until they find it. They will be saved from these Ringwraiths by elves, another markedly foreign race that inhabits the greater world outside, and all of this will take place within the boundaries of the cosy microcosm of the Shire, made up by this nineteenth-century narrative blend of rural bliss, prosaic people, irreverent jokes and a general fairy-tale/fable atmosphere *à la* Beatrix Potter or Kenneth Grahame,[146] where the genuinely evil monsters and the dark side of the fantastic are so out of place. Tolkien must have been acutely aware of the narrative obstacles derived from these circumstances, and he uses various strategies to carry out the delicate movement from the Shire to the exterior world, where mythic, epic and romance narrative elements may be integrated with less friction.

In the first place, the narrator disposes of certain characters that help him modify the narrative world of the Shire and make a little more room for the monsters. Bilbo is already known to us from *The Hobbit*, a story that has acquainted us with the idea of the hobbit-adventurer who leaves the Shire to roam unknown and dangerous parts of the world, having fantastic adventures

---

146 We know that Tolkien appreciated both Beatrix Potter (Tolkien 1966:43) and Kenneth Grahame (*Letters*, letter 77; Tolkien 1966:91). Tolkien (1966:43) considered that most of Beatrix Potter's stories belong to a genre somewhere between the fable and the fairy tale, and that it is their inherent morality that brings them close to the latter category. A combination of novelistic rules of credibility and nineteenth-century fairy tale, such as the one we find in the opening chapters of *The Lord of the Rings*, would fall closer to Tolkien's definition. As for Kenneth Grahame, the influence of *The Wind in the Willows* can also be seen in the episode taking place in the Old Forest, which is very similar to chapter 3 ('The Wild Wood'), of Grahame's tale.

as he goes along.¹⁴⁷ Bilbo reminds us that the Shire is in fact a part of the much bigger Middle-earth, inhabited by a great number of strange and wild creatures, where both dangers and considerably more ceremonious and solemn cultural traits are part of everyday life. The Ring, the most important inheritance from Bilbo's adventures, is so prominent a theme in the first two chapters, 'A Long Expected Party' and 'The Shadow of the Past', that it can almost be seen as the true protagonist of this part of the story.

In these chapters Gandalf, another important character taken from *The Hobbit*, talks and acts in accordance with the novelistic narrative standards of the Shire, but he also contributes to the idea of the land of the hobbits as an exception to the 'rules'. In his long digression about the Ring in the second chapter, Gandalf reminds us of a number of events from the previous narrative, such as the meeting between Bilbo and Gollum. He also informs us of the dangers connected with the possession of the Ring, underlining its absolute relevance to the global conflict between the great forces that operate in Middle-earth.

Frodo is a new character, but he is significantly associated to the Ring from the first chapter, when he inherits it from Bilbo. Apart from Frodo's initial identification with the Ring, Tolkien presents him as an unusual, restless, sensitive hobbit, not fully integrated in the lifestyle of The Shire.¹⁴⁸ For this reason, Bilbo as Frodo's 'precursor', the association with the Ring and the personality of Frodo make the reader expect the appearance of some sort of unusual adventure related to his person.

---

147 Shippey (2003:71) talks of Bilbo as having two essential sides, saying that he "knows almost nothing about Wilderland, and cannot even skin a rabbit, being used to having his meat 'delivered by the butcher, ready to cook'. Yet he has a place in the ancient world too, and there is a hint that (just like us) all his efforts cannot keep him entirely separate from the past." Shippey (2003:72) concludes that Bilbo has "not entirely lost his passport into the ancient world, and can function in it as our representative, without heroic pretensions but also without cynical ironies."

148 See Segura (2004:190). Bobes Naves (1993:180) points out that the hero's self-imposed alienation from his fellow country-men is a typical feature of novels set in provincial towns (the most famous example of how this chronotope can be used in the novel is found in Flaubert's *Madame Bovary*). Frodo himself admits that "there have been times when I thought the inhabitants too stupid and dull for words, and have felt that an earthquake or an invasion of dragons might be good for them." (*LotR*, 76). In this way, while in the Shire, Frodo is portrayed as a character with certain affinities to romance – being associated to the realm of the fantastic thanks to the Ring – but also to novel paradigms, especially in his attitude towards the world that surrounds him and towards 'truth', as we shall see.

Last but not least we have Sam Gamgee, Frodo's gardener. Sam is without doubt one of the most novelistic characters of the whole story, but he has been absorbing Bilbo's adventure stories ever since he was young, and he is eager to become acquainted with the mysteries of the world beyond the borders of the Shire. We have already seen how he ventures to question the limits of the prosaic local vision of his countrymen in the scene at the inn in which he tries to talk about dragons and walking trees, and his father, not quite pleased with this tendency, says of him:

> '[...] Crazy about stories of the old days he is, and he listens to all Mr. Bilbo's tales. Mr. Bilbo has learned him in letters – meaning no harm, mark you, and I hope no harm will come of it.
>
> *'Elves and Dragons*! I says to him. *Cabbages and potatoes are better for me and you. Don't go getting mixed up in the business of your betters, or you'll land in trouble too big for you,* I says to him.' (*LotR*, 36)

Sam presents us with a split attitude towards reality: the prosaic, which seemingly comes from his upbringing (typical of the Shire) as well as his social class; and the open-minded, which admits the possible existence of certain phenomena regarded supernatural by the people of the Shire (typical of Bilbo).

Collectively, the characters of Bilbo, Gandalf, Frodo and Sam confirm the *possibility* of high adventure and the inclusion of dark, fantastic elements in a narrative that starts off in a nineteenth-century blend of bourgeois fairy tale and humoristic and rural novels, in a community marked by a narrow-minded concern for material interests and respectability.

However, Tolkien disposes of more narrative tools than just characters to help him render coherence to the presence of the darker and "grander" elements that anticipate the narrative wealth of the exterior world. My analysis of the inter-traditional literary dialogue in this part of the story will focus on the strategies that Tolkien uses to integrate romance elements in the nineteenth-century blend, as the hobbits move together with the reader along the road that leads towards the rest of Middle-earth.

The Black Riders in the Shire

The exceptionally limited power and competence of the Black Riders as agents of Sauron during their sojourn in the Shire has been the subject of both hostile and reconciliatory critical approaches.[149] From my point of view, none of these approaches has yielded very satisfactory explanations. At this stage of the story, the Black Riders seem almost incompatible with the powerful and terrible creatures we come across further on in the narrative, and this incongruity is not easily accounted for. Manlove (1978:181), in his characteristically naïve analysis of Tolkien's works, attributes this inefficiency of the Black Riders to sheer incompetence on behalf of the author, arguing that Tolkien is unable to stick to his initial narrative propositions, while Shippey (2003:105) admits somewhat apologetically that they are less powerful here than in any other part of Middle-earth, adding laconically that "[i]t seems likely that [...] Tolkien found the transit from familiar Shire to archaic Wilderland an inhibiting one."

Tolkien himself tries to explain the initial weakness of the Riders in one of his letters, stating that they have an intrinsically limited physical power over the brave, and that their real strength lies in the fear they inspire in their victims. In the same letter, Tolkien also claims that the Witch King of Angmar could not be as powerful at this stage of the story as he later would become (in *The Return of the King*), alluding to the transformational effects taking place when Sauron gives him the military command over the troops, something which would render him an additional, demonic force. (*Letters*, letter 210)

This argument sounds very much like a reconstruction with the benefit of hindsight; an attempt at rationalising the intuitive narrative strategies the author employed when trying to fit in the Black Riders in the narrative zone of the Shire. In the first place, even if it would be true that the Ringwraiths should become more feeble the further away from Mordor they come, hence making their limited power in the Shire coherent with their conception, it still would not make much sense that Sauron should send a pack of ghosts with limited physical power over the brave to recover something as supremely important

---

149 See Manlove (1978), Shippey (2003), and Gasque (1968).

as the One Ring. A more credible scenario, given Sauron's pragmatic ruthlessness, would put another kind of malevolent warrior on display; someone as implacable as the Black Riders but more inconspicuous, cunning and subtle, for instance the ambassador who appears in the chapter 'The Black Gate Opens', especially as we know that Sauron has such subalterns at his disposal.

For my part, I believe that the reason for the weakness of the Black Riders in the Shire is due to the initial, happy-go-lucky kind of aimlessness of the author when he first launched the hobbits out of the Shire and into the exterior world. At first, Tolkien believed that he was writing a sequel to *The Hobbit*, but to his surprise, his narrative world had changed since he last visited it and he found himself immersed in a far darker, vaster, deeper and wider world than the fairy-tale atmosphere that haunted the version of Middle-earth present in the earlier narrative would give room for. The progressive discovery of this "new" world would eventually lead him on over many hundred pages and culminate in the narrative we today know as *The Lord of the Rings*, but the fact remains that Tolkien did not know where the road would lead him when he wrote the first drafts of the initial episode, and this includes the later role of the Black Riders. During the subsequent re-elaborations of the text that took place once the whole manuscript was finished, he must have become aware of the problems they entail as powerful and supernatural beings within the boundaries of the Shire, and this was probably the reason why he decided not to elevate them to their full status as the most powerful agents of the Dark Lord until the third book, leaving the original descriptions of them much as they were. However, even in this "lighter" version their presence becomes a serious narrative challenge, the demands of which Tolkien meets with not a little skill.

Gasque (1968:155) considers that the Black Riders are presented ambiguously at first, "so that we have believed in them as real men before they are confirmed as Wraiths." This point of view is a more fruitful starting point than the opinions we have seen earlier, although it does not explain all the facets of the problem, as we shall see.

From the chapter 'Three Is Company' and on there is a significant change in the narrative, due to the narrator's shifting focus, which is now directed towards a more romance-oriented perception of reality.[150] In order to achieve a balanced and coherent dialogue between novel and romance, the narrator frequently makes use of what we might call 'light effects'. When the chapter begins, the narration is firmly rooted in the characteristic blend between the nineteenth-century humoristic and rural novel and the fairy tale, the narrative trademark of the Shire, with a narrator putting an ironic emphasis on the gossipy inclination of the villagers:

> One summer's evening an *astonishing* piece of news reached the Ivy Bush and Green Dragon. Giants and other portents on the borders of the Shire were forgotten for *more important matters*: Mr. Frodo was selling Bag End, indeed he had already sold it – to the Sackville-Bagginses! (*LotR*, 79)[151]

Shortly after, Gandalf leaves the Shire and Frodo waits in vain for his return. Finally, he decides to begin his journey without the wizard, accompanied by Sam and Pippin. After finishing his last dinner at Bag End, Frodo goes for a short walk in the neighbourhood. Night is falling, and the progressively weakening light affects Frodo's perception of his home:

> The sun went down. Bag End seemed sad and gloomy and dishevelled. Frodo wandered round the familiar rooms, and saw the light of the sunset fade on the walls, and shadows creep out of the corners. (*LotR*, 82)

The description is a clear anticipation of the first appearance of a Black Rider, a few lines later. Significantly, in this first encounter, Frodo can only vaguely hear the voice of the Rider, which intuitively seems to him "strange" and "unpleasant", and it is a relief to him to hear the footsteps move down the road, away from Bag End. The first description of the twilight brings about this strangely threatening atmosphere, closer to romance than to the novel, based as it is on purely subjective impressions in turn affected by an almost supernatural sensibility, pushing the narrative from the daylight realm of order and familiarity towards the chaotic, fearful and uncontrolled landscapes of the night.[152] A moment later, Frodo tries to rationalise his instinctive fear, turning

---

150 For introductory studies on the perception of reality in romance literature, see Vinaver (1971), Stevens (1973), and Beer (1977). The common idea is that the treatment of space and time is subordinated to the experiences of the protagonist, and that reality is often presented as dreamlike and vague; space becomes a scenery in which rational perception fades, and time is split up in fragmentary, unconnected moments (Vinaver 1971:5).
151 My italics.
152 Night is related to "chaos, death, regression, anxiety, secular fear" and is "a symbolic realm full of monsters." De Paco (2003:323). My translation.

back toward his familiar house where he meets Sam Gamgee, with whom he talks in a way that once more recalls the interaction between Pickwick and his servant Sam Weller:

> 'Sam!' he called. 'Sam! Time!'
>
> 'Coming, sir!' came the answer from far within, followed soon by Sam himself, wiping his mouth. He had been saying farewell to the beer-barrel in the cellar.
>
> 'All aboard, Sam?' said Frodo.
>
> 'Yes, sir. I'll last for a bit now, sir.' (*LotR*, 83)

The journey begins. The narrator holds the romance elements in check by sticking to the nineteenth-century narrative blend in the meticulous descriptions of the landscape and the exact chronology of the events, which are mixed with a certain inclination towards the fable and the fairy tale, as in the use of parenthesis and the sudden, seemingly uncalled-for focalisation on behalf of a fox watching the sleeping hobbits as he passes by.[153]

The next meeting with a Black Rider will alter this atmosphere once more. This time, the appearance of the Rider does not take place at dusk or at night (though it is hinted at when the narrator mentions that the sun is on its way down),[154] but its mere presence produces an uncanny reaction in Frodo, who, inspired by his fear, feels an almost irresistibly strong need to put the Ring on his finger. As Gasque observes in the quotation above, the description of the Rider is thoroughly ambiguous:

> Round the corner came a black horse, no hobbit-pony but a full-sized horse, and on it sat *a large man*, who seemed to crouch in the saddle, wrapped in *a great black hood and cloak*, so that only his boots in the high stirrups showed below; *his face was shadowed and invisible.*
>
> When it reached the tree and was level with Frodo the horse stopped. The *riding figure* sat quite still with its head bowed, as if listening. From inside

---

153 See Segura (2003).
154 In the first draft, this scene begins in the middle of a sentence, without previous reference to space and time (Tolkien 2000:47). The fact that the final draft presents us with a scene taking place at nightfall might be due to a significant change in the text: in the first draft, it is *Gandalf* who appears on the horse. Only when the Black Rider had replaced the wizard, Tolkien indicated the references to dusk and night, perhaps as a means of preparing the appearance of the Ringwraith with a more "romance-friendly" ambience.

the hood came *a noise as of someone sniffing to catch an elusive scent*; the head turned from side to side of the road. (*LotR*, 88)[155]

On the one hand, the narrator describes the Rider as a man, but on the other, the person is shrouded in mystery, hidden under his clothes with his face concealed. In the following paragraph, the Rider is referred to as a "figure", while the sniffing sound and the head (not *his* or *her*, but *its* head, as if the creature were sexless or belonged to the animal world) turning from side to side leave us with an uncertain impression as to the Rider's identity, making us ask ourselves whether we are dealing with a man or an animal, or perhaps a monstrous combination of both. The threatening atmosphere is very much present in this scene, and the almost supernaturally motivated fear that Frodo feels for the Rider makes us associate the black colour of the clothes with its symbolic significance: violence, death, and evil.[156]

The fact that these symbolic associations are more immediate here than those of, for example, the grey colour of Gandalf's cloak in the scene describing his arrival at Hobbiton in the first chapter,[157] indicates the degree to which the appearance of the Black Riders adds a strong flavour of the romance tradition to the narrative, as well as the necessity to construct a dialogue to fit in this new element. However, it is also important to notice that the descriptions are still ambiguous. Tolkien offers a dialogue between the novel and the romance traditions which ends with a return to the territory of the novel. We are not convinced of the human characteristics of the Rider, but there is still nothing in the descriptions that clearly indicates that he should belong completely to the realm of the supernatural. Rather, the description shows something – a man, a strange animal or perhaps something else – which at any rate is markedly alien to normal hobbit experience: the Ringwraith is "dressed up" as a person because

---

[155] My italics. It is interesting to notice that in the first draft, in which it is Gandalf who appears on the horse, he too is ambiguously presented. The subsequent modifications altered the initial descriptions, making the horse black instead of white, the man upon it large and not small, and eliminating the description of an actual nose that protrudes from within the hood, sniffing (Tolkien 2000:54).

[156] It is also interesting to notice that Miller (2000:283), when discussing the figure of the "Black Knight" in the epic and romance traditions of the Scandinavian and Germanic north, says that in these traditions, black "also marks [...] the monster, who is simultaneously made black, anomalously shaped, and inhumanly hideous."

[157] See *LotR*, 37. On the one hand, Gandalf wears not grey only: his hat is blue, and his scarf is silver. On the other hand, the wizard arrives in plain daylight and he is welcomed by hobbit-children.

of the need to adapt him to the narrative zone of the Shire. At the same time, the description leaves a clear romance mark on the narrative.

It is Sam who brings the narrative back to the novel tradition when he retells his father's conversation with the Black Rider at Bag End (the same conversation that Frodo barely overheard before leaving), providing a new point of view that underscores the human potentiality of the Black Rider:

> *What sort of a fellow was he?* says I to the Gaffer. *I don't know*, says he; *but he wasn't a hobbit. He was tall and black-like, and he stooped over me. I reckon it was one of the Big Folk from foreign parts. He spoke funny.* (LotR, 89)

As a result of tossing the Rider back and forth between possible interpretations, the ambiguity of the figure is still present, but as Sam's father is given the last word, our final interpretation is inclined towards a novel-conceived reality.

The next time the Rider approaches the hobbits, night has already fallen and a pale "unearthly" starlight makes the descriptions of the landscape less precise. At this occasion, Tolkien does not insist on the ambiguity of the Rider, whose human characteristics are considerably toned down:

> The sound of hoofs stopped. As Frodo watched he saw *something dark* pass across the lighter space between two trees, and then halt [...] The *black shadow* stood close to the point where they had left the path, and it *swayed from side to side*. Frodo thought he heard the sound of *snuffling*. The shadow bent to the ground, and then began to *crawl* towards him. (LotR, 92)[158]

In this description, the stress falls on the infrahuman characteristics of the Rider, emphasising the threatening sensation and an animal-oriented behaviour. To begin with, the Rider is no longer mounted on his horse, it is not only the head but the whole body that turns from side to side, the verb "sniff" is changed for "snuffle"; and when the figure moves it "crawls" over the ground towards Frodo. Again, the influence of the weak light guides the narrative toward romance paradigms, revealing, even if it is only partially, the monster that resembled a human being during the day.

The repeated apparitions of the Black Rider during the first stage of the journey, the ambiguity of the descriptions and the threatening atmosphere brought

---

158 My italics. This description is identical to that of the first draft (Tolkien 2000:58).

about by his presence also recall the mysterious knight that appears time and time again to Ralph, the hero of William Morris's *The Well at the World's End*, in the first chapters of that book. However, this prose romance is closer to the romance tradition and does not dialogue with the novel – and even less with the nineteenth-century blend we have mentioned – in the same way as *The Lord of the Rings*.

The elves in the Shire

Luckily for the hobbits, dusk is also an adequate atmosphere for the introduction of more benevolent romance beings, such as the elves. When Gildor Inglorion arrives a moment after the re-appearance of the Black Rider, the descriptions suddenly acquire far more positive symbolic associations, such as the songs,[159] the laughter, and the light in their eyes and around their feet. Frodo justifies the presence of the elves attending to novelistic rules of probability, explaining to the others that they (the elves) sometimes cross this part of the Shire, but facts are that the reader is witnessing the first instance of what Tolkien calls "eucatastrophe", which, given the arbitrary character of such miraculous turns of events, must be excluded from one of the basic premises of the realist novel, namely that of credibility. Both improbable coincidences and a miraculous saving grace play an important part in the structural framework of romance narratives in general,[160] and the fact that the narrator feels obliged to justify its presence denotes the still strong novelistic influence on the events taking place in the narrative zone of the Shire, even in its nocturnal, more 'romance-friendly' version.

---

159 Concerning songs and declamations of poetry in *The Lord of the Rings*, Segura (2004:122) notes that they function as an interlacement of the different cultural traditions that exist in Tolkien's imaginary world. Gildor's song doubtlessly contributes to enhance the dialogue between novel and romance. Regarding the elves and their relation to the romance treatment of space and time, all through *The Lord of the Rings*, the episodes in which elves play a prominent role bring about some sort of distortion in ordinary perception of space and time (in the Shire, Rivendell and Lórien), paving the way for transcendental experiences. In the Shire, where the narrative *mélange* novel/romance does not permit any major deviations in either direction, these experiences are reduced to mere sensations, as when Sam, the day after meeting the elves, seems to lack words to describe what he feels about them.
160 Stevens (1973:4) divides the fantastic elements in romance narratives in four categories: the exotic; the mysterious; the strictly magic (the marvellous controlled by man); and the miraculous (the marvellous controlled by God). Eucatastrophe leans close to the last category, albeit without any explicit mention of any divine influence on the course of the events.

The elves as such are also related to the tradition of medieval romance. Shippey (2003:55-65) concludes that the medieval poem *Sir Orfeo* is the text that inspired Tolkien most when creating the elves, while at the same time acknowledging many other analogues to romance narratives, such as *Pearl* and *Sir Gawain and the Green Knight*, and their presence substantially modifies the narrative towards these domains. The gratuitous appearance of an 'adventure', the indistinct landscape of medieval romance and the elves' slightly archaic diction – "we too are only tarrying here a while, ere we return over the Great Sea" (*LotR*, 93) – contribute to the general influence of romance paradigms on the narrative, which from this moment on becomes a *mélange* of the romance and novel traditions. This mixture is born out of the tension between the elves, the night and the monstrous enemy, on the one hand, and the hobbits and the Shire – even in its nocturnal shape – on the other.

As a result, Sam and Pippin, a lot more novelistic in attitude and conception than Frodo, become difficult to integrate in this environment, and the efforts of Pippin to adapt his speech to that of the elves sound artificial and forced: "'O Fair Folk! This is good fortune beyond my hope,' said Pippin. Sam was speechless." (*LotR*, 94)[161] Pippin's comment shows that a basically novelistic character cannot suddenly alter his natural speech in accordance with the diction of another tradition without considerable friction. If this radical change in tone has not been previously prepared for by means of an efficient narrative transition of some sort, such a clash is doomed to seem incongruous. In terms of the inter-traditional dialogue, we may consider Pippin's intervention an 'arrested intruder', given that it reflects a romance influence on his person which is not incorporated into the dialogue with sufficient narrative fluency. One of the reasons for this failure is that his sudden reverential attitude and formal speech do not match any previous assimilation of romance elements – as opposed to Frodo, Pippin has up until this moment been consistently immune to any tradition except for the blend of the nineteenth-century novel and fairy tale.

The hobbits are invited by Gildor to join the elves and they walk together to a glade in the woods. During this nightly walk, the narrator suggestively combines vague and exact descriptions in his constant references to a palpable

---

161 In the original draft, this comment belongs to Frodo, and not to Pippin (Tolkien 2000:60).

geography, at the same time omitting any specifications regarding distances and the chronology of events. The novel/romance *mélange* persists in the subsequent conversation between Gildor and Frodo, during the course of which the hobbit manages to keep his discourse on a level above the colloquial tone he has employed in his interaction with Sam and Pippin, but without yielding totally to the ceremonious diction of romance. Gildor not only uses a more archaic speech than Frodo, but he also explicitly acknowledges the possible influence of the hand of fate on their encounter:

> 'In this meeting there may be more than chance; but the purpose is not clear to me, and I fear to say too much.'
>
> 'I am deeply grateful,' said Frodo, but I wish you would tell me plainly what the Black Riders are. If I take your advice I may not see Gandalf for a long while, and I ought to know what is the danger that pursues me.'
>
> 'Is it not enough to know that they are servants of the Enemy?' answered Gildor. 'Flee them! Speak no words to them! They are deadly. Ask no more of me! But my heart forebodes that, ere all is ended, you, Frodo son of Drogo, will know more of these fell things than Gildor Inglorion. May Elbereth protect you!'
>
> 'But where shall I find courage?' asked Frodo. 'That is what I chiefly need.' (*LotR*, 98)

In this dialogue we notice the difference in attitude towards reality showed by Frodo, on the one hand, and Gildor, on the other: while the words of the elf are shrouded in mystery and have an air of vagueness about them, expressing irrational beliefs, such as forebodings based on intuition, Frodo wants to find out concrete things, for practical purposes. A romance attitude is mingled with a novelistic impulse, firmly rooted in a tangible reality, and we do not perceive any clear direction in the dialogue.

This *mélange*, in which romance elements are given more room than before, is not in any way opposed to the nineteenth-century blend of novel and fairy tale that composes the essence of the daylight version of the narrative zone of the Shire, it is rather a logical extension of it. The integration of the idea of destiny and forebodings in the framework of a rural novelistic narrative set in a nineteenth-century milieu is not a new one; it has an antecedent in Thomas Hardy, whose novel *Far From the Madding Crowd* we have already mentioned as a possible source of inspiration for certain aspects of the Shire (though it must be said that there is no evidence that Tolkien ever read Hardy).

In this context, it is interesting to notice that E.M. Forster (1963:90) considers that Hardy puts an excessive emphasis on the element of causality: "[...] the flaw running through Hardy's novels [is that] he has emphasized causality more strongly than his medium permits." The comment – which could also be applied to other nineteenth-century writers about rural life, such as Emily Brontë or Nathaniel Hawthorne (though the latter portrays rural *New* England) – suggests that Hardy breaks with what Forster perceives as a fundamental premise of the realist novel, namely that of presenting a plausible portrait of people whose lives depend both on circumstance and chance, rather than one based on other grounds (whether in the shape of a divinely defined, and hence predestinate, plan for the course of events or the overarching influence of a plot-centred narrative in which the characters conform to the story rather than the other way around).

The use that Tolkien makes of the idea of destiny, taking its presence into account while not fully acknowledging it as *the* supreme controlling force, likewise moves the narrative toward the periphery of the realm of the novel, but, as in the cases of Hardy, Hawthorne and Brontë, without obliterating its influence. This is an important part of the process that creates the *mélange* between novel and romance in this episode. The outcome is a narrative zone which, being compatible with the daylight version, can act as a mediator between the Shire and the outside world, preparing the reader for what is to come in later chapters.

The next day, the elves have disappeared and we are back in the daylight version of the narrative zone of the Shire. Accordingly, Pippin is given plenty of room to exhibit his most irreverent joking side, including comments that could have been taken straight out of *Three Men in a Boat* – "'I didn't want to leave you any [food], but Sam insisted'" –, and he harasses Frodo with questions related to purely practical issues, such as the route to follow. Frodo, however, is still in deep thoughts after the nocturnal meeting with the elves and seemingly needs more time to shift back to the carefree holiday atmosphere which surrounds the hobbit excursion at daytime.

After dismissing Pippin, Frodo turns to Sam, with whom he spends some time talking about the elves. Only after this is he allowed to be drawn back toward the narrative territory of the novel, mainly through the renewed conversation with Pippin. During the ensuing dialogue between romance and novel, the romance aspects of Frodo gradually fade as the novel paradigms become more dominant.

The rest of the journey through the lands of the Shire remains anchored in the nineteenth-century blend, which is reaffirmed during the dinner at Maggot's house, a character whose diction, behaviour and local knowledge shows a marked resemblance with the portraits of farmers in Hardy and other rural novelists of the era. Nightfall alters the narrative once more towards romance standards, though the narrator allows himself to play a cheap trick on the credulous hobbits (and the readers, by now), based on a limited perception of reality produced by the darkness and the fog, having Merry appear in the shape of a Black Rider. This false concession to romance brings the narrative dangerously close to the satirical devices used by Jane Austen in *Northanger Abbey*, in which the author ridicules the conventions of the gothic novel by having apparently supernatural phenomena rationally explained, and the trick would have pushed the delicate balance between romance and novel (which, as I have argued, is essential to the construction of the Shire as a narrative zone) too far towards the territory of the novel and the satire if it had not been counterbalanced by the reminder that the danger, though 'supernatural', is at least *potentially* real, as shown by the sudden appearance of a real Black Rider on the opposite side of the river a few moments later.

At the same time, the fact that Tolkien *does* include the joke in the first place shows just how deep into the territory of the nineteenth-century blend of novel and fairy tale the narrative has delved, and in the next chapter we find the hobbits comfortably settled in a bourgeois cottage, bathing, chatting, singing and dining in the carefree spirit of the Pickwickians, Jerome's holiday-goers, or the animals in Grahame's *The Wind in the Willows*.

The opinion of Gasque (1968:155), who emphasises the credulity of the hobbits, and above all that of Sam, as the key to the reader's acceptance of the elves, is just a part of the intricate fabric of narrative strategies that Tolkien had to weave in order to integrate these elements in the narrative zone of the Shire. More important is the lingering influence of the first drafts of this part of the story, when Tolkien still thought he was writing a sequel to *The Hobbit*, and the subsequent revisions to make the narrative zone of the Shire, largely inherited in spirit from the first story, fit into a larger literary chronotope dominated by a profound *mélange* between earlier narrative traditions, such as myth and epic.[162]

Romance, whether in the shape of the adventure novel, the pseudo-medieval novels of Morris, the gothic novel or the original nineteenth and early twentieth-century fairy tales and fables, proved an efficient narrative vehicle to put traditions in dialogue, and Tolkien would later exploit it further for the incorporation of new traditions, as in the episode of the Old Forest and the Barrow Downs, when the narrative engages in a dialogue with myth, and in Bree, when the reader and the hobbits are put on the threshold to the epic world. It is possible that the problem of how to integrate the Black Riders and the elves in the narrative microcosm of the Shire triggered his discovery and later use – conscious or not – of romance as the most eloquent mediator between the different narrative traditions that take part in the narrative dialogue in *The Lord of the Rings*.

4.2. The Tom Bombadil-digression: from myth-making to map-making

When the hobbits cross the border of the Old Forest, they enter a lugubrious and thoroughly strange region which has very little to do with the Shire, which precedes it in the story, and even less with Bree, which is to follow. Within the framework of *The Lord of the Rings* as a whole, the episode constitutes an exception to the general dynamics of the intertraditional dialogue in which no narrative paradigm is allowed to obliterate the presence of the others.

---

162 Segura (2004:125) considers that Tolkien, when writing this part of the narrative, realised that it was necessary to eliminate the authoritative and impersonal tone of the omniscient narrator that he had begun with. This is shown in the progressive evolution of the style, from the nineteenth-century blend of the rural/humoristic novel and fairy-tale/fable of the first chapters, towards the prose romance that comes to dominate the narrative once the hobbits arrive at Bree.

I believe that it is not too rash to say that in the Old Forest, the sense of both time and space is radically altered, making the episode lean very close to the realm of myth.

The reason why Tolkien did not edit out the episode is not easily accounted for, since the digression does not exert any significant influence either on the characters or the plot[163] (except for the sword that Merry finds in the tomb and later uses to kill the Witch-King of Angmar). Gasque (1968:155) feels that it is "charming but slightly unconvincing" because Tolkien has not prepared it sufficiently and because it takes place just before the adventure in Bree. That claim, apart from lacking any credible or convincing support, is actually quite frivolous, since Tolkien *does* prepare the transition, and very carefully at that, as we shall see. Shippey (2003:109) considers that in *The Lord of the Rings*, "landscape and the beings attached to it are in a way the heroes," and that the digressive episodes in the story exist due to Tolkien's wish to connect the imagined world with our own, because

> they suggest very strongly a world which is more than imagined, whose supernatural qualities are close to entirely natural ones, one which has morover been 'worn down', like ours, by time and by the process of lands and languages and people all growing up together over millenia.

This description, while fitting for the portrayal of Ithilien, for instance, is not really valid for the Old Forest, which has not been worn down by time, languages and people – in fact, like Lórien, it is a place which to some extent exists *outside* time.

Rosebury (2003:32) takes the argument one step further and claims that in the Tom Bombadil-episode, "what looks like excess from the point of view of a plot-based structure is wholly necessary for a different kind of structure," alluding to the author's need to create a feeling of intense sympathy for Middle-earth and its peoples (by extensive and careful portrayal) in order to make the reader care sufficiently about their potential destruction.

---

163 Tolkien was always enigmatic about Tom Bombadil's function in the story, saying that "I put him in because I had already 'invented' him independently [...] and wanted an 'adventure' on the way. But I kept him in, and as he was, because he represents certain things otherwise left out" (*Letters*, 192), and "[...] even in a mythical Age there must be some enigmas, as there always are. Tom Bombadil is one (intentionally)" (*Letters*, 174).

While I agree with Rosebury on this, I believe that the interpretation may be invested with further significance if we connect Tolkien's strategy with his particular creative impulse in order to make it illuminate the narrative techniques that the author uses to integrate the different parts of Middle-earth into a coherent whole. If we believe Tolkien when he says that his story-telling creativity is based on discovering feasible contexts for his invented languages (*Letters*, 264), the narrative as such necessarily becomes an exploration of Middle-earth itself, as if the writer were filling empty spaces on a map as the writing progressed. In short, if the exploration of context – that is, physical, cultural, and historical space – *as such* is a central part of *The Lord of the Rings*, the development of the plot is, if not secondary, then at least only of equal importance to the presentation of the discoveries. This is partly shown by the writer's decision to keep the Tom Bombadil-episode in the larger narrative in spite of its apparent redundancy within that framework. The question of *why* Tolkien keeps it is in turn intimately related to *how* he does it, because the exploration and discovery of Middle-earth is to a great extent based on the exploration of the limits of the intertraditional dialogue.

Tolkien must have been keenly aware that his narrative universe, as presented in the Shire, had to change in order to be able to accommodate Tom Bombadil: he needed to create a different context for that character and the world associated with him. To have him appear singing and chanting spells at, for example, *The Green Dragon* of the first chapters, would have given rise to a narrative distance too wide to bridge and brought about a break rather than a fusion of the different narrative traditions involved,[164] which is what we often find in modernist literature and poetry written in the mode of ironic myth, such as Joyce's *Ulysses* or Eliot's *The Waste Land*. Tolkien was also interested in integrating mythic paradigms in his narrative, but he avoided resorting to irony to handle the dialogue. Therefore, the transition from Crickhollow to the House of Tom Bombadil is both prepared and executed with great care. In this process, the dialogue between romance, myth, and – in the end – the novel, which establishes the limits of different characters and events

---

164 In 'The Adventures of Tom Bombadil', Tom Bombadil does interact with Shire-people without ironic clashes, but the folk-tale atmosphere of those narrative poems makes them very different in tone from the portrayal of the Shire in *The Lord of the Rings*.

in different spaces, is frequently used to make room for this transcendent realm within the 'earthly' boundaries of Middle-earth.

Dreams, mists, hedges, tunnels and gates: the borders of romance

The narrator begins preparing the reader for the change of scenery long before the hobbits reach the forest. In the previous chapter, during the dinner at Frodo's new house in Crickhollow, Fredegar Bolger speaks repeatedly of the superstitions that surround the Old Forest, claiming that the forest is just as perilous as the Black Riders, and even if Merry denies the supposed dangers of the trees, he insinuates that they have a will of their own.[165]

After that, Frodo's dream directs the reader's attention to a strange space, similar to that of a nightmare and symbolically charged with elements such as the sea, the dark moor, the lonesome white tower and the sound of thunder. Flieger (1997:99) considers that Frodo's adventure outside the Shire is for him a kind of dream, "as if [he] has fallen wide asleep into a dream so vivid that ordinary waking life takes on the evanescent quality of a dream in comparison." According to Flieger, there would be several possible starting points for this dream, as the moment when the hobbits cross the Brandywine and enter the house at Crickhollow; when Frodo wakes up suddenly from his dream; or when he hears the ominous clang of the gate shutting behind them at the edge of the Old Forest. Flieger (1997:198-199) concludes: "They are from now on until the end of the journey in a world far removed from ordinary daylight experience."

I personally consider that the starting point for the invitation to a narrative dialogue with romance elements comes when the hobbits go to bed and Frodo starts dreaming. The sudden wakening moment on the first line of the following chapter does not bring about any drastic changes from one kind of reality to another: it is still dark, and once the hobbits leave the house, they trot along through a blurry, half-seen landscape in which the mist "seemed to open reluctantly before them, and close forbiddingly behind them" (*LotR*,

---

[165] "'I have been in several times – usually in daylight, of course, when the trees are sleepy and fairly quiet.'" (*LotR*, 122)

124). The atmosphere suggests mystery, with a prominent presence of border elements in the descriptions, something which was already present in Frodo's dream.

The limit of the Old Forest is marked by a tall hedge, a tunnel that leads through it and, at the end of the tunnel, a gate. As the gate closes behind the hobbits, Merry explicitly mentions that they have entered another region: "'There!' said Merry. 'You have left the Shire, and are now outside, and on the edge of the Old Forest.'" (*LotR*, 125)

Miller (2000:147), when discussing the motif of a hero crossing a border and entering a dangerous zone, says that the movement usually implies a change of several basic conditions present in the previous narrative:

> [...] the hero finds and penetrates into threatening or unknown places and terrains, with the near certainty of encountering alterity in the form of either hostile human, animal, or supernatural forces.

If we add to the concept of the border that the dangerous zone is a deep and dark forest, the situation is likely to generate a series of well-known expectations. The symbolical meaning of the forest in Western culture has always been related to the idea of mystery and threat. In the Western narrative tradition, to go into a forest is often to enter a universe full of spells, dangers and adverse elements (De Paco 2003: 199). One well-known example, taken from medieval romance literature, is the Forest of Broceliande, which is the place where knights typically go to find adventure.

Trees and sleep: romance space consolidated

Once the protagonists find themselves within the limits of the forest and walk through the mist, the mysterious atmosphere of the dream retains its qualities in a natural way, even after the sun has come out. From the first moment, the hobbits have the impression that the trees are observing them disapprovingly. Apart from this, the orientation becomes more and more difficult as the day wears on, and when they try to avoid the Withywindle, it seems as if the very trees put obstacles in their way to make them head for the river:

> After an hour or two they had lost all clear sense of direction [...] They were being headed off, and were simply following a course chosen for them – eastwards and southwards, into the heart of the Forest and not out of it. (*LotR*, 129-130)[166]

The blurry and vague romance landscape, similar to that of a dream (Vinaver 1984:5; Jewers 2000:93), has convinced us of the *possibility* of the rumours being true, though the narrator is still not ready to acknowledge this supernatural state of affairs with categorical statements. Instead of rushing on headlong towards the realm of romance, the narrative retains the dialogue with the novel, alternating the vagueness of the romance tradition with more realistic descriptions, as in the moment when the hobbits finally reach the Withywindle. I believe that the presence of these persistent novel-elements may be explained by a conscious strategy aimed at underscoring the contrast between the situation before and after the spell cast by Old Man Willow. The effect is that the atmosphere of a dream is made even stronger than it already was and the narrative moves further away from the territory of the novel. As opposed to Thorpe's view,[167] I do not believe that it is the realism of the previous descriptions *as such* that helps Tolkien integrate the Old Man Willow sequence in the storyline, but rather the narrative device of sleep.[168] The realism is there mainly to enhance the idea of the border: if Tolkien wishes to create an effect of unreality to be able to integrate the supernatural events that are to follow in the narrative, the new ambience must replace a more sober reality. The hobbits fall asleep before the Old Man Willow and Tom Bombadil enter the narrative, and it does not seem as if they really wake up until they leave the Barrow-downs behind, thirty pages later.

The dream – Old Man Willow's spell – brings about the final invitation to romance which ends up placing the narrative firmly within the realm of this tradition, and this allows for a confident and unabashed telling of the subsequent fantastic events – the straightforward descriptions of Merry and Pippin

---

[166] Regarding the mysterious behaviour of the trees, Tolkien says that "The Old Forest was hostile to two-legged creatures because of the memory of many injuries" (*Letters*, 419), an opinion which reinforces the forest's role as a community of trees with a will of their own.
[167] Thorpe (1992:315) says that the realistic descriptions of the arrival to the river makes it possible for Tolkien to incorporate the 'Old Man Willow' – episode into the narrative. Why this should be so is not further explained.
[168] In Flieger's (1997:200) opinion, "sleep is the operative word in the Willow man sequence."

being swallowed by the willow, and Tom Bombadil casting a counter-spell to let them out. By now, Tolkien has prepared the reader sufficiently to be able to describe these things as if they happen *de facto*: the accumulation of the two dreams (each one further increasing the sensation of unreality), the idea of the border and the strange characteristics of the forest, have all contributed to taking the reader far away from the everyday-reality of the Shire. The effect is that the narrator can operate on a much more uninhibited romance level compared with the previous chapters.

Manlove (1978:182) speaks of Tom Bombadil's timely arrival as yet another example of what he calls an improbable coincidence. In Manlove's opinion, these "improbabilities" are not coherent with the narrative premises that Tolkien establishes in the first chapters. This may well be so, but Manlove's critical stance is based on the assumption that a literary work that breaks with a reader's initial expectations must necessarily be bad. To begin with, this is not a very serious approach to the literary value of any novel, and in the case of *The Lord of the Rings* it is particularly misplaced. While it is true that the story starts out in a narrative paradigm closer to the novel tradition than any other, it is never a purely realistic novel universe that is presented to us, but a novel tradition mixed with ingredients of fairy tale, romance and even the fable, as we have seen in the previous section. In the Old Forest, we find ourselves in a very different reality, much closer to romance, where improbable coincidences and fantastic events may occur at will, but Tolkien does not place us there arbitrarily. He introduces the romance elements in the novelistic narrative with immense care and skill, using particular strategies for making the transition as smooth as possible, until it is completed and integrated in the larger whole. This is the reason why the episode should not disturb any reader (at least from the point of view of narrative coherence) who is conscious of the dynamics of the intertraditional dialogue in *The Lord of the Rings*.

Thus, the two dreams, the border and the descriptions of the setting, enable Tom Bombadil to introduce himself without any novelistic inhibitions, exhibiting his supernatural powers with the natural ease that corresponds to characters of romance-oriented narratives. But there are two other things about Tom Bombadil that place him with at least one foot in the tradition of myth:[169] his intimate connection with the natural world, and the sense that he belongs to a strange, almost transcendental realm, which is both inside and outside the framework of normal time, as we shall see.

Tom Bombadil and Goldberry: nature and myth

Tom Bombadil's peculiar relationship to the natural world is hinted at from the start: the song that he sings when he first appears in the forest is full of references to natural phenomena, such as the wind, birds, hills, sunlight and starlight, branches of trees, and water.[170] Furthermore, in the narrator's description of him, his movements are compared with those of a cow that crashes through the underbrush in order to reach the river, and the colour of his face is likened to that of a red, ripe apple. Henceforth, the mythical aspects of Tom Bombadil will be closely related to his direct communion with a nature unadulterated by routine-blunted perception.[171] This can be seen when the hobbits approach Tom's house and their perception of the surrounding nature is altered, making the landscape take on dream-like qualities: "They began to feel that all this country was unreal, and that they were stumbling through an ominous dream that led to no awakening" (*LotR*, 136). Shortly after this, they arrive at Tom's house, paradoxically located "up, down, under hill"; that is, in no particular place but in all at the same time,[172] and they hear the voice

---

169 Shippey (2003:105-106) says of Tom Bombadil that "he seems in fact to be a *lusus naturae*, a one member category," and regarding his language of wonder, he claims that "There is an ancient myth in this feature, that of the 'true language', the tongue in which there is a thing for each word and a word for each thing, and in which signifier then naturally has power over signified – language 'isomorphic with reality' once again." Tolkien himself says of Tom Bombadil that if "you take your delight for things for themselves without reference to yourself, watching, observing, and to some extent knowing, then the questions of the rights and wrongs of power and control might become utterly meaningless to you" (*Letters*, 179). Both views reinforce the mythic character of Tom Bombadil, who is above the concepts of good and bad, and who operates in perfect harmony with the natural world.
170 Quella Kelly (1968:179-180) identifies Tom Bombadil's voice with that of nature: "Sound and sense is important in Tom's poetry because he, like nature, is nonrational [...] Non-sensical words and syllables which are pleasing to the ear or which simply fill out the measure are a normal part of his discourse [...] his timelessness permits him to be as repetitious and diffuse as the luxuriant nature for which he speaks."
171 In fact, Tom Bombadil can be seen as a personification of Tolkien's idea of "Recovery" as expressed in his essay 'On Fairy-Stories' (Tolkien 1966:77).
172 Tolkien himself did not seem to be very sure of the exact location of Tom's cabin, or at least, the different drafts offer contradictory descriptions, the cabin being situated sometimes on the south side of the Withywindle, sometimes on the north, as Christopher Tolkien points out (*Shadow*, 114, 327-328).

of Goldberry, "as young and as ancient as Spring, like the song of glad water flowing down into the night from a bright morning in the hills" (*LotR*, 137). Tolkien himself does not say that the setting is primordial or mythic, but it certainly seems as if he is bent on creating just that feeling.[173]

However, the transition that takes the narrative from romance towards myth is not completed until the hobbits reach Tom Bombadil's house, where the connection between this strange character and nature, transcendence and universal questions concerning the human condition is considerably reinforced. Again, Tolkien uses the vehicle of the border as one of the means to carry out the transition. In the first line of the chapter 'In the House of Tom Bombadil', the narrator explicitly mentions that the hobbits walk over the threshold, and this is also the moment that marks the completion of the transition, landing us very close to the realm of myth. As soon as they are inside the house they meet Goldberry, and Frodo experiences a strange sensation bordering on religious revelation, which makes him recite verses previously unknown to him:

> 'Fair lady Goldberry!' said Frodo at last, feeling his heart moved with a joy that he did not understand. He stood as he at times had stood enchanted by fair elven-voices; but the spell that was now laid upon him was different: less keen and lofty was the delight, but deeper and nearer to mortal heart; marvellous and yet not strange. 'Fair lady Goldberry!' he said again. 'Now the joy that was hidden in the songs we heard is made plain to me.
>
> > *O slender as a willow-wand! O clearer than clear water!*
> > *O reed by the living pool! Fair River-daughter!*
> > *O spring-time and summer-time, and spring again after!*
> > *O wind on the waterfall, and the leaves' laughter!* (*LotR*, 138-139)[174]

---

[173] In one of his letters, Tolkien claims that "We are not in 'fairy-land', but in real river-lands in autumn," though it should be noted that the next sentence continues: "Goldberry *represents* the actual seasonal changes in such lands." (*Letters*, 272, my italics). The insistence that the land is 'real' may of course also be due to the fact that Tolkien, in this letter, was criticising Forrest J. Ackerman's script for a projected screenplay, in which he perceives a linguistic treatment leaning too far toward a childish fairy tale.

[174] Greene (1992:45) places Goldberry in the tradition of visionary and prophetic poetry, saying that *The Lord of the Rings* shows this school of poetry translated into prose, developing "the tradition of the English novel by injecting it with strains of visionary, romantic and mythic literary practice." Further on in her essay, Greene adds: "[i]n Tolkien's writings about the legendary Third Age, his images retain this complexity of visual structure [...] They are possible in terms of nature, but strange and burdened with symbolic meaning [...] The reader is left with the impression that [Goldberry's] power is so fundamental that there is no need for any display of sovereignty [...] Tolkien has combined the complex symbolism of the elaborate pictorial images of Spenser and Milton with observation of real things found in this world [...]" (Greene 1992:47-48).

When describing Frodo's feelings, the narrator offers an example of meta-dialogue as he allows Frodo to reflect on the different imprints that the elves and Goldberry leave on his mind, emphasizing the natural reverence that the latter inspires.

In Frodo's first dream in Tom Bombadil's house, a man is saved by an eagle from the top of a high tower. Later on we learn that the man is Gandalf and the tower Orthanc, Saruman's stronghold, and that the event really happened. Frodo is thus given a dream vision that transcends both space and time. The following night, he is given another vision in which the scenery is later revealed to us as Valinor, a primordial, mythic region that belongs to another dimension. Flieger (1997:204) believes that the ambiguity of the descriptions of the nights in Tom Bombadil's house "makes it a solid reinforcement of the premise that some dreams transcend, rather than replace, waking experience". This state of mind, in which a mortal is given glimpses of a primordial universe beyond this world, is one of the aims of myths, in any version of it (Eliade 2000:27; Campbell 1997:218).[175]

Furthermore, Tom Bombadil's discourse covers all imaginable topics, good things as well as evil, as he sums up the history of the universe for the hobbits, taking them to "strange regions beyond their memory and beyond their waking thought" (*LotR*, 146). He claims that he is the first being on Earth and plays with the Ring as if he were beyond good and evil. Apart from this, Frodo loses his sense of time at Tom Bombadil's house, and he feels strangely compelled to confess his fears to him. All these influences are clear invitations to the mystical and transcendent realm of myth, or at least to something very close to it, and the transition is completed without hardly any narrative dialogue from the moment the hobbits walk over the threshold of Tom's house.

However, it is important to notice that we have not entered a *purely* mythical narrative zone. Frodo makes repeated inquiries into the nature of Old Man Willow, the true reasons for Tom's sudden appearance at the right moment, and about Tom's identity, which shows a novelistic impulse to explain the mysterious and incomprehensible events with references to plausible (from

---

175 See chapter 2, section 2.4., of the present study.

the point of view of the hobbits) cause-and-effect relationships. These clear invitations back to the novel are rejected both by Tom and Goldberry, who refrain from giving detailed information and maintain a detached attitude towards novelistic verisimilitude: "Just chance brought me there, if chance you call it" (*LotR*, 141), and "He is the Master of wood, water and hill" (*LotR*,139). Still, the *intention* to uphold a connection with novelistic standards of realism is very much present, and this is significant from the point of view of the intertraditional dialogue, which yields very little space to any pure generic paradigms in this work.

More dreams, fog, and gates: romance and myth in the Barrow-downs

After leaving the house of Tom Bombadil, the hobbits head for Bree, but as they cross the Barrow-downs they become involved in an adventure which in many ways is similar to the incident with Old Man Willow, and which is also marked by a dialogue between romance and myth. Once again, the narrator prepares the reader for romance by using the device of sleep and an altered perception of the physical space. The hobbits fall asleep in the shadow of a great standing stone, and when they wake up, the world seems to have changed completely:

> They found that they were upon an island in the fog. Even as they looked out in dismay at the setting sun, it sank before their eyes into a white sea, and a cold grey shadow sprang up in the east behind. The fog rolled up to the walls and rose above them, and as it mounted it bent over their heads until it became a roof: they were shut in a hall of mist whose central pillar was the standing stone. (LotR, 153)

Both their sleep and the mysterious behaviour of the fog help create the blurred and imprecise setting which is typical of romance and therefore also apt for the fantastic events that are about to take place in quick succession: after losing his friends in the fog, Frodo passes two standing stones and enters another world, or at least another time, in which he is abducted by a barrow-wight who places him next to the other hobbits inside a tomb. The wight commences a lugubrious chant, and a hand reaches towards the sword that lies on Sam's chest, with the evident intention of sacrificing him ritually. Frodo attacks the arm with another sword and sings a rhyme that Tom Bombadil has previously taught them to use in the event of danger. Tom appears as if by magic, rescues the hobbits and brings out the treasures from the tomb into the daylight.[176]

Once again, we seem to have left Middle-earth completely and entered an otherworldly realm in which a dreamlike reality and supernatural events become prominent, along with the presence of Tom Bombadil, who appears instantly when called for (like the gods in the Classical epic tradition), as a force of light and order waging battle against darkness.[177] Merry's dream, the sharing out of the magic swords, and the visions that Tom sends into the heads of the hobbits, speaking of the remote past in which the swords were forged and showing a man with a star on his brow, also add to the transcendence of the experience.

The Road: novel on the way back to Bree and Middle-earth

Evidently, this cannot go on for much longer if Tolkien wants to resume the journey and tell us about the meeting between the hobbits and Strider in Bree. Hence, the narrator needs to find a way to re-establish the dialogue with the novel. This dialogue begins when the travellers finally descend the hills and approach the same road that they had previously left in Buckland, when they decided to cut across the Old Forest. The descriptions now become much more detailed, including concrete geographical references, and the effects of the rain links the two seemingly separate universes we have traversed during the previous chapters by means of a common meteorological situation, as if nothing had happened and no borders had been crossed:

> At this point [the road] ran nearly from South-west to North-east, and on their right it fell quickly down into a wide hollow. It was rutted and bore many

---

[176] St. Clair (1992:65), Miller (2000:144), and Day (2003:138), all mention the Scandinavian saga tradition as possible sources for this episode, referring to sacrificial rites and the paralysing power of the un-dead inhabitants. The motif as such may of course have come from this tradition, especially as we know that Tolkien enjoyed and admired the Scandinavian sagas, but in terms of narrative style, I find it closer to the gothic novel, especially in its almost obsessive attention to closed and oppressive spaces which seem to have a life of their own. If we look for analogues with any particular work from this tradition, the hand that walks on its fingers recalls the strange ghost that terrifies the inhabitants of the old castle in *The Castle of Otranto*, by Horace Walpole, whose different body parts appear on their own, among others a hand with a gauntlet on it (Walpole 1998:102-104). The gothic treatment of the tomb sequence in *The Lord of the Rings* is also more consistent with the general narrative pull towards romance paradigms that takes place here.

[177] In Quella Kelly's (1968:182) words, the wight's song is "a negation of life and nature; a denial of Tom Bombadil and Goldberry."

signs of the recent heavy rain; there were pools and pot-holes full of water. (*LotR*, 162)

The road thus marks the end of the digression which has taken us into a blank area on the map of Middle-earth. For this reason, the continued presence of Tom Bombadil implies a serious narrative obstacle in this well-defined and detailed setting, given that he has acted like an undisputedly supernatural – if not divine – being only a few pages before. The narrator solves the problem by emphasising the descriptions of physical space, increasing the protagonism of the landscape, and by limiting the references to Tom Bombadil considerably. When they reach the road and Tom finally speaks, he uses a much more novelistic discourse than before, now deprived of rhymes and vague references, and filled with details that evoke a 'real' place:

> [...] four miles along the Road you'll come upon a village, Bree under Bree-hill, with doors looking westward. There you'll find an old inn that is called The Prancing Pony. Barliman Butterbur is the worthy keeper. (*LotR*,163)

As soon as Tom Bombadil disappears, the narrator allows Sam to return to the narrative with a brief comment on the queer qualities of the former. Sam then begins to inquire about more prosaic issues, such as the atmosphere of *The Prancing Pony* and the character of the Breelanders.

It would seem as if the two characters cancel each other out: where one is (that is, where one acts or talks), there is no room for the other. There are hardly any references to Sam at all during the whole digression, save a mention that he did not remember having any particular dreams in the house of Tom Bombadil (something which underscores his lack of integration, in that it places him outside the sphere of influence of the traditions of romance and myth at this stage of the narrative). Sam, being firmly tied to the novel tradition, and Tom Bombadil, with deep roots in myth, cannot interact explicitly in this digression without marring the fluency of the intertraditional dialogue.

The important thing at this stage is to acknowledge the importance of the narrative dialogue as a means to carry out the transition from homely Shire to half-homely Bree, situated on the threshold of the austere grand world, by way of the unfamiliar Old Forest. In this dialogue, the return to the road becomes a very efficient invitation to the novelistic tradition. The road marks the end of the romance/myth digression as a mythic space and it also constitutes a real geographical border, running over a well-defined landscape with clear horizons and directing the hobbits to very concrete places with no mysterious connotations. The influence of the novel on the narrative is now so strong that it affects even Tom Bombadil, as we have seen, and the sole fact that Sam gets his voice back is a sure sign that the narrative standards have become perfectly readjusted to the tradition of the novel.

As we have seen, the major part of the digression is informed by narrative standards of romance, which acts as a mediator to incorporate the mythic episodes. It is interesting to notice that romance digressions and their formal lack of function from the perspective of a plot-centered structure were also frequently used by the Italian school of epic poetry. Quint (1985:179-182), when discussing the different traditions at work in Renaissance epics (his example is Tasso's *Gerusalemme Liberata*) points out that the movement from an epic plot towards a romance plot in the same literary work often takes on the character of a digression in which "time is broken down into unrelated moments isolated from one another and from any larger historical or narrative plan." In Quint's view, these authors often use the device of a boat that carries the hero over a stretch of water to frame the digression.

In *The Lord of the Rings* something similar happens, but while the formal devices used to integrate romance and myth – hedges, dreams, roads and mist – trigger the different stages in the narrative evolution of the digression, the dialogue they help establish allows Tolkien to explore, reveal and integrate the Old Forest and the Barrow-downs in the larger narrative.

In this integrative process, the digression anticipates the grander world and the grander narrative, by presenting somewhat lighter versions of future horrors and magnified creatures. We will come across parallels to the Old Forest, Tom Bombadil and the Barrow-wights further on in the story, in the shape of Fangorn forest, Treebeard (a character who combines both Bombadil and Old Man Willow to a certain extent), and the Dead that haunt the Paths of the Dead. Interestingly, the roles of all the later parallels are all much more clearly defined, contextualized and deprived of their dream-like quality, than the former. This shows two distinct stages in the narrative: the 'innocent',

Shire-based stage, and the more mature Middle-earth based stage which begins when the hobbits reach Bree, and which calls for a higher standard of internal coherence. This difference in narrative treatment also reflects Tolkien's initial lack of knowledge about the grander epic world that awaited his protagonists beyond Bree (*Letters*, 216-217).

The fact that the adventure survived the revision indicates that, for Tolkien, the discovery and revelation of the world had become just as important as the advancement of the plot. Perhaps it is when he decides to include the episode that he first discovers that word-making, map-making, myth-making, and plot-making go hand in hand in this work. As Rosebury argues, the slow unfolding and presentation of the wonders of Middle-earth contribute to a great extent to the successful development of the plot. According to Tolkien, at the core of this process is the word, but in the process of contextualization of that word, the intertraditional dialogue, which shapes and integrates the context in the grander narrative universe, plays a crucial role.

4.3. Aragorn's heroic evolution

Aragorn, depending on the interpretations we choose to make, can be regarded as a character from the traditions of the novel, the romance, or the epic.[178] Veugen's (2005:181-182) attempt at summarising Aragorn's heroic evolution, from a hero of the high mimetic mode to the hero of romance, is interesting, but at the same time grossly simplifying, as Veugen (2005:182) herself admits: "this transition is not as gradual or lineal as presented here. It is closely tied in with the overall story."

The transition *is* tied in with the overall story, but much more closely than Veugen seems ready to admit. I believe that the simplification referred to above is a direct result of strictly applying Frye's theory of modes to the analysis of *The Lord of the Rings*. As the story unfolds, we perceive that Aragorn is much more than just a character moving from the high mimetic mode towards

---

178 See, for example, Flieger (1981), who sees him as a figure from romance, while Kocher's (1974) analysis often shows him as a novel-character of flesh and bones. Shippey (2003) and Veugen (2005) tend to emphasize his romance and epic sides.

the mode of romance. He is continually informed by the novel, romance and epic traditions. What is more, this profound *mélange* yields a number of situations that outline the limits of the different traditions in dialogue, as we shall see.

The following analysis is an attempt to disclose the different stages in the heroic evolution of Aragorn from the point of view of the intertraditional dialogue, and at the same time to provide a glimpse of how the limits of this dialogue condition the narrative universe, the chronotope of Middle-earth, as it is presented in *The Lord of the Rings*.

Aragorn in Bree: Epic and the Adventure Novel

At the *Prancing Pony* in Bree, when Frodo lands after his clumsy manoeuvre while singing, the Ring has slipped on his finger and he disappears. This event gives rise to a change of tone in the narrative, marked by the explicit inclusion of elements that the hobbits perceive as decidedly foreign. The most prominent of these is Strider, who enters the scene to tell Frodo that he knows more about the Ring than the hobbits may think.

The figure of Strider reinforces the mysterious and threatening atmosphere that surrounds Bree and the inn. He has still not turned into the romance and epic hero that he will later become, but offers all the ambiguity of a novel character. At first, this may have been a consequence of Tolkien's lack of knowledge about Aragorn when he first wrote the episode.[179] The study of the evolution of this narrative, *The Return of the Shadow*, makes it clear to us that Tolkien's original idea was that the hobbits should meet a kind of adventurer-hobbit in Bree, called "Trotter", who would later guide them through the Outside World. However, the character of Aragorn became more dominant and Tolkien changed the name to Strider, given that the distance between a hobbit adventurer called Trotter and the later, epic/romance hero Aragorn was too great.

The name Trotter is also interesting from another point of view. The same name, attached to a character related to a somewhat similar episode, also appears in

---

[179] Regarding Tolkien's first inclusion of this character in the story, he wrote: "Strider sitting in the corner at the inn was a shock, and I had no more idea who he was than had Frodo" (*Letters*, 254).

Dickens's *The Pickwick Papers*. In that episode, Pickwick and his servant Sam Weller arrive at a rural inn late at night, after a long journey. They travel *in cognito*, and Sam, calling himself Walker, strikes up a conversation with the servant of another gentleman, with the aim of extracting information which may be helpful to Pickwick. The other servant introduces himself as Trotter and tricks him with an apparently innocent attitude.[180]

The common features of the two episodes – the late arrival at a rural inn, the invented names, the similarity between characters, the search for information and the ambiguous character of Trotter/Strider – may imply that Tolkien was looking for a model in sources close to the world of the Shire, a narrative zone to which he may have thought that his characters had returned. However, he had to modify the narrative substantially when he discovered the potential of Aragorn. The result of the modifications is that Aragorn in Bree represents a *novelistic anticipation* of the Great Epic world which is waiting for the hobbits further on in the narrative. Tolkien was surely aware that it would have been absurd to introduce Aragorn as a genuinely epic hero in the almost burlesque environment of *The Prancing Pony*, and that the evolution towards epic characteristics should be gradual and carefully elaborated.[181]

The first step is the change of name, from Trotter to Strider, but there is plenty more evidence of Strider's potential as a character who transcends the limits of the novel. It is of course true that Strider is still very far from the epic hero he will later become,[182] but in the narrator's first descriptions of him, we may find hints of several epic features. Miller (2000:135) claims that the epic hero feels comfortable in the wilderness, which is definitely the case with Strider: the first descriptions reveal that he is *"weather-beaten"*, that his boots are worn and covered with mud, and that he wears *"a travel-stained cloak of heavy dark-green cloth."* (*LotR*,172) Apart from this, Strider has dark

---

180 See chapter 16 in Dickens (2003: 211-228).
181 Segura (2004:130) also comments on the change of tone in the narrative from the moment Aragorn enters the scene, which is when it shifts more towards the heroic tone of the epic.
182 Miller (2000:8, 198, 230), when discussing the epic hero's personality, claims that he should never try to hide his true identity; that he will be recognised as the hero he is due to his heroic presence, even if nobody knows who he is; and that his speech is not primarily associated to a manifestation of intelligence, subtlety or sophistication, but rather used as an extension and/or anticipation of his physical power.

hair with flecks of grey, something which Miller (2000:295) identifies as a sign of threat and a connection with the supernatural.[183]

This description emphasizes Strider's ambiguity and narrative potential, without exceeding the limits of what is permissible in the narrative zone of Bree, a border town in all senses, where the strangeness of the Outside World should be adequately blended with the more familiar Shire-related affairs.

In the chapter 'Strider', the hobbits have the opportunity of chatting privately with him, and it is here that the text shows a more exhaustive exploration of the limits of this character in the narrative zone of Bree. Strider begins in novelistic terms, providing the hobbits with a plausible explanation for his presence in Bree, marked by a colloquial tone, and revealing that he is very much conscious of the lack of heroic standards in his physical appearance:

> '[...] Well, I have a rather rascally look, have I not?' said Strider with a curl of his lips and a queer gleam in his eye. 'But I hope we shall get to know each other better. When we do, I hope you will explain what happened at the end of your song. For that little prank–' (*LotR*, 180)

Shortly after this, when Strider talks about the Black Riders, his diction becomes 'tainted' with a much more formal and serious tone, though it still retains certain colloquial features. The theme as such makes the narrator manipulate the light, which fades until an 'apparent' darkness dominates the room. In this romance-imbued atmosphere, Strider offers his help, something which Sam refuses violently, while the perspicacious Frodo notices the change of tone in his discourse: "'[...] I think you are not really as you choose to look. You began to talk to me like the Bree-folk, but your voice has changed.'" (*LotR*, 182)

Frodo, when explicitly mentioning this fact, is implicitly acknowledging both Strider's heroic potential and his inter-traditional flexibility. His observation gives the narrator license to continue elevating Strider's tone and heroic

---

183 In Miller's view, Hagen of Tronegge's (of the Nibelungenlied) strange and contradictory connotations are considerably reinforced by the grey flecks in his hair: "[...] a man's hair, when it is not naturally but prematurely gray [implies] a character not quite wholly human, and perhaps inflated with strange instinct or uncanny power [...] The colour/noncolour appears to threaten, by obscuring, the bright effulgence of the hero, and in the best interpretation will display, at least in the north, an otherworldy and inhuman connection."

stature, but instead, he chooses to return to the path of the novel, having the comical and slightly ridiculous inn-keeper Barliman Butterbur reappear with a letter from Gandalf that he has just remembered. The letter corroborates Strider's status as friend, but Sam is still not convinced: "'You might be a play-acting spy, for all I can see, trying to get us to go with you. You might have done in the real Strider and took his clothes. What have you to say to that?'" (*LotR*,187)

Aragorn replies by arguing that if stealing the Ring had been his aim, he would have taken it already. After speaking, he accompanies his discourse with a momentary manifestation of his epic potential:

> He stood up, and *seemed suddenly to grow taller. In his eyes gleamed a light, keen and commanding.* Throwing back his cloak, he laid his hand on the hilt of a sword that had hung concealed by his side. They did not dare to move. *Sam sat wide-mouthed staring at him dumbly.*
>
> 'But I am the real Strider, fortunately,' he said, looking down at them with his face softened by a sudden smile. 'I am Aragorn son of Arathorn; and if by life or death I can save you, I will.' (*LotR*, 187)[184]

With such a reply, Aragorn is appealing both to a novelistic reasoning based on logic – which Sam is asking for – and to the powerful arguments of the epic hero, whose physical appearance and arrogant, violent attitude inspires a natural respect: his body seems to grow taller and his eyes shine with undisputable authority. The combination of these two attitudes – one based on reason, and the other on his (temporarily) awe-inspiring presence – convinces the hobbits, though it is Strider himself who concludes that he will be their guide. He keeps up this double attitude for some time, talking about his broken sword, the dangers they will have to face on the road, and Gandalf's mysterious disappearance, in formal and solemn terms that well fit the gravity of the situation, but mixed with exact data regarding time and place, due to a novelistic impulse of rendering verisimilitude to the spatial-temporal relationships. However, little by little, the narrative equilibrium begins to lean dangerously towards the epic, and since this is not admissible in Bree, the narrative needs to introduce a novelistic counterbalance. Pippin's prosaic comment is more than efficient for that purpose:

---

184 My italics.

> Pippin yawned. 'I am sorry,' he said, 'but I am dead tired. In spite of all the danger and worry I must go to bed, or sleep where I sit. Where is that silly fellow, Merry? It would be the last straw, if we had to go out in the dark to look for him.' (*LotR*, 189)[185]

The problem is that such a statement turns the narrative dialogue upside-down, instead of just altering its course towards a more balanced dialogue between the novel and the epic. Pippin trivialises the situation to such an extent that Aragorn's reaction must necessarily be the same as that of Sam a moment before – wide-mouthed bafflement – and the narrative effect would be exclusively comic. Tolkien achieves the appropriate balance and rescues the dialogue by having Merry (the most intertraditionally flexible of the hobbits, after Frodo) reappear at the inn with news about the Black Riders. From this moment and on, a more natural and less tense interaction between the hobbits and Aragorn is established: the hobbits keep their novelistic and colloquial discourse, but without ridiculing the situation's epic gravity, while Aragorn adapts his solemn speech somewhat to the level of the hobbits.

> Strider looked at Merry with wonder. 'You have a stout heart,' he said; 'but it was foolish.'
>
> 'I don't know,' said Merry. 'Neither brave nor silly, I think [...]' (*LotR*, 189)

Through this dialogue between the epic and the novel, which is a fundamental feature of the chapter 'Strider', the two traditions end up in a kind of narrative compromise. However, the characteristics of the narrative zone of Bree – a border region with more elements of the novel than of the epic – make the dialogue lean more towards the novel. This is particularly clear in the figure of Aragorn, whose epic dimension is considerably reduced. Far from being granted the overwhelming protagonism of the epic hero that he will later enjoy, in Bree Aragorn is portrayed as a character with certain affinities to the role of the intimidating helper-friend from the tradition of the nineteenth century British adventure novel.[186]

---

185 Shippey (2003:212), when discussing hobbit jokes, considers that they "reflect and by intention deflect the modern inhibition over high styles which we and they share." The statement also describes the effects of the hobbits' prosaic (novelistic) replies in the face of the more ceremonious and solemn discourse of other traditions.

186 According to Toda Iglesia (2002:129), this type of friend usually appears as a spy or guide, using his extensive knowledge of the resources and dangers of the foreign terrain to make the hero's progress easier.

When discussing this type of character, Toda Iglesia (2002:108) underscores two basic features: his intimate association with amulets and magic artefacts, and his physical ugliness. Tolkien may or may not have been aware of these conventions, but it is interesting to notice that Aragorn will later exhibit certain traits which will take him far beyond the limitations of the role of the 'intimidating friend' of the adventure novel, and that the analogues with the magic artefact are reduced to a broken sword, shrouded in mystery and still not explicitly recognised as 'magic', while the ugliness becomes a somewhat shabby, though noble, physical appearance.

In Toda Iglesia's view, in terms of genre, the British nineteenth-century adventure novel is an attempt to mediate between the narrative traditions of the epic, the romance and the novel, but it is also an expression of the Victorian era with its particular rites of passage undergone by young British men in remote areas of the empire.[187] This *mélange* should make it a perfect model for the narrative zone of Bree, a border region mixing the Shire and the Outside World, with certain Victorian connotations.[188] At the same time, it becomes a highly efficient narrative vehicle for the first stages of the journey in which the hobbits are initiated in the customs and the characteristics of the strange and dangerous Outside World.

Strider's way of talking and acting the day after the events at the inn reflects the conclusion that Tolkien may have reached with regards to the narrative treatment of this character: Aragorn still has to renounce his fully epic traits and remain in the realm of the novel. Upon leaving Bree, Strider says: "I am afraid we shall have to try to get one pony at least. But so ends all hope of starting early, and slipping away quietly! We might as well have blown a horn to announce our departure." (*LotR*, 194)

---

187 Toda Iglesia (2002:23-33) highlights the combination of these traditions as one of the prime trademarks of the adventure novel, while arguing that the didacticism would be intimately associated to the imperialist ideology of the Victorian era.
188 Bree, because of its historical relationship and geographical proximity to the Shire, retains at least some characteristics of the latter. The construction of the Shire as a narrative zone is deeply indebted to some literary expressions of the Victorian and Edwardian eras, as we have seen in section 4.1. (pages 119ff). Lobdell (2004:1-24) also discusses the influence of the Edwardian adventure novel on *The Lord of the Rings*.

A purely epic hero would not have expressed himself with the extreme indetermination of the first sentence – rather: "Bring a steed to Aragorn, son of Arathorn, heir of Gondor, or my wrath shall fall upon this village," or something of the kind – and he would definitely not have tried to hide or escape from his enemies. The main point of an epic hero's existence is to invest his name with glory, so one of his absolute priorities should rather be to announce to everybody that he sets out to carry out great and impressive deeds.[189] As Strider implies in the quotation above, the way in which they have to leave is neither purely epic nor successful from the point of view of the more pragmatic novel-hero, and this seems to him deeply unsatisfying. While they do attract the attention of the villagers, it is not because they want to, but because prosaic circumstances (the loss of the ponies) *make* their departure so conspicuous. Aragorn is not comfortable in this role, and his complaint is marked by the frustration of a hero with epic aspirations who is obliged by the limits imposed by the narrative dialogue to assume a role with considerably less power over his environment, and who finds that he is unsuccessful even in the comparatively easy and trivial novelistic task[190] of "slipping away quietly" from a sleepy town.

Rivendell: Romance and Epic

In the chapter 'The Council of Elrond', Strider's importance in the narrative is steadily increased, until his role as one of the main protagonists of the story is firmly established. He finally emerges as Aragorn, a character with deep roots in the novel, romance and epic traditions.[191] This, however,

---

189 Normally, the epic hero of the pre-Christian era considers it to be of prime importance to make his name known to the world through great deeds, since it is his only way of being included in the songs and in this way to achieve immortality. The idea that this should be the main objective of all heroes is taken for granted, whereby the protagonists will always know what their duty is. The notion of fighting is intimately related to the ambition of overcoming his mortality, the great enemy of all (see chapter 2, section 2.1). The reference to the horn is also associated to the hero of the epic and *chanson de geste* traditions, which will be discussed when analysing the character of Boromir.

190 Compared with the epic hero, the 'intimidating friend' of the tradition of the British nineteenth-century adventure novel is faced with different predicaments and can allow himself to be pragmatic about the relationship between honour and success, in this case avoiding an open confrontation with the enemy in order to escape unseen.

191 Flieger's 1981 essay 'Frodo and Aragorn: The Concept of the Hero', in Isaacs and Zimbardo (2004, second edition) was, together with Shippey's (2003:121-122) observations, first published 1983, one of the first serious reflections on the negotiation of narrative traditions in the character of Aragorn in this part of the tale. Both interpretations remain not only valid, but they are still among the best studies of the Rivendell episode up to this date.

is achieved only after a long negotiation of the limits of the intervening narrative traditions.

From the point of view of the intertraditional dialogue, it is interesting to notice Aragorn's persistent difficulties to take on the epic hero's stance, even when he seems to assume several of the corresponding features. This can be clearly seen in his dialogue with Boromir, in which he is ostensibly invited to become more 'epic' in his manners, as we shall see.

Flieger (1981:48) claims that when Aragorn shows his sword, he "publicly puts off the Strider-figure, assuming his rightful identity and all it implies." In my opinion, the statement is only true if we interpret Aragorn's "rightful identity" as a profound *mélange* of the novel, romance *and* epic traditions. In fact, the scene underscores just how difficult it is for him to shoulder the epic personality that the situation seems to require: facts are that he refrains from announcing himself as the true king (and much less from doing so *triumphantly*, as an epic hero would), and this very 'un-epic' hesitation makes it necessary for Elrond to reveal his identity.

This revelation implies a direct threat for Boromir, since Aragorn's kinship with Isildur would give him the right to claim the throne of Gondor, governed by Denethor, Boromir's father. He is not convinced by Aragorn's subsequent words about the sword and challenges him with his reply: "[...] the sword of Elendil would be a help beyond our hope – if such a thing could indeed return out of the shadows of the past". (*LotR*, 264)[192]

However, Aragorn is still surprisingly reluctant to give in to this invitation to heroic (epic) standards. When Boromir challenges him, Bilbo of all persons cuts in to recite an allegorical poem about Aragorn's birthrights. Only when his heroic stature has been certified by two different sources does Aragorn begin to answer Boromir in a more epically adequate manner, returning both the challenge and the boasting.

This reluctance is not so much due to limitations of the narrative zone of Rivendell, in which an epic or a *chanson de geste* hero may be fully projected

---

[192] Regarding the boasting and the challenging, Miller (2000:234-237) states that "two warriors implicitly recognize each other as men of a similar terrible kind through boasts."

(as Boromir's example has shown us), but it is rather a consequence of characterisation. Tolkien establishes a fundamental difference between the two rivals: Boromir's pride is matched against Aragorn's humility.[193] This dichotomy seems to arise as a consequence of Tolkien's wish to make a different kind of hero out of the raw material that Strider has given him; a hero who is not fully epic, but that combines certain aspects of pagan courage – which Tolkien admired in the pre-Christian Scandinavian and Germanic cultures[194] – with characteristics of the Christian hero, such as patience, humility and unyielding faith.[195]

Tolkien is thus interested in establishing a contrast between Aragorn and Boromir which underscores the spiritual integrity of the former and the moral fragility of the latter. In this process, the behaviour of Boromir helps defining the particular heroic features of Aragorn, and this is something that the narrator will exploit all through the journey from Rivendell to Amon Hen, as we shall see.

Aragorn receives the sword that belongs to him by birthright. From this moment on, Aragorn's identity will be intimately connected to his sword, and this will consolidate our new conception of him as an epic and romance hero *in spe*, in part because his mission is to recover his kingdom,[196] in part because the sword contributes to a conception of Aragorn as an epic hero with a basically Christian (romance) ethos. As symbols, the hilt of the sword symbolizes the material world, while the blade represents the materialisation of the spiritual dimension, and in the Christian tradition, swords are related to the spirit and

---

193 Shippey (2003:121), when discussing the difference in linguistic flexibility between Aragorn and Boromir, emphasizes the former's capacity of using colloquial speech compared to "Boromir's slightly wooden magniloquence." This difference in diction is also indicative of Aragorn's humbleness as opposed to Boromir's pride.
194 See Tolkien (1997:20-28).
195 Milton is a forerunner to Tolkien here, since one of his strategies for character-drawing in *Paradise Lost* was to highlight the contrast between the Christian hero's authenticity and the falsehood of the secular epic hero. In Steadman's (1969:15-16) opinion, "Milton juxtaposed Christian and secular ideals of heroic virtue within the same narrative framework and thus brought out the distinctive qualities of both [...] The new [Christian heroic patterns] serve as a yardstick to measure – and castigate the old." This is particularly clear in the treatment of Adam and Satan.
196 According to Miller (2000:134), the normal structure of the epic hero's adventures is the following: "hero is exiled, comes back to the centre that sent him away, or to other centres of enclosed, rigid, restricting, old, and impacted power [...] he reacquaints the settled people with his name, or with a name." The same structure dominates the myth central to Arthurian romance: the fertilisation of the Waste Land and the mythic paradigm that governs Aragorn's action, the "hero-king myth" as labelled by Veugen (2005:180-181).

word of God, with a will of their own. According to De Paco (2003:252), the habit of giving them names would be a result of this.[197]

The *mélange* between the epic mission and the Christian ethos found in the figure of Aragorn is also implied by the contrast with Boromir in the scene where the Fellowship departs from Rivendell:

> Aragorn had Andúril but no other weapon, and he went forth clad only in rusty green and brown, as a Ranger of the Wilderness. Boromir had a long sword, in fashion like Andúril but of less lineage, and he bore also a shield and his war-horn.
>
> 'Loud and clear it sounds in the valleys of the hills,' he said, 'and then let all the foes of Gondor flee!' Putting it to his lips he blew a blast, and the echoes leapt from rock to rock, and all that heard that voice in Rivendel sprang to their feet. (*LotR*, 296)

While Aragorn's mission thus is typical of both the romance and the epic traditions,[198] it is interesting to see that the sword – the word and spirit of God in the Christian iconography – is the only weapon he needs. His simple clothing is also indicative of his humble stance compared to the more extravagantly dressed Boromir, who also carries a shield to protect himself – a detail hinting at his lack of faith – and a war-horn to announce his departure and make the world acquainted with his name and deeds.

All through the journey towards Lórien and Amon Hen, the narrator continues defining Aragorn's heroic role by comparing him with Boromir, whose lack of self-control, patience and faith stands out unfavourably against the calm backdrop of Aragorn's (and Gandalf's) Christian virtues. Boromir is continuously played out as a hero with initially good intentions, but led astray by distrust, as when he protests against Gandalf's decisions: "All choices seem ill, and to be caught between wolves and the wall the likeliest chance. Lead on!" and "thither we are going against my wish. Who will lead us now in this deadly dark?" (*LotR*, 317, 323, respectively). However, the scene that best shows his lack of

---

197 Aragorn calls his sword Andúril, which means "the flame of the West."
198 In Kocher's (1974:128) view, the starting point for Aragorn's most difficult trials is the departure from Rivendell. In truth, from Rivendell and on Aragorn will be subjected to increasingly difficult tests that will end up involving the destiny of the whole world. That issues of supreme – even universal – importance for large communities should be at stake is typical of epic narratives, such as the *Iliad*, the *Aneid*, or *Paradise Lost*.

faith, patience, self-control and prudence is when he becomes tired of waiting for Gandalf to find the magic word at the Gates of Moria and throws a stone in the lake. This imprudence wakes up the *kraken*, a monster that threatens to kill the whole Fellowship, and may well be interpreted as a punishment in response to Boromir's moral weakness.

At the same time, Aragorn repeatedly shows that he is just as strong, skilful and courageous as the Gondorian in battle. At Caradhras, when Boromir volunteers to open up a path through the snow, Aragorn joins him. (It is significant that it is Boromir who later boasts of the feat: "'But happily your Caradhras has forgotten that you have Men with you,' said Boromir […] 'And doughty Men too, if I may say it […].'"(*LotR*, 309). Later on, when fighting the wolves, Aragorn and Boromir are shown as equally brave and strong; during the first battle with the orcs, the narrator says that "Boromir and Aragorn slew many" (*LotR*, 343), and in the decisive moment at the bridge of Khazad-dûm, both heroes try to help Gandalf while the rest are paralysed by fear: "'"He cannot stand alone!' cried Aragorn suddenly and ran back along the bridge. 'Elendil!' he shouted. 'I am with you, Gandalf!' 'Gondor!' cried Boromir and leaped after him" (*LotR*, 349). In this way, Aragorn is consolidated as the most complete hero of the two.

Lórien: Romance

Lórien is a narrative zone which, due to its close connection to romance paradigms, is particularly ill suited for a further exploitation of the epic potential of Aragorn and Boromir, who will both lose protagonism in favour of Frodo and Sam. At Cerin Amroth, Aragorn exhibits an assimilation of the romance tradition in the scene where he recalls his first meeting with Arwen. The bloodstained epic hero we have seen a few pages before has now become a love-sick romantic who, contemplating a flower with a dreamy look in his eyes, utters a few sentimental words and takes Frodo's hand as they leave.

In this scene, Aragorn's epic potential is almost annihilated. His previous refusal, at Rivendell, to yield completely to the epic paradigms of characterisation; his Christian/romance traits (with love at the centre), and the invitation by the physical space, particularly adequate for the inclusion of romance elements,[199] make his romance conversion so credible that the reader even begins to suspect that he will leave his epic pretensions and turn into a solid romance knight. The scene anticipates his future flirts with this tradition – which will eventually lead to a complete transformation into the romance king once the war is won – but as he 'sobers up' after this interlude, his epic potential is not completely lost in the process.

From Amon Hen to Fangorn: Novel, Epic, and Romance

In the scene describing the death of Boromir at Amon Hen, apart from the evident analogy with *Le Chanson de Roland*,[200] we can also see a parallel between the heroic couples Aragorn/Boromir, on the one hand, and Hector/Achilles on the other. While Hector as a character is marked by both his sense of responsibility and his battle courage, Achilles is intimately connected with uncontrolled and destructive wrath. From my point of view, it is not the homeric version of these heroes that comes closest to the treatment of the heroic couple Aragorn/Boromir, but rather Benoît de Sainte-Maure's *Le Roman de Troie*, which, according to King (1987:231), is also the first version that emphasizes the difference between the villain and the courtly knight in the characters of Achilles and Hector:

> Benoit's Achilles can't play the courtly game well because he is the plaything of his own twin sexual and aggressive passions [...] Hektor channels his energies in a more productive way: he has achieved wisdom and the courtliness that goes with it.

The parallels to the scene of Boromir's death is significant, because Tolkien's treatment also reminds us of Aragorn's romance (and Christian) potential, even in the moments most heavily informed by epic or *chanson de geste* standards, such as Boromir's heroic feats waging battle on the orcs and his subsequent (and,

---

199 Regarding the connection between the elves and the tradition of medieval romance, Shippey (2003: 55-65) considers that the medieval poem *Sir Orfeo* is the text that inspired Tolkien the most for the creation of this race. Lórien also has a clear connection to the Middle-English poem *Pearl*, in which the poet tries to cross a river to join his dead daughter, who shows him the splendours of Paradise on the other side. Similarly, as the members of the Fellowship cross the Silverlode they enter an immaculate and paradisiac realm (Shippey 2003:218). See also Kaufmann (Lobdell 1975:143-152).
200 The analogy with the protagonist of *Le Chanson de Roland* is evident: like Roland, Boromir blows the horn in order to make his allies aware of the attack, but it is too late – he, too, dies with many wounds after killing an incredible number of enemies likened to insects. Even the friends of both are similar: Olivier is marked by his wisdom, as Aragorn is, while Roland is characterized by his impetuosity, courage, strength and fury in battle. See Day (2003:173).

of course, highly appropriate) death. The scene shows Aragorn's double affinities as he forgives Boromir both because of his traditionally heroic death and his repentance:[201] his reaction is motivated by pity and forgiveness – Christian virtues – on the one hand, and, on the other, by the epic hero's ethos, centered on the virtue of a death on the battlefield, being the epic hero's most efficient method of investing his name with lasting glory.[202]

The chapter 'The Departure of Boromir' shows, among other things, the persistent limitations of Aragorn as a traditional epic hero. From the moment we first met him, in Bree, we have perceived his inherent epic potential, which to a great extent has been held in check by the other members of the Fellowhip: the hobbits, who have brought him into dialogue with the novel; Gandalf, who has eclipsed him as a leader; and Boromir, whose egotism and lack of moral strength Aragorn has been made to counterbalance with a constant exhibition of his combination of epic and romance/Christian virtues, and whose presence and remarks have questioned his protagonism.

At this stage of the narrative, all these characters have conveniently disappeared, and Aragorn is presented with an opportunity to put his full epic potential on display: the most recent action has been marked by *chanson de geste*-standards; and the comrades that remain – Gimli and Legolas – do not imply an obstacle for his epic fulfilment because of their narrative neutrality.

In short, everything seems to indicate that Aragorn will finally turn into a pure epic hero, and when he makes the decision to follow the orcs, the narrator elevates the tone to the high diction of the epic:

> '[...] With hope or without hope we will follow the trail of our enemies: and woe to them, if we prove the swifter! We will make such a chase as shall be accounted a marvel among the Three Kindreds: Elves, Dwarves, and Men. Forth the Three Hunters!'

---

201 See Kocher (1974:132): "Aragorn shifts none of the blame to Boromir, whose sincere repentance and heroic death in battle [...] completely redeem him in Aragorn's eyes."
202 The Scandinavian saga tradition, which may be interpreted as a 'lighter' and more domestic version of the older epics and the medieval chanson de geste, also shows this ethos, mainly because of its strong connections to Norse mythology and its emphasis on earthly fulfilment by heroic deeds that persisted even after the Scandinavian kingdoms were officially converted. Tolkien found the combination of pagan courage and the Christian ethos in Beowulf particularly attractive. See Tolkien (1997).

> Like a deer he sprang away. Through the trees he sped. On and on he led them, tireless and swift, now that his mind was at last made up [...]. (*LotR*, 440)

Aragorn's tone and boastful attitude, together with the wish that the heroic feats be turned into a matter of legend and the physical strength conferred by his new-found determination, all help setting the scene for a further exploitation of his epic side. It remains to be seen, however, whether the nature of the mission meets the demands of the epic.

During the first part of the hunt for the hobbits, Aragorn, Gimli and Legolas cover a distance of forty-four leagues (around two hundred kilometres) on foot in only four days, crossing the great plains of Rohan. In spite of this impressive feat, they do not manage to hunt down the orcs. Aragorn and Gimli believe that their failure is due to Saruman's influence (*LotR*, 448), but there may be other reasons involved: the rescue of Merry and Pippin is not an epic mission. Aragorn, the king in exile, is getting farther and farther away from Minas Tirith, where he should be going to fight the Enemy and claim kingship. And for what reason? To save two hobbits, who at this moment seem totally insignificant for the outcome of the conflict between Sauron's forces and those of the Free People. Such a mission is bound to fail from the point of view of a purely epic narrative tradition.[203] Aragorn himself seems to acknowledge this constraint when they interrupt the chase momentarily for want of light, but even so, he wants to go on:

> [...] Gimli murmured [...]: 'Would that the Lady had given us a light, such a gift as she gave to Frodo.'
>
> 'It will be more needed where it is bestowed,' said Aragorn. 'With him lies the true Quest. Ours is but a small matter in the great deeds of this time. A vain pursuit from its beginning, maybe, which no choice of mine can mar or mend. Well, I have chosen. So let us use the time as best we may!' (*LotR*, 446)

Éomer and the Riders of Rohan attempt to put Aragorn back on the epic track, killing off the orcs and offering him horses in exchange for a promise to go straight to Edoras as soon as he has confirmed the absence of hobbits among

---

[203] The epic greatness of the hunt is related to the physical feat, not to its objective. Because of this, the mission fails from a result-oriented epic standpoint, while it is a success from the point of view of the romance, which emphasizes the knight's spiritual education.

the dead orcs. During the meeting with Éomer, this character inspires him to speak and behave like an epic hero (Kocher 1974:133), proudly affirming his rank in almost boastful words. But instead of joining the *rohirrim* in the war against Saruman he stubbornly rejects the offer and decides to continue the search for the hobbits.

After finding the funeral pyre for the orcs empty of hobbit-remains, Aragorn, Gimli and Legolas camp below a tree at some distance from the forest of Fangorn. Both the nightfall, and the ensuing darkness that blurs ordinary perception of reality, and the proximity of the legendary Fangorn Forest invite the romance tradition into the dialogue and make the strange behaviour of the sheltering tree coherent and even feasible:

> It may have been that the dancing shadows tricked their eyes, but certainly to each of the companions the boughs appeared to be bending this way and that so as to come above the flames, while the upper branches were stooping down; the brown leaves now stood out stiff, and rubbed together like many cold cracked hands taking comfort in the warmth. (*LotR*, 462)

Shortly after this, a silent old man appears, only to vanish instantly again, without leaving any trace.

The world has become mysterious with the nightfall, and the strange events reinforce the presence of romance paradigms in the narrative dialogue, which will incline the balance towards this tradition on the following day, as the adventurers enter the Forest of Fangorn to look for the hobbits.

As they lose the horses and leave the realm of Rohan behind, Aragorn also loses his epic bearings quite clearly, and delves into a romance territory that leads him further away from his 'true' quest.[204] The atmosphere in the forest is oppressive and the orientation becomes increasingly difficult. Gimli is the first to acknowledge the minimal prospects of success of their enterprise and tries to convince Aragorn to change his mind:

---

204 See Quint (1985:179-182) on the narrative movement towards romance standards in an epic narrative. Quint discusses an episode from Tassos's *Gerusalemme Liberata*, in which Reinaldo, the protagonist, allows himself to be led astray from his historical (epic) mission and experience a romance adventure in which the events suddenly become disconnected from each other and from the global plot. When Reinaldo sobers up and returns to the road of the main action, the epic presents him with a clear objective and organises the events in a coherent narrative.

'If we do not find them soon, we shall be of no use to them, except to sit down beside them and show our friendship by starving together.'

'If that is indeed all we can do, then we must do that,' said Aragorn. 'Let us go on.' (*LotR*, 512)

There is a significant difference between the attitude of Aragorn, who feels that it is his duty not to lose faith, and that of Gimli, which is more pragmatic and realistic. Aragorn's obstinate stance will be rewarded by the reappearance of Gandalf (which is portrayed much as a haphazard encounter with a romance wizard), but – and this is important – only after he has shown an unbreakable faith in the success of the mission, little less than impossible to begin with, that he has chosen.[205]

The assertion, on behalf of a spiritual authority such as Gandalf, that he has successfully passed a moral test, gives Aragorn the final license to abandon the hunt for the hobbits and embark on epic ventures:

[...] 'Come, Aragorn son of Arathorn!' he said. 'Do not regret your choice in the valley of the Emyn Muil, nor call it a vain pursuit. You chose amid doubts the path that seemed right: the choice was just, and it has been rewarded. For so we have met in time, who otherwise might have met too late. But the quest of your companions is over. Your next journey is marked by your given word. You must go to Edoras and seek out Théoden in his hall. For you are needed. The light of Andúril must now be uncovered in the battle for which it has so long waited. [...]' (*LotR*, 522)

In this way, everything is finally set for a full exploitation of Aragorn's epic potential: his romance/Christian virtues have been tested and confirmed, and he has been granted permission to carry out epic deeds.

Meduseld and Helm's Deep: Epic.

It has been a commonplace in Tolkien criticism to compare the arrival at Meduseld, Théoden's fortress, with the parallel episode in *Beowulf*, where the eponymous hero enters Heoroth, the home of the Danish king Hrothgar, to

---

205 Hope is one of the main virtues in Tolkien's moral universe. As we have seen, the way Tolkien merges different traditions clears the way for the applicability to modern times, expressing something that we might call a 'meta-narrative myth of hope for the twentieth century'. As Aragorn is one of the most important representatives of this myth, it is important that he should not lose faith in the mission and yield to the less spiritually informed ambitions of the purely epic hero.

help him fight the monster Grendel.[206] Apart from the sequence itself, the verses sung by Aragorn as they pass the grave mounds of the dead kings of Rohan also evoke the Northern heroic world, because of their similarity with the elegiac Old English poem 'The Wanderer'.[207] Aragorn's version reads like this: "Where now the horse and the rider? Where is the horn that was blowing? / Where is the helm and the hauberk, and the bright hair flowing?" The similarity with the original is undeniable: "Where is the horse now, where the hero gone? / Where is the bounteous lord, and where the benches / For feasting? Where are the joys of the hall?" (Hamer 1970:181)

We are thus entering a territory close to Northern Europe during the early Middle Ages, of whose narrative traditions *Beowulf* is the most notable representative, and this is reflected in Aragorn's behaviour as they approach Meduseld. At the gates, he engages in a violent argument with the doorwarden, showing us a side of his personality far removed from the suffering romance knight, ready to face the risk of failure and humiliation for the sake of spiritual growth, that we have seen only a few pages before: now, he refuses to leave his sword outside the Hall and defies both the doorwarden and the king by proudly affirming his identity, up to a point where armed combat seems inevitable:

> 'It is not clear to me that the will of Théoden son of Thengel, even though he be lord of the Mark, should prevail over the will of Aragorn son of Arathorn, Elendil's heir of Gondor.' (*LotR*, 533)

Aragorn's formerly humble attitude has been replaced by the arrogant and challenging stance of the epic hero (Miller 2000:234), invited by the physical space, the action and the characters. It is only after Gandalf's insistent mediation that Aragorn finally accepts the doorwarden's conditions.

The scene that shows Théoden's conversion and Gríma's subsequent downfall is marked by a strong emphasis on Christian virtues, such as hope, mercy, forgiveness and generosity,[208] all of which are diametrically opposed to the

---

206 For example, St Clair (1992:64), Tolley (1993:155-156), and Shippey (2003:124).
207 Quella Kelly (1968:170-200) concludes that there are similarities between the poetry of Rohan and Old English poetry in intonation, alitteration, repetition and word-order.
208 Théoden is convinced by Gandalf's message of hope, while Gríma is forgiven and offered a place in the cavalry at the king's side. He rejects the offer with disdain but is nonetheless given a horse and freedom to leave.

warrior ethics of the pre-Christian epic hero. Perhaps as a consequence of this, Aragorn hardly intervenes in the dialogue; he cannot mar his new and full-grown epic identity by falling into the 'pit' of mercy.

However, Tolkien has not finished torturing the recently converted epic hero with foreign influences. Éowyn, the king's niece, enters the scene, hopelessly falling in love with Aragorn. The episode is nothing more than a brief interlude, but it is enough to remind us of Aragorn's courtly – romance – side, given that he acts with her as a typical knight of medieval romance would; courtly and kindly but always true to his lady.[209] At the same time it is significant that Éowyn should be a basically epic heroine,[210] something that reduces the analogue with the courtly love scenes from the medieval romance tradition to a minimum, albeit it does not entirely suppress them.[211]

In the following chapter, 'Helm's Deep', the dialogue between romance and epic is particularly evident in the different attitudes towards war shown by Gimli and Legolas, on the one hand, and Aragorn, Éomer and Théoden on the other. For the former, the battle is an entertainment, good sport that inspires competitiveness:

> 'Twenty-one!' cried Gimli. He hewed a two-handed stroke and laid the last Orc before his feet. 'Now my count passes Master Legolas again!'
>
> [...] 'Good!' said Legolas. 'But my count is now two dozen. It has been knife-work up here.' (*LotR*, 559)[212]

As opposed to this romance attitude, Aragorn and Théoden exhibit an epic disposition towards the battle. For them, war is a serious matter and despera-

---

[209] Courtly love and its consequences – in this case, the constant testing of Aragorn's fidelity on behalf of Éowyn – is one of the most prominent themes in medieval romance. The most well-known example is, perhaps, *Sir Gawain and the Green Knight*, in which the protagonist is afflicted by constant invitations to adulterous love that he must resist. On the influence of this work on *The Lord of the Rings*, see Miller (1991) and Chance (1986).
[210] Éowyn shares many features with the amazons, the female warriors of the *Iliad* and the *Aneid*, and with Brynhild of *Völsungasagan* / Brunhilda of the *Nibelungenlied*. For a more exhaustive exploration of these analogues, see Day (2003:157) and Fenwick (1996).
[211] Miller (2000:46-47) states that "the femenine element in romance epics breaks and reforms the narrative frame." This is an effect that will be more clearly appreciated in the next meeting between Aragorn and Éowyn.
[212] Compared to the austere epic hero, the romance knight shows a far more leisurely attitude towards battle, marked by what we might call an enthusiastic desire for competition and good sport.

tion is only grimly held in check by the desire to gain immortality through impressive deeds that are to be sung by poets:

> 'The end will not be long,' said the king. '[...] When dawn comes, I will bid men sound Helm's horn, and I will ride forth. Will you ride with me then, son of Arathorn? Maybe we shall cleave a road, or make an end as will be worth a song – if any be left to sing of us hereafter.'
>
> 'I will ride with you,' said Aragorn. (*LotR*, 562-563)[213]

Isengard: Novel

The ease with which Aragorn shifts to the novel tradition during the sojourn at Isengard is also worth a comment. In this episode, Merry and Pippin take on the role of masters of ceremony: they bring food and pipe-weed to the weary travellers and organise a kind of novelistic picnic at the gates of Orthanc – much like a group of tourists would at the gates of some medieval castle – in the jocose and carefree tradition of Jerome's humoristic holiday novels,[214] before filling in the informative gaps for their friends and for the reader.

Gimli's interventions reinforce the presence of the novel tradition, as he asks, in a similar humoristic tone, for food and a comfortable place to eat it, a story well told[215] and pipe-weed to enhance the pleasure of listening to it. Aragorn remains rather austere at first, but as he sits down to enjoy the lunch he shows a clear tendency to soften the rigidly epic stance that has dominated his personality during the last chapters:

---

[213] In Miller's (2000:220) view, "[the epic hero is] playing out a suicidal scenario [accepting] a confrontation from which he cannot possibly escape alive [...] he presents himself as victim, but he will not go quietly, and most often he will not go alone [...] [He] dooms himself and his men." Aragorn shows indulgence and even sympathy for Legolas and Gimli's competition (*LotR*, 561), but he does not take part in it. Dickerson (2003:42) claims that the competition between the elf and the dwarf is not the central event in the treatment of this episode, given the comparatively limited space it is given by the narrator, while Chance (2001:221) underscores the analogues between the descriptions of the battle and descriptions found in Old English heroic poetry, such as *The Battle of Maldon* or *Brunanburh*, that share many features with the Nordic current of epic poetry represented by *Beowulf*.

[214] *Three Men in a Boat* and *Three Men on the Bummel* come to mind. There are many similarities beween the interaction of the characters in these novels and that of the hobbits, especially during the first part of the journey through the Shire.

[215] With a story well told, Gimli refers to novelistic standards of 'truth' – a chronologically and geographically coherent and full picture – as shown by his subsquent questions.

'Now let us take our ease here for a little!' said Aragorn. 'We will sit on the edge of ruin and talk, as Gandalf says, while he is busy elsewhere. I feel a weariness such as I have seldom felt before.' He wrapped his grey cloak about him, hiding his mail-shirt, and stretched out his long legs. Then he lay back and sent from his lips a thin stream of smoke. (*LotR*, 586)

Now, invited to take part in a novelistic discourse by the hobbits, the action (picnicking) and the type of conversation (prosaic and colloquial, basically aimed at filling in the missing gaps of the plot), the 'Beowulfian' hero leaves the epic issues for Gandalf and Théoden, covering his shining armour with the travel-stained coat and making himself comfortable on the ground to smoke and chat. He admits his double personality with a natural ease, assuming once more the stance of a character from the adventure-novel.

Minas Tirith: Epic and Romance

When Aragorn arrives at the fields of Pelennor, commanding a fleet of ships with black sails,[216] it is in the midst of general despair. His behaviour as he shows his true identity, unfolding the standard[217] and carrying out prodigious feats of arms, is decidedly epic, but as he prepares to enter the city, his attitude changes radically: he is suddenly reluctant to enter the city in triumph and hides his banner, removes the star from his brow and covers his mailcoat with the elvish cloak. His official reason for doing so – to avoid trouble with the people of the city – is of a certain relevance as it shows his romance/Christian prudence, but there may be other motivations involved, related to the limits imposed by the intertraditional dialogue.

---

[216] Day (2003:161-162) considers that the main connection between Aragorn's return and Theseus's homecoming after his adventure in Crete is the despair that strikes the inhabitants of the city when seeing the black sails. This and other analogues enhance the connections between Minas Tirith, on the one hand, and the classical Athens and Troy on the other, reinforcing Aragorn's own relationship to the main narrative traditions associated to that epoch: epic and heroic poetry, and myth. See Greenman (1992).

[217] The unfolding of standards and banners symbolizes, according to De Paco (2003:181) the exaltation of the bearer's identity, but also the victory of Christ after his glorious resurrection. Tolkien has yet again succeeded in finding a symbol closely related to Aragorn that is capable of integrating both epic (pagan) and Christian aspects, at least if we interpret Aragorn's ride through the Underworld of the Paths of the Dead as a kind of death and resurrection that culminates in a glorious return. The connection between Aragorn and Christ will be reinforced as he enters Minas Tirith, as we shall see.

Miller (2000:119-120) argues that the city is easily turned into a serious threat for a battle-waging epic hero: on the one hand, it puts constraints[218] on his previously unlimited range of action, and on the other – more important – it inhibits his normal behavior, necessarily violent and aggressive:

> In the heroic tradition [...] the city is a trap for heroism. So is marriage, which usually means submission to the ideal systems of contractual kingship, continuation, and social rules [...] In the usual epic scenario, the hero is prepared to go to any lengths to avoid the fate of Héktor – not death, but death on the defensive, trapped in the constricting bonds and artefacts of culture, rather than death on the offensive, assaulting that culture.

It is evident that Aragorn's aim is to take command of the city, marry Arwen and become king of Gondor and of all the Free People. However, he still has to command his troops in the final battle against Sauron, and to enter the city in triumph, and then defend it as the official patriarch, would diminish his potential as an epic hero according to the epic conventions as outlined by Miller above. In the end he prefers to enter the city *incognito*, with the exterior signs of his epic identity hidden and his armour covered.

There may be further reasons for his prudence. By hiding the epic side of his identity, he also paves the way for the subsequent action, in which he acts as the healer and revitalizer of the kingdom.[219] As in the case of Éowyn's pleas for love in Édoras and at Dunharrow, and the unfolding of the banner as Aragorn approaches Minas Tirith, Aragorn's entrance in Minas Tirith to heal the wounded and ill does not imply a complete rejection of one narrative

---

218 The cities of early Mediterranean civilizations (for example, Troy), were normally protected by walls that surrounded the whole urban area. Minas Tirith has a similar structure, but with seven walls instead of only one, which means that the further towards the centre (where the Citadel and the tower of Ecthelion, the steward's residence that the new king must take back, are located) Aragorn comes, the more constricted he will become.

219 See Kocher (1974:140): "On the plains of Pelennor, [Aragorn] overcomes the enemies of Gondor by arms. But Gondor itself he overcomes by love." Flieger, in her essay 'Frodo and Aragorn: the Concept of the Hero', in Isaacs and Zimbardo (1981:49-50), links Aragorn's double role of healer and renewer to the romance tradition. This is particularly evident in the scene in which Aragorn heals Faramir and Éowyn. Here, the theme of the new king who arrives to heal the kingdom – his name Envinyatar means 'Renewer', as Aragorn himself points out (*LotR*, 897) – and that of Éowyn's unrequited love, reinforce the presence of the romance tradition, which can be appreciated in the descriptions of the effects of *athelas*, which brings a virginal air to the room, "as if it had not before been breathed by any living thing and came new-made from snowy mountains high beneath a dome of stars." (*LotR*, 902)

tradition in favour of another,²²⁰ but rather a *significant* narrative movement towards the tradition of romance that at the same time retains its connections with the epic.

Victory: Romance

From the episode of the Fields of Cormallen and on, Aragorn's intertraditional flexibility is almost completely reduced to his romance side. The scene showing him seated on a throne in the clearing of the forest of Ithilien with the sword on his knees, acting like a benevolent and wise king, is a proper introduction for what is to come.

The romance continues dominating the narrative when the heroes return to Minas Tirith. At this stage, Aragorn appears as the revitalising king of medieval romance: wise, strong, still young and with healing powers: "ancient of days he seemed and yet in the flower of manhood; and wisdom sat upon his brow, and strength and healing were in his hands, and a light was about him." (*LotR*, 1004) This time he enters the city triumphantly, and the narrator emphasizes the renewed splendour of the streets. However, Aragorn the romance king lacks a queen to become complete and to fulfil the mythical pattern. The problem is that the White Tree of Gondor is dead, and Aragorn cannot get married until it flowers again.

Gandalf enters the scene once more, and acting as a divine messenger he takes Aragorn to Mount Mindolluin, where he explains to him what should be done, showing him a sapling that against all odds has sprouted from the rocky ground. Aragorn plants the sapling where the old tree used to stand and marries Arwen on the day of the summer solstice. Both things are intimately connected to the medieval and renaissance world-view, where the king and queen are at the centre, and in direct union with God.²²¹ As we have seen, virtually everything in this episode is related to the concepts of fertility and renewal (the marriage, the flowering tree and a general renaissance of the

---

220 Regarding the theme of healing in the epic tradition, Miller (2000: 325-326) says that Achilles has the ability to heal, but he does not use it because "the [epic] hero's business is always to deal out death." The point is that even if healing is not a priority for an epic hero, it is not totally foreign to him.
221 In the Christian (and hence, romance) iconography, the tree symbolizes a bridge between heaven and earth, as does the union between the king and queen. (De Paco 2003:145, 347).

arts and culture in the city²²²) which by analogue with the central myth in Arthurian romance – we may well call it the fertilisation of the Waste Land – puts the narrative in close contact with medieval romance.

One of the reasons for this may be that Aragorn, after the triumph at the Black Gate, takes on the role of king, whereby he loses his epic traits, perhaps since the figure of the king and all it implies in terms of responsibility and stability are opposed to the attitude and fundamental ambitions required of the epic hero (Miller 2000:140-141). In this way, Aragorn is reborn together with the birth of the Fourth Age, but at the same time he is reduced to the stereotype of the Renewer king and becomes so inflexible that he can no longer take part in the intertraditional dialogue.²²³

4.4. Rivendell: narrative mélange

A border rehabilitated

Rivendell, Elrond's house, is in many ways similar to Bree. Like Bree, from the point of view of narrative tension, this narrative zone represents a return to safety and rest after exhilarating and breathtaking adventures. Geographically, it is a border region, situated close to the Misty Mountains, which is the most conspicuous line of division between East and West in Middle-earth. As for its cultural characteristics, it also offers a wide range of traditions. However, while Bree is a town visited mainly for commercial reasons, due to its proximity to the Road, Rivendell, located far from any trading route, is the object of pilgrimage for people in search of knowledge and spiritual ease.²²⁴ This

---

222 See Day's (2003:172-174) comparison between Aragorn and Charlemagne. That the central myth of *The Lord of the Rings* should be the founding of the city, as Moorman says in 'The Shire, Mordor, and Minas Tirith', in Isaacs and Zimbardo (1968:203), is to reduce the scope of applicability too drastically; but it makes sense if we expand the implications of that enterprise to the bringing of hope to a spritually wounded culture by the use of intertraditional elements.
223 In Kocher's (1974:142) words: "Aragorn the man recedes to Aragorn the King."
224 Day (2003:52) establishes two basic analogies for Rivendell: on the one hand, Oxford during the Great War, because it is "a safe refuge and a place of learning and long meditation for the world-weary," where the common language is English (compared to Westron in Rivendell) while the scientific languages are Greek and Latin (Sindarin and Quenya in Rivendell); and on the other hand Delphi, which means 'crack' or 'cleft' (to be compared with the elvish name for Rivendell, Imladris, which means 'profound cloven valley'), where the oracle, like Elrond, gives advice to travellers before journeys and other ventures. (Day 2003:52-55)

difference in socio-economic *raison d'être* will have a decisive influence on the intertraditional dialogue, making the presence of romance, epic and myth much more prominent in Rivendell than in Bree.

When it comes to the setting, while both places are located in border areas, Rivendell offers more possibilities for a 'free' and unrestricted incorporation of different traditions. It is more remote from the Shire than Bree, and the familiar elements will thus fade with a certain ease as strange and foreign influences begin to dominate the narrative zone.

As for the characters, instead of a middle-aged, business-minded innkeeper, we find an ancient, wise half-elf of global political importance presiding over the house. As a result, the 'clientele' of Rivendell is infinitely more sophisticated than that of *The Prancing Pony*. There is also a greater variety of characters at Rivendell than in Bree, and they act and speak as official representatives of different cultures. Regarding the thematic aspect of this narrative zone, the characters in Rivendell are given plenty of space to talk about the history of Middle-earth and debate the issue of the Ring during the Council.

For this reason, it is also of prime importance for Tolkien to rid this narrative zone of the ballast inherited from *The Hobbit*, given that Rivendell is a place that has first been portrayed there. In the earlier story, Rivendell is frequently referred to as "the Last Homely House", and takes on much of the role which in *The Lord of the Rings* has already been assigned to Bree, namely that of being the ultimate threshold to the strange and dangerous Outside World. In the later narrative, the narrator uses the term "the Last Homely House" only twice, first at the very beginning of the episode, when Frodo has just woken up, and the second time at the end, as they leave. The episode is thus framed by two identical denominations of its setting, but by the time the reader, who is familiar with the version of Rivendell presented in *The Hobbit*, comes across the epithet for the second time, it has come to mean something entirely different. Instead of a world (however vaguely) reminiscent of the cosy Shire, being just another stage on a comparatively frivolous adventure, the treatment of Rivendell as a narrative zone is now clearly marked by the solemn matters that are being discussed there – if it is 'homelike' in any sense, it is because it represents the end of the hobbits' previous life as they knew it. It is after Rivendell that the hobbits really begin to change.

Technically speaking, Rivendell's change in character is brought about by a process of 'rehabilitation' that Tolkien elaborates for this narrative zone in *The Lord of the Rings*. The process involves a restriction on the inter-traditional dialogue, because it implies a recognition of the fixed personality of certain characters that have appeared in the earlier narrative, such as Glóin, Bilbo and Elrond. Except for Gandalf, who already in *The Hobbit* was portrayed as a character with considerable intertraditional flexibility, the people who have been presented to us in that story are difficult to incorporate in a narrative that depends on the intertraditional dialogue to such an extent as *The Lord of the Rings* does, given that in the previous story they travel in Middle-earth without hardly establishing a dialogue with it, and it would be absurd to radically alter their personality at this stage.

The chapter 'Many Meetings' is partly used as a starting point, from which Tolkien tries to find the tone that differs most adequately from the one used to portray these characters in the first book, because without an efficient change, their inclusion in the following chapter, 'The Council of Elrond', will present a serious obstacle for the fluency of the intertraditional dialogue. The result of the process is that Tolkien preserves part of the original tone, but without exploiting the stereotypical traits of each race or community for comic ends,[225] as he did up to a certain point in *The Hobbit*, and in this way they are 'updated' and integrated in the new narrative zone without much difficulty or narrative incoherencies.

When Frodo wakes up in Rivendell after the adventurous journey, the atmosphere of the narrative zone is very similar to the one Tolkien used to describe the Last Homely House in *The Hobbit*. This brief return to the nineteenth-century narrative *mélange* of the initial chapters provides a eucatastrophical contrast to the more serious, almost ominous tone which has dominated the journey from Bree. Gandalf is the same old wizard as ever, smoking his pipe

---

225 Except, perhaps, for Bilbo, who is often used to deflate the epic and prophetic tone of Gandalf, Elrond and others, partly in order to pave the way for Frodo's heroic evolution, as we shall see.

at the bedside and talking about the events of the outside world as if they belonged to a remote place. Because Frodo asks the pertinent questions, Gandalf is able to fill in the informational gaps and put a novelistic frame around the space-time relationships and the construction of the plot.

However, Gandalf will grow in status in this narrative zone, until we get a glimpse of the 'divine messenger' that he will eventually become. This growth begins at the dinner on the night before the Council, when Frodo sees him next to Elrond: "[...] Glorfindel, and even Gandalf, whom he thought he knew so well, were revealed as lords of dignity and power" (*LotR*, 243). Elrond, on the other hand, appears just like we have seen him in *The Hobbit*, as a benevolent and wise king of romance, respected by everybody: "Venerable he seemed as a king crowned with many winters, and yet hale as a tried warrior in the fulness of his strength. He was the Lord of Rivendell and mighty among both Elves and Men." (*LotR*, 243)

Frodo feels rather misplaced due to the presence of so many important and renowned persons, but he is more at ease when speaking with Glóin, one of the dwarves that accompanied Bilbo in the adventure narrated in *The Hobbit*. The courteous diction of Glóin is very similar to that of Thorin Oakenshield as he is portrayed in the earlier story, and comments such as "Allow me to congratulate you on your recovery" (*LotR*, 244) produce a slightly comical effect that brings us closer to the general tone of the first book. However, Tolkien does not further exploit the comical potential of the dialogue between an ancient dwarf and a modern hobbit, and the narrator adopts a more neutral attitude in the portrayal of the former.

After the dinner, the guests move on to the Hall of Fire, where Frodo meets Bilbo. Neither the passing of time nor the accumulated knowledge of the different traditions of Middle-earth seem to have altered this character's personality much. When we meet him now, he is very much like the jolly hobbit we have seen in the first chapters of *The Lord of the Rings*, as his initial remarks indicate: "'Hullo, Frodo my lad!' said Bilbo. 'So you have got here at last. I hoped you would manage it. Well, well! So all this feasting is in your honour, I hear. I hope you enjoyed yourself?'"(*LotR*, 247)

At the same time, it is clearly not the innocent, carefree Bilbo of *The Hobbit* we meet. Despite the light tone of his speech, there is something unsettling about his behaviour (which was also present in the first chapter), motivated by the presence of the Ring – Bilbo seems to turn into some sort of monster with greedy eyes when he sees it.

These initial modifications in the characterization of Gandalf, Glóin and Bilbo, however slight, contribute to the 'rehabilitation' of Rivendell, shaping it as a narrative zone which ends up being distinctly different from that of *The Hobbit*.

Defining the heroes

In the chapter 'The Council of Elrond' we see how Gandalf, Elrond and Glóin acquire a more sombre dimension. After the chapter 'Many Meetings', in which the narrator admits, up to a certain point, the limitations of the characters who have been shaped in the narrative universe of *The Hobbit*, Tolkien takes us, in 'The Council of Elrond', very far from the nineteenth-century narrative blend and reveals the amplitude of Middle-earth through reports about events in different parts of the world, given by many different speakers.

Unlike the world presented in *The Hobbit*, the narrative zones of *The Lord of the Rings* as a whole make up a more realistic setting, with much more plausible and coherent political, economical and social relationships. It is also a world seriously threatened by a common enemy. Both differences will affect the evolution of the characters that we have already met in *The Hobbit*, who during the Council tell stories from different places that significantly enhance the coherence and spatial-temporal depth of the tale,[226] and contribute to the more solemn and sombre tone that begins to dominate the narrative.

At the same time, the importance of Frodo, Aragorn and Gandalf is gradually increased, until their roles as the main protagonists of the work are firmly

---

226 Shippey analyses the Council of Elrond, saying that it represents a "violent 'culture-clash'" and that it provides "an image of the 'life-styles' of Middle-earth the solider for its occasional contrasts with modernity." (Shippey 2003:122) In *Author of the Century* (Shippey 2002:68-77), he offers a more extensive analysis of the different voices in the Council, highlighting Elrond's archaic speech, the Scandinavian traits of Glóin's discourse, the "pseudo-archaic" language of Boromir, the linguistic flexibility of Aragorn and Gandalf, and the modern rhetorics of Saruman.

established. The chapter also anticipates the direction of their different heroic evolutions. Frodo will henceforth be identified with the Ring and therefore also with the end of the Third Age, of which he will become a symbol. Aragorn, as we have seen, will turn into something as complex as a pagan epic hero with a Christian ethos, and Gandalf will end up assimilating several features of what we might call a 'divine messenger'. This evolution will be subtly but appreciably reaffirmed in the following chapter, 'The Ring Goes South'.

The reader (through Frodo's eyes) has already acknowledged the awe-inspiring importance of Gandalf when finding him at Elrond's side at the dinner table the night before, but it is not until the Council that he makes public his true role in the ensuing global conflict.[227] It is significant that Elrond should leave the last word to Gandalf,[228] and that the wizard then takes charge of the Council, summarising the most important issues concerning the conflict generated by the Ring during no less than fifteen pages, ending his discourse by formulating the most relevant and pressing question: What shall we do with the Ring?

While it is very clear that Gandalf is the one in charge of defending the liberty of the 'Free Peoples' against the threat of Sauron, it seems as if he would prefer others to make the final decisions and to act. According to Tolkien, the function of the wizards, "maintained by Gandalf, and perverted by Saruman, was to encourage and bring out the native powers of the Enemies of Sauron" (*Letters*, 180), which well fits the discreet role Gandalf plays when it comes to decision-making, because in these situations, Gandalf habitually acts like a heroic tutor. This particular role, whose most important function is to inspire, not to act for others, can also explain quite a few apparent inconsistencies of the plot. One question frequently raised after seeing Peter Jackson's adaptation was "Why didn't Gandalf just send for the Eagles to carry the ring to Orodruin?" The answer is precisely because he is not meant to; that it is beyond his power as a character. And these limits are largely set by the intertraditional dialogue.

---

[227] Tolkien states in one of his letters that Gandalf was "an 'incarnate' angel [...] an emissary from the Lords of the West." (*Letters*, 202). Day (2003:126-129) finds several parallels between Gandalf and Hermes, Odin and Alcuin.
[228] Elrond introduces him with the following words: "[...] I call upon him last, for it is the place of honour, and in all this matter he has been the chief." (*LotR*, 267)

One example of the way the different narrative traditions interact in order to establish the limits of the others can be found towards the end of the debate that follows Gandalf's final question, when his discourse turns moralising as he defends the idea of throwing the Ring into the fire of Orodruin on moral grounds, with reference to faith and hope:

> 'Despair, or folly?' said Gandalf. 'It is not despair, for despair is only for those who see the end beyond all doubt. We do not. It is wisdom to recognize necessity, when all other courses have been weighed, though as folly it may appear to those who cling to false hope.' (*LotR*, 286-287)

Elrond corroborates the feasibility of the idea in terms of ancestral wisdom – "such is oft the course of deeds that move the wheels of the world: small hands do them because they must, while the eyes of the great are elsewhere" – (*LotR*, 287), but Bilbo alters the almost biblical tone of the narrative, volunteering to take on the mission. This interference gives rise to a more novelistic dialogue with Gandalf that ends with Bilbo's wish to choose the members of the expedition, so that they may finish the Council and take a lunch-break:

> 'Elves may thrive on speech alone, and dwarves endure great weariness, but I am only an old hobbit, and I miss my meal at noon. Can't you think of some names now? Or put it off till after dinner?' (*LotR*, 288)

This time, Bilbo is far too prosaic for his proposal to be considered, the comment being so out of place that it may almost be considered an *arrested intruder*. However, his intervention manages to reduce the prophetic and solemn tone brought to the narrative by Gandalf and Elrond's words, altering it enough for Frodo to be able to assimilate his heroic role in more novelistic than epic or mythic terms: "'I will take the Ring,' he said, 'though I do not know the way'" (*LotR*, 288). Frodo's offer reveals his adherence to several traditions: on the one hand, he now becomes a hero with an epic/mythical mission; and on the other he admits his limits as such in a more novelistic fashion.[229]

In the next chapter, 'The Ring Goes South', Gandalf, Aragorn[230] and Frodo consolidate their new identities, that have been publicly exposed during the

---

[229] Sale (1968:255) writes that the scene shows that "Frodo is fitting into some ancient pattern, but he himself does not know how or why." According to De Paco (1993:133), the traditional symbolism of a ring is that of shared destiny. From this moment, Frodo's fate will be strongly linked to the Ring and to the end of the Third Age that this object comes to represent.

[230] For a full discussion of Aragorn's heroic evolution, see section 4.3.

Council. Shortly after the Council, Gandalf partakes in a conversation with the hobbits with the same intertraditional flexibility as before, but now the narrator makes an effort to distance the wizard from them. For example, it is significant that he should stand outside the building, talking to them through an open window, and also that when he speaks, he should excuse himself for using expressions more appropriate for hobbits: "If you want to know, the only real eye-openers, as you put it, were you and Frodo; and I was the only one that was not surprised." (*LotR*, 289)

As for Frodo, his new identity is closely linked to the Ring, as we have already seen. The Ring is in turn intimately connected to the end of the Third Age, and Frodo will embody this 'event' insofar as he assimilates – both on a personal level and in his narrative account – the different traditions present in Middle-earth during this historical epoch. In Rivendell, where Frodo's destiny and new identity have been publicly announced, we may discern the first explicit signs of assimilation.[231] On the last day of Frodo's stay in Elrond's house, Bilbo takes him to his room to equip him for the adventure. As Flieger (1981:54) points out, the procedure is dispatched with a highly prosaic tone that reduces the epic potentiality of the scene, and Frodo accepts the sword and the mithril mail-coat that Bilbo gives him almost against his will, saying that they would give him a strange look. However, Bilbo insists and Frodo ends up wearing both, though he covers the mail-coat with his normal clothes. Bilbo's next comment, in spite of the carefree tone, announces an important change in Frodo: "'Just a plain hobbit you look,' said Bilbo. 'But there is more about you now than appears on the surface.'" (*LotR*, 295)[232]

The procedure marks a double starting point for Frodo: on the one hand, it is the moment when he leaves everything known behind in order to face an uncertain destiny, but it also shows that from now on, Frodo's heroic evolution will be fundamentally internal.

In short, Rivendell as a narrative zone admits an open dialogue between all the traditions of Middle-earth, both because it is a border region and because of

---

231 Up until this moment, Frodo has been singled out from the rest of the hobbits because of his special sensitivity and transcendental dreams, which is but an anticipation of his projected assimilation of different traditions that begins to take shape at Rivendell.
232 Flieger (1981:55) believes that this is the moment when Frodo begins to acquire new epic traits.

the multicultural origins of the guests. The big difference compared to Bree is brought about by its function as an elvish sanctuary of wisdom, inhabited by an ancient people capable of transcending the 'terrestrial' existence.[233] The result is a continuous *mélange* of different traditions, in which, roughly speaking, the hobbits represent a novelistic interpretation of reality, whereas the elves softly erase the borders of that reality. Boromir brings an epic stance to the dialogue (with particular emphasis on the *chanson de geste*-variety) while Gandalf and Elrond come close to mythic paradigms due to their longevity and the strong blend of prophetic and moralising messages in their discourse. However, none of these generic elements is allowed to clearly dominate the dialogue.

Gandalf's long digression during the Council is emblematic of the narrative zone of Rivendell in that it covers many of the narrative traditions present in Middle-earth. Tolkien makes an extensive use of the enormous inter-traditional flexibility of this character, making him reproduce voices as different as those of Isildur, Saruman, the Gaffer, Radagast, Gwaihir, Barliman Butterbur and even Sauron (when reading the inscriptions on the Ring). Bilbo becomes an *arrested intruder* when he asks for a dinner-break, but the intrusion helps to vivify the predominant note of this episode – the *mélange* – given that it tones down the solemn prophetic and moralising discourses of Gandalf and Elrond until we reach a level where this discourse is able to interact with the other traditions, as Frodo's subsequent intervention shows.

For all this, I would say that the novel has a slightly stronger presence than the other traditions in this narrative zone. In the first place, the intense polyphony which is present throughout the whole episode is typical of the novel (Bakhtin 1989:117-148). Furthermore, the game of separating the pieces of the plot puzzle and then putting them back together again at chosen moments – as during the Council, when Gandalf finally explains his failure to show up in the Shire at the appointed time – is also a typically novelistic narrative strategy aimed at enhancing the tension and ensuring dramatic effects.

---

233 Frodo, when hearing the elvish songs, is given visions: "far lands and bright things that he had never yet imagined opened up before him" (*LotR*, 249). Segura (2004:78) also relates the elvish songs to transcendental experience, while Hein (1998:188) argues that Frodo "[t]hrough the elven language [...] has caught sight of a high, ethereal reality, one more appropriate to dream than waking, that envelopes his entire being. He has been enchanted by [...] a mythic reality momentarily glimpsed."

4.5. The Mines of Moria: generating applicability

As the Fellowship approaches the gates of Moria, romance elements begin to establish an increasingly intense dialogue with the novel, which has dominated the narrative since the departure from Rivendell. Already on the slopes of Caradhras, the descriptions of nature become more subjective: night turns "deadly dark", the wind is "bitter" and the mountain sides are "grim" (*LotR*, 305). Gandalf, Gimli and Boromir affirm that the blizzard is the doing of the Enemy, and strange voices are heard in the wind. Gandalf uses his 'magic'[234] to make a fire, though it is not enough to repel the snow and the cold. After a short debate, they decide to try their luck in the ominous Mines of Moria, in spite of their bad reputation. Shortly afterwards they are attacked by wolves. Gandalf holds them back with a spell of fire, and the carcasses of the wolves disappear as if by magic. Gandalf believes that this is due to the influence of Sauron: "'It is as I feared,' said Gandalf. 'These were no ordinary wolves hunting for food in the wilderness [...].'" (*LotR*, 317)

The Fellowship arrives at the gates of Moria at dusk. After some fruitless attempts, Gandalf finally manages to find the word which opens the gates and, as this happens, a monster appears in the lake next to the entrance. The Fellowship successfully escapes into the tunnel beyond the gates, and the monster shuts the doors behind them with such vehemence that the ceiling comes down, blocking the exit.

In terms of the intertraditional dialogue, these romance elements establish a dialogue with the novel, but as the Fellowship enters the Mines and everything is set up for another romance détour, like the one that took place in the Old Forest, the influence of this tradition disappears almost completely. Instead, a dialogue between novel and myth ensues, giving rise to a vast range of possible interpretations. I will now focus on one of the many possible interpretations offered by the text, in order to show how the intertraditional dialogue yields applicability for Tolkien's narrative.

---

234 According to Tolkien (*Letters*, 200), the Enemy uses its magic to dominate people and things, with subjugating and terrible effects (their wizards dedicate their labours to industrial and bellicose enterprises), while Gandalf and the elves use it "for specific beneficent purposes. Their goetic effects are entirely artistic and not intended to deceive." The 'sensationalist' kind of magic, with immediate and surprising results, is only sparingly used, and when it happens, it is usually more subtle than the fire-spell referred to above. However, it is significant that the magic of Gandalf and the elves normally appears in episodes heavily informed by romance standards in 'medievalized' settings (such as Lórien and Fangorn), while the Enemy's magic (for instance, that of Saruman), is more easily interpreted in modern terms.

The Mines of Moria and the Twentieth Century

The dramatic entrance in the Mines of Moria is more symbolically charged than the episode that takes place in the Old Forest, which is also preceded by a transition towards romance and a clear marking of the border. But, while in the Old Forest the clang of the gate coincided with a voluntary entrance to a new territory where different rules shape the narrative, at the gates of Moria the protagonists are attacked by a monster and forced to enter. As they do so, the ceiling collapses, eliminating all possibility of a return. It is up to the reader to decide how to interpret this, or not to interpret it at all, since the text itself does not guide us towards any given reading. One possible interpretation, however, is based on analogues with the Great War and its aftermath.

According to the British authorities, the hostile attitude of Germany that culminated in 1914 with the attack on Belgium, compelled Britain to take part in the conflict later known as the Great War. Once this happened, Europe was drawn into a spiral of violence: the mass destruction of the First World War was succeeded by the imperialism of opportunistic totalitarian regimes that eventually paved the way for the even bigger conflict of the Second World War.

Something similar happens to the Fellowship of the Ring in Moria: while they know that they are probably heading for war sooner or later, the *kraken* compels them to enter the mines hurriedly and prevents them from going back. This will give rise to the first open confrontation with the Enemy, which later on will lead to more armed conflicts on a bigger scale. Before the War of the Ring is over, the hobbits will have experienced the feeling that the old world is gone – both because of what happens in the Mines, where Gandalf and the Balrog fall into the abyss, and the apocalyptic mass-destruction of the war.

Gandalf's words reinforce the analogue:

> 'Well, well!' said the wizard. 'The passage is blocked behind us now, and there is only one way out – on the other side of the mountains. I fear from the sounds that boulders have been piled up, and the trees uprooted and thrown across the gate. I am sorry; for the trees were beautiful, and had stood so long.' (*LotR*, 326-327)

The intrusion of the novel

With the episode of the Old Forest fresh in memory, we might expect the narrative to turn toward mythic paradigms at this stage, not only because of the preceding transition from novel to romance, but also because of the implied similarities with the Underworld – or King Mino's labyrinth with the minotaur at its center – from classical mythology, or with Hell from Christian iconography. However, the devices that were used to soften the transit from familiar Crickhollow to the mythic realm surrounding Tom Bombadil's house and the Barrow-downs – dreams, sleep and vague descriptions of the physical space – are now absent. We have already seen how at Rivendell, the antecedent of *The Hobbit* was exorcized from that narrative zone, and it is perhaps the need to present a coherent, plausible and clear vision of the Misty Mountains, as opposed to the fairy-tale caves à la *The Princess and the Goblin* that were present in the earlier narrative, that makes the narrator adopt a novelistic tone as the Fellowship enters the Mines.

Now, the protagonists carefully count the steps of the first stairway, and Gandalf estimates the distance to the exit at the other side to some forty miles (*LotR*, 327). After this follows a description of the members of the Fellowship and of the architectural wonders of the mines, and the sound of the footsteps of each character (except Gandalf). All of this contributes to invest the physical space with novelistic verisimilitude.

This surprising turn is an example of an *intrusion*; that is, an unprepared transition that works from the point of view of narrative fluency. That this return to the novel should work may be due to the fact that the presence of mythic and epic elements is more reduced at the initial stage of this narrative zone, compared to, for example, the situation at Rivendell in which Bilbo's plea for lunch in the midst of an epic debate about the fate of the world becomes an *arrested intruder*.

The influence of novelistic paradigms continues almost until the end of the journey through the Mines. When the Fellowship arrives at a crossing, Gandalf (not sure of which road to follow) orders the others to rest. Pippin throws a stone down a shaft and apparently rouses something that had better been left alone. This makes Gandalf angry. However, Gandalf's irritation may also be due to another reason, explicitly admitted by the wizard himself: he is grumpy because he has not smoked for a long time (*LotR*, 331). This admittance brings him closer to a novelistic character, affected by trivial needs, than to the messenger of the Valar that we glimpsed at Rivendell, and that will return before the episode ends.

The next day, after having walked for eight hours, covering a distance of fifteen miles "as the bird flies," that the narrator estimates to some twenty 'real' miles, Gimli sings a song, clearly tinged with romance traits, about the legend of Durin and the first dwarves that settled in Moria. Gandalf embodies the novel's impatience with romance idealization as he counters Gimli's narrative of greatness and nobility with an account of the true reasons why the dwarves came there in the first place: they were simply greedy for *mithril*.[235] Now, he says, the jewels have been stolen by orcs and the lower levels of the mines are flooded – the old romance space has been profaned by a destructive modernity.

Novel and myth in dialogue

In this way, the journey through the Mines of Moria situates the reader in a very concrete, detailed and palpable space, traversed by characters of flesh and blood, with real limitations, in spite of the narrator's golden opportunity to 'legitimately' enhance the romance features of the narrative with the justification of the darkness and the confusion offered by the labyrinth. The problem, now, is that the text has become committed to the cohesion and verisimilitude of the realist novel for the portrayal of the Mines, and the encounter with the Balrog, which is to follow, requires a movement towards the territory of myth. This transition is not an easy one, especially as the narrator has already once renounced the resources offered by romance. The problem is partially solved by the presence of a novelistic device – a diary written by dwarf settlers[236] – with mythic contents, though plausible in the context of Middle-earth in general, and the Mines of Moria in particular.

---

[235] Regarding the relationship between dwarves of different narrative traditions and their attraction to the mineral world, see Shippey (2003:61).

[236] Segura (2004:163) highlights Tolkien's consistent use of written documents, such as letters, inscriptions and diaries, in *The Lord of the Rings*, as a means to provide the reader with missing information and enhance the verisimilitude of the narrative.

The diary is found in a room that hosts the tomb of Balin, where we see the traces of a long-lost battle in the shape of arms and skeletons. The book itself is meticulously described in order to underscore its ancient appearance:

> [The book] had been slashed and stabbed and partly burned, and it was so stained with black and other dark marks like old blood that little of it could be read. Gandalf lifted it carefully, but the leaves crackled and broke as he laid it on the slab. (*LotR*, 339)

Gandalf contributes to the sensation of authenticity that surrounds the book by stating that the pagination shows that the two initial pages are missing, and the reading as such reveals the narrator's ambition of investing the document with as much realism as possible.[237]

> '*We drove out orcs from the great gate and guard* – I think; the next word is blurred and burned: probably room – *we slew many in the bright* – I think – *sun in the dale. Flói was killed by an arrow. He slew the great.* Then there is a blur followed by *Flói under grass near mirror mere.* The next line or two I can't read. Then comes *We have taken the twentyfirst hall of North end to dwell in. There is* I cannot read what. A *shaft* is mentioned. Then *Balin has set up his seat in the chamber of Mazarbul.*' (*LotR*, 339)

The ancient diction of the dwarves and the realism of the complicated reading of an incomplete document is combined with the ominous feeling that surrounds the final stage of the dwarves' adventure in Moria, the tragedy of which is testified by the skeletons and the desolate state of the mines. The reader will remember the sounds that were heard after Pippin threw his stone down the shaft, so the reading of the diary sets the scene for a situation which implies a real threat, in spite of the fact that the opponents are orcs; that is, creatures controlled by a figure of mythic stature (Sauron). In this way, Tolkien creates a narrative atmosphere capable of hosting a dialogue between novel and myth, giving rise to a smooth and efficient transition without having to resort to strategies such as dreams or descriptive manipulation of the physical space.

The transition towards myth is initiated immediately after Gandalf has situated the reader spatially:[238] at this moment, the Fellowship becomes aware that the

---

237 In Flieger's (2005:75) words, Tolkien uses the book of Mazarbul as an "attempt at verisimilitude by artifact."
238 Gandalf tries to be as accurate as possible about their location: he concludes that they are in the twenty-first hall on the North-end, which is why they should take the Western exit and descend towards the south, given that they are "on the seventh Level, that is six above the level of the gates." (*LotR*, 341)

orcs are approaching, whereby they find themselves in a situation identical to the one described in the diary – trapped in the *Chamber of Mazarbul*. Together with the orcs comes a powerful being, whose identity is still unfamiliar to us, that Gandalf must repel with his magic in order to escape. Gandalf's words insinuate that it is something out of the ordinary, and with supernatural powers: "What it was I cannot guess, but I have never felt such a challenge. The counter-spell was terrible. It nearly broke me." (*LotR*, 345)

Little by little, the narrative begins to lean closer to myth, and the descriptions combine realism with a high degree of symbolic meaning:

> Before them was another cavernous hall. [...] They were near its eastern end; westward it ran away into darkness. Down the centre stalked a double line of towering pillars [...] Their stems were smooth and black, but a red glow was darkly mirrored in their sides. Right across the floor, close to the feet of two huge pillars a great fissure had opened. Out of it a fierce red light came, and now and again flames licked at the brink and curled about the bases of the columns. Wisps of dark smoke wavered in the hot air. (*LotR*, 346-347)

We are in a real place, but the connotations of the underground abyss and the fire – Hell and apocalypse – are not left unnoticed.[239] The members of the Fellowship arrive at a bridge that spans another abyss where Gandalf must stop the monster he previously challenged, which now appears in all its mythic splendour:

> It came to the edge of the fire and the light faded as if a cloud had bent over it. Then with a rush it leaped across the fissure. The flames roared up to greet it, and wreathed about it; and a black smoke swirled in the air. Its streaming mane kindled, and blazed behind it. In its right hand was a blade like a stabbing tongue of fire; in its left it held a whip of many thongs. (*LotR*, 348)[240]

As we can see, the dialogue between novel and myth, which is achieved by incorporating mythical elements in a credible way, and by the parallels between the situation described in the diary and the present state of affairs, ends in a narrative dominated by mythic paradigms mainly due to the symbolically charged descriptions of the physical space and of the Balrog.

---

[239] According to De Paco (2003:98), the abyss usually represents the dark primordial chaos before Creation, and the infernal darkness of the last days.
[240] Tolkien (*Letters*, 180) himself says of the balrogs that they were "primeval spirits of destroying fire, chief servants of the primeval dark Power of the First Age."

The Bridge of Khazad-dûm: the meeting between Christian and pagan traditions

At this stage of the narrative, two supernatural powers are brought face to face: the Balrog, described as a shadow that wields a sword shrouded in red flames in one hand and a whip in the other, and Gandalf, with a sword of white fire and a staff. The weapons as such tell us a good deal about the type of duel that is being portrayed, opposing two types of authorities by means of traditional symbols – the punishment, as represented by the Balrog's whip, and the guidance and protection symbolized by Gandalf's staff[241] – as well as the association with the fire, that may be of divine or demonic origin (De Paco 2003:259). The colour of their swords may also be significant: the red colour of rage and Hell illuminates the Balrog's sword, while the white colour of Gandalf's blade, which furthermore has a name of its own,[242] recalls light and the forces of Good.[243]

Apart from the Christian symbolism, there are more ingredients that add to the applicability of the scene. Day (2003:36-38) highlights the similarity between the Balrog and Surt,[244] the guardian of the gates of Muspellheim (territory of the giants in Norse mythology) – the battle at the bridge being analogous to the fight between Surt and Frey, the god of the Sun and the rain, on the bridge Bifrost, that marks the onset of Ragnarök (the twilight of the gods). To this analogue we may add that in *The Lord of the Rings*, a horn is also sounded – Boromir blows his as he sets out to aid Gandalf – and the bridge collapses.

That Caradhras should deny the passage of the Fellowship over the mountains, close to the sky, is also significant for the transmission of this *mélange* of pagan

---

[241] In De Paco's (2003:301) words, the whip symbolizes authoritative command and punishment, while the staff is "a magic weapon, an instrument used to mediate between the visible and invisible worlds, a symbol of the teacher's tutorship" (De Paco 2003:323). My translation.
[242] Its name – Glamdring – is explicitly mentioned by the narrator twice during the battle. Regarding the tradition of giving names to swords and its relationship to Christian belief, see page 160.
[243] Miller (2000:285) points out that the colour red is always dangerous, "reflecting the doubled potencies of blood and fire [...] the 'hot blood' of the furious warrior-hero [and] the destructively heated potentiality of the warrior." De Paco (2003:198) relates white colour to indifferentiation, transcendental experience, innocence, and holiness. The analogue with the Biblical Archangel Michael, the messenger of the Last Judgment who usually appears as a warrior with a sword, also contributes to emphasize Gandalf's role as messenger of the Valar in the episodes leaning most heavily towards mythic narrative paradigms.
[244] See also Noel (1977:101).

and Christian traditions. The blizzard makes them descend to a subterranean space, with more immediate connections to the idea of the Christian Hell,[245] something which prevents the Christian connotations of the duel from disappearing in the dialogue. A battle with spirits of the air would more easily have given rise to a different interpretation, because of their intimate relationship to the Christian Heaven.

The journey through the Mines of Moria that culminates in the battle between Gandalf and the Balrog can thus be seen as an event that produces a vast and suggestive applicability, based on a combination of different narrative traditions (the mythic tradition being a combination of Norse and Christian symbolism). The outcome is the expression of a meta-narrative myth that underscores the need to resist defeatism in times of hopelessness by resorting to both Christian and pagan stances. The expression of such a myth is of course not restricted to the Mines but completed when the whole narrative comes to an end. However, the journey through the Mines of Moria illustrates very well on its own Tolkien's particular version of ironic myth, with an undogmatic reversal of its defeatism based on a combination of pagan and Christian virtues, relating the tale by means of applicability, not allegory, to twentieth-century concerns.

4.6. Gandalf: messenger of the Valar

Gandalf's fall at the bridge of Khazad-dûm, apart from reinforcing his particular identity,[246] is also the starting point for the development of Frodo and Aragorn's independency as heroes in their own right. Through the wizard's mediating attitude, which does not impose but suggests and leaves the final decision to others,[247] his constant appeals to hope and his generous sacrifice

---

245 Dufau (2005:115), persuasively explains that Moria can be interpreted as a place that erradicates the essence of the Self: "Moria shelters an anti-space that baffles all attempts at self-location [...] The traveller is bound to lose whatever bearings he used to have. How could he find a language of being in such a place since the concept of language refers to a system of signs? [...] The self cannot evolve in collapse and breaking: it dies in such places." The idea of chaos and the destruction of one's essence is, of course, compatible with the Christian idea of the soul's destruction in Hell. Obertino (1993) highlights the parallels between Moria and pagan epic tradition in the *Aeneid*.
246 The fact that Gandalf disappears every once in a while is another trait inherited from *The Hobbit*, and it is also important for his own identity as a messenger of the Valar whose ambition is to bring out the best in Sauron's enemies.
247 For instance, in the debate held by the members of the Fellowship regarding the route to follow after having been defeated by Caradhras. (*LotR*, 312-315)

at the bridge, he provides them with an example, emphasized by his own apparent death, of Christian virtues that are added to the epic courage and strength of Aragorn and the novelistic practicality of Frodo, which will be a fundamental inspiration for both from this moment on.

That this should be so is indicative of Gandalf's status as a moral authority of mythic dimensions. When the wizard is present, he tends to eclipse the others. As Hughes (1981:78-79) says: "If Gandalf becomes too competent, too able to control the action, too ready a deus ex machina, his character will limit the imaginative possibilities of hobbits and men too much". As we have seen in the discussion of Aragorn's heroic evolution, when Gandalf comes back after his 'rebirth' in the Misty Mountains, he takes over the narrative once more, completely overshadowing Aragorn. As a matter of fact, it is necessary that he should disappear every once in a while, to leave room for the others to ponder his words and act accordingly – or not. But is he a *deus ex machina* when he is present, or does he retain some of his previous, human fallibility? We will now concentrate on Gandalf's return and see how his mythic dimensions, considerably reinforced from Fangorn and on, interact with the other traditions in Middle-earth to shape his unique character.

Gandalf in Fangorn: romance wizard

When Gandalf returns after the fall in Moria, he enters the scene in the shape of a romance wizard, shrouded in mystery, who begins by paralyzing the adventurers with a magic spell and continues by talking to them in such an ambiguous way that for a long time they remain uncertain of his identity and intentions. When he finally reveals who he is, he jumps theatrically on top of a rock, takes off his grey coat and raises his staff, exhibiting his white, radiant clothes. Another spell makes Gimli's axe fall from his hands, while Aragorn's sword catches fire and Legolas's arrow is consumed by flames.

The effect of all this is a spectacular and bombastic visual image of Gandalf, which is very difficult to reconcile with the wizard's previously austere and restrained character. The problem is that this image does not coincide with the later Gandalf either: he immediately cools down, forgets about his games and begins talking to Aragorn and the others in a tone which is practically identical to the one that used to mark his speech before he fell in Moria.

Why does Gandalf present himself to the others in such an absurdly 'romance' way? Possibly, due to the demands of the intertraditional dialogue, a reason Tolkien himself seems to acknowledge: "I think the way in which Gandalf's return is presented is a defect [...] That is partly due to the ever present compulsions of narrative technique." (*Letters*, 201)[248] Though Tolkien mainly refers to the need to express in few words what has happened to Gandalf, the mysterious game-playing and the apparently gratuitous character of the meeting may also be due to the romance ambience that permeates the forest of Fangorn, and the mythical connotations of the return.[249]

The treatment of the ensuing dialogue is novelistic in the sense that it serves to fill in informational gaps, but at the same time, Gandalf's presence is marked by clear connections to a mythic reality: the narrator insists on the light that surrounds him, and some of his observations reveal his intimate association with a supernatural moral consciousness, as when he refers to the battle against Sauron for the soul of Frodo at the top of Amon Hen, and the mysterious assertion that Boromir "escaped" before he died: "Galadriel told me that he was in peril. But he escaped in the end. I am glad. It was not in vain that the hobbits came with us, if only for Boromir's sake". (*LotR*, 517)

Escape from what? And what did the hobbits have to do with it? One possible interpretation is that the answer is related to the same motivations that made Aragorn forgive Boromir after his treason: a *mélange* of Christian (romance) and pagan heroic (epic) ethics. Boromir's soul was saved due to his repentance, and the hobbits provided him with a just cause that helped him achieve heroic redemption in battle.

This paradoxical *mélange* – the need for a pagan (epic, in the context of the intertraditional dialogue) courage in the face of impending disaster and death, without any hope for posthumous rewards other than one's lasting reputation,

---

[248] In the same letter, a little further on, Tolkien adds: "the return of G. is as presented in this book a 'defect', and one I was aware of, and probably did not work hard enough to mend." (*Letters*, 201-202)

[249] See Miller (1989).

and the Christian (romance) humility based on virtues such as hope, mercy, forgiveness, and generosity – marks Gandalf's message, and is a clear inheritance from *Beowulf*. This combination was already present in Moria, connected to twentieth-century concerns by means of an enhanced applicability, as we have seen, and we will see more of the same as they move towards the epic scenarios of the War of the Ring.

Rohan and Gondor: Christian virtues, pagan courage

As they prepare to leave Fangorn, Gandalf gathers the lost horses, that return together with Shadowfax (whom Gandalf has summoned by means of telepathic skills[250]), and he encourages the others to engage in the epic ventures of heroic warfare: "'I see a great smoke,' said Legolas. 'What may that be?' 'Battle and war!' said Gandalf. 'Ride on!'" (*LotR*, 527)

At Meduseld, Gandalf speaks first with Gríma, King Théoden's counsellor, who also works as a spy for Saruman, having deceived the king for a long time.[251] Gandalf knows this and seizes the opportunity to inculcate the message of hope in Théoden by means of a manifestation of his supernatural powers, concentrating all the light in the hall on himself. Thunder and lightning accompany the vision, Gríma's voice is effectively quenched and Gandalf points to a high window:

> [...] There the darkness seemed to clear, and through the opening could be seen, high and afar, a patch of shining sky. 'Not all is dark. Take courage, Lord of the Mark; for better help you will not find. No counsel have I to give to those that despair. Yet counsel I could give, and words I could speak to you. Will you hear them? [...]' (*LotR*, 537)

The works of the divine messenger are fruitful: Théoden is convinced and even physically rejuvenated, while Gríma is forgiven and offered a place in the cavalry next to the King. Even as he rejects the offer, they give him a horse

---

250 Burns (2006:104-106) points out the similarities between Gandalf and Shadowfax, on the one hand, and Odin and Sleipner, on the other.
251 This character has a parallel in Unferth, one of the warriors at Hrothgar's court in *Beowulf*, but he is also in many ways similar to Gagool of Haggard's *King Solomon's Mines*, as Tolley (1993:155-156) points out. This double analogue is significant, given that Gríma will later appear together with Saruman, a decidedly novelistic character (especially after his fall). When that happens, he easily adopts a personality much closer to the latter tradition.

so that he may leave Rohan. Christian virtues are again imposed on the more savage warrior ethics, that would have had Gríma executed for his treason, but at the same time it is worth noticing that the whole point of waking Théoden from his defeatist slumber is that he should engage his troops in the War of the Ring.

The battles that follow do not primarily show Gandalf's ties to the epic tradition, in spite of his interventions on the battlefield, but establish his increasingly firm links with the role of divine messenger, whose main function is to inspire spiritual strength and hope in Sauron's opponents. At Minas Tirith, he corrects Denethor when the steward insinuates that Gandalf lusts for the power over Gondor, explaining that he aims at preserving all valuable things in the world for the future, not only those of Gondor: "For I also am a steward. Did you not know?" (LotR, 789)

Gandalf's concerns are universal, not regional or national, and related not only to the present but also to the future, and he insists on the need to embrace such a responsibility in his conversations with Denethor: "'You think, as is your wont, my lord, of Gondor only,' said Gandalf. 'Yet there are other men and other lives, and time still to be. And for me, I pity even his slaves.'" (*LotR*, 845) Gandalf is a steward of the creative powers of the world, a steward of spiritual values and virtues who guides and protects the Free Peoples that fight against Sauron's destructive power.

The rescue of Faramir, during which Gandalf chases away the shadows brought by Sauron's forces with the white light that emanates from his person and his hand, reinforces the movement towards myth within Gandalf, as does the scene in which the wizard stops the Witch-king of Angmar from entering Minas Tirith – an episode that synthesizes the struggle between the forces that feed the primordial fears of night and those that cling to the hope brought by the light of the new day.[252]

That Gandalf should follow Pippin to prevent Denethor from burning his son Faramir alive, instead of trying to defeat the Nazgûl on the battlefield, is

---

[252] In Shippey's (2002:212-216) opinion, it is the interaction between nature (symbolized by dawn and the crowing cock) and the horns of Rohan that makes the eucatastrophe possible and adds a mythic dimension to the episode.

significant. He is not, in the first place, an epic slayer-hero, but a divine messenger, and the suicidal madness of Denethor provides him with an excellent opportunity to make use of this condition, not by feats of war, but by providing others with a moral example.[253]

The scene in which Gandalf and Denethor debate over the body of Faramir is closely connected to mythic paradigms, symbolizing the struggle between hope and despair, life and death, as the following dialogue shows:

> 'He [Faramir] will not wake again,' said Denethor. 'Battle is vain. Why should we wish to live longer? Why should we not go to death side by side?'
>
> 'Authority is not given you, Steward of Gondor, to order the hour of your death,' answered Gandalf. 'And only the heathen kings, under the domination of the Dark Power, did thus, slaying themselves in pride and despair, murdering their kin to ease their own death.'
>
> [...] '[...] The West has failed. It is time for all to depart who would not be slaves.'
>
> 'Such counsels will make the Enemy's victory certain indeed,' said Gandalf. (*LotR*, 887)

Denethor's suicide and moral fall is also symbolized by the collapse of the House of the Stewards, and the servants loyal to the Steward are convinced by Gandalf's words about the influence of Sauron on their leader (the bond between Sauron and Denethor has been revealed when the Steward showed the corrupting palantír that he has used to communicate with the Dark Lord). This connection, now broken, shows the mythic character of Gandalf's intervention, an interpretation further reinforced when he resucitates Faramir.[254]

There is also another mythic component related to Denethor's behaviour that is worth mentioning. The white tree, the emblem of Gondor, has withered, symbolizing the main mythic paradigm of medieval romance:[255] the land has

---

253 Miller (2000:31) writes that what he terms "mythological epic" tends to elevate the hero "to an awesome height, running the risk of devaluating his heroic feats." Tolkien avoids this effect by having Gandalf return to the citadel instead of taking him out on the battle-field.

254 Regarding the presence of Christian myth in the episode, Denethor shows (because of Sauron's influence) a certain similarity to Satan as he is portrayed in *Paradise Lost*. In Steadman's (1969:17) description of this Miltonic character, Satan represents "a leadership that misleads, a magnanimity that strives for unmerited honours, accomplishes acts of destruction instead of 'acts of benefit' and turns out to be vainglorious ambition and pride."

255 See section 2.4 (page 67).

become sterile because of the king, who now is old and ill and has to die for a new king to replace him and bring fertility to the land. From this point of view, it is symptomatic that the result of the confrontation between Gandalf and Denethor should be that the Steward dies while Faramir lives and falls in love with Éowyn.

At the same time, it is Denethor's lack of "Northern courage" that causes his fall. Saint Clair's (1996:65) analysis of this character links him to the pagan Njal of the eponymous Icelandic saga – Njal, who is intelligent, cunning, brave and perceptive, also loses his best-loved son and dies on the pyre: "[He is] what Denethor might have been without the palantír." In another interpretation, Shippey (2003:130) underscores the lack of Northern courage in Denethor, though he attributes this flaw to the effects of a civilized culture.

In the third place, the associations between Denethor's death and the cultural apocalypse brought by the Great War, together with the transitory spirit that followed, are also clear.[256] Gandalf claims, after Denethor's death, that the old Gondor has ceased to exist, for better or worse (*LotR*, 889), while Aragorn, after the victory on the fields of the Pelennor, says that the sun descending toward a great fire is "a sign of the end and fall of many things, and a change in the tides of the world. [...]" (*LotR*, 895). None of them is able to predict the future course of events, but, judging from the way things turn out in the end, the apocalypse ends up bringing hope and vigour to those who did not lose faith while the darkness lasted. In this way, the scene of the funeral pyre at the Houses of the Dead is made up of several layers of applicability, giving shape to yet another example of the meta-narrative myth of hope for the twentieth century that the narrative articulates.

After the arrival of the Riders of Rohan and Aragorn at Minas Tirith, Gandalf takes on the role of supervisor and counsellor. At the Houses of Healing he is always present, but now he only flanks Aragorn, so that the latter may fulfil the prophecy about the true king who will show the authenticity of his lineage by healing the wounded and dying.

---

256 For a discussion of the sundering effects of the Great War on the literary imagination of the age, see chapter 3, page 75ff, of the present study. The symbolical connotations of the suicide are related to the destruction of the world (De Paco 2003:356).

In the council held in the chapter 'The Last Debate', the wizard's opinion will remain influential, but he always leaves the final decision to the mortals. His speech is marked by parables and sayings expressed with an almost evangelical diction, that exemplify his moral counsel regarding duty – "[...] it is not our part to master all the tides of the world, but to do what is in us for the succour of those years wherein we are set, uprooting the evil in the fields that we know, so that those who live after may have clean earth to till" (*LotR*, 913) – with a strong emphasis on the need to make altruistic sacrifices:

> '[...] it may well prove that we ourselves shall perish utterly in a black battle far from the living lands; so that even if Barad-dûr be thrown down, we shall not live to see a new age. But this, I deem, is our duty. And better so than to perish nonetheless – as we surely shall, if we sit here – and know as we die that no new age shall be.' (*LotR*, 914)

Though the altruistic motivation be Christian, Gandalf obviously appeals to the qualities of Northern courage, offering no salvation but just the grim satisfaction of knowing, in the moment when they "perish utterly" – that is, with no further hope of salvation – that they have done their duty.

The seven thousand men that Aragorn finally mobilizes for the war against Mordor are so obviously inferior in number to Sauron's forces that the attack seems almost ridiculous. Prince Imrahil compares it with a child that threatens an armoured knight "with a bow of string and green willow" (*LotR*, 916). This imagery recalls the famous biblical story of David and Goliath, and the outcome of the battle is also the same: against all odds, the smaller force wins. However, as in the episodes taking place in the mines of Moria and at Minas Tirith, the *mélange* of Northern courage and Christian duty is also complemented by the possibility of investing the applicability with a twentieth-century dimension: not only is it an obvious counter-attack on the defeatist attitude in general, it is also a rebuttal of Graves's poem 'Goliath and David', which criticizes the innocence of the biblical parabole in the light of the poet's experiences in the Great War, expressing exactly the cynical spirit and helpless disillusionment of the post-war period that Tolkien abhorred.[257]

---

[257] The poem first appeared in Graves's collection *Goliath and David* (1917). In Shippey's (2003:335) words, one of the main differences between Tolkien and other writers of the era lies in the former's refusal to accept the break with the past after the war: "[...] unlike many men of his age, he had not been alienated even by the Great War from the traditions in which he had been brought up. Unlike Robert Graves, his near-contemporary and fellow-Fusilier, he never said 'Goodbye to All That'."

As the battle rages at the Black Gate, Gandalf appears like a wrathful god of the old epics, coldly supervising the destruction of lives: "Upon the hill-top stood Gandalf, and he was white and cold and no shadow fell on him" (*LotR*, 984). This epic grimness is not relieved by the appearance of the Eagles, as the wizard announces that the Final Judgment, or the moment in which a more general destiny will be decided (the word 'doom' significantly, and perhaps deliberately, leaves room for both interpretations) has come – "Stand, men of the West! This is the hour of doom!" He finally announces the success of Frodo's mission and takes off towards Orodruin mounted on Gwaihir, Lord of the Eagles.

The figure of Gandalf now acquires an almost divine status, both in his description, emphasizing the white colour and the absence of shadows from his person, and in the announcement of the hour of doom. The scene suggestively combines the vision of the war-hungry gods of the classical epics and Norse mythology with an image closely resembling the Archangel Michael, messenger of the divine judgment (the scene at Khazad-dûm also shows Gandalf like this). The arrival of the Eagles reinforce the double inheritance: the descent of Eagles in biblical tradition is synonymous with "the descent of grace on the mortals" (De Paco 2003:106, my translation), which may be applied to what actually happens when they arrive at the Black Gate. At the same time, Gandalf's dependence on these birds makes him similar to the figure of Odin (Burns 2006:71-72).

This combined myth, embodied by Gandalf and with an applicability to twentieth-century concerns, establishes a dialogue with romance as the heroes return to Minas Tirith. Gandalf, being now an acknowledged spiritual authority, presides over the ceremony of coronation, blessing the new king in the name of the Valar: "Now come the days of the King, and may they be blessed while the thrones of the Valar endure!" (*LotR*, 1004) The only problem left is that Aragorn needs a queen to fulfil the mythic scheme of medieval romance, and the white tree is still dead.

As Gandalf shows Aragorn the sapling of the new tree on Mount Mindolluin, his mission on Middle-earth is brought to an end. As a consequence, this is the last time he assumes the role of the divine messenger, but it is also the most explicit: he now prophesies the future of Middle-earth, having contributed significantly to putting it on a clearly defined course (as opposed to what happened after the Great War in the twentieth century), recognizing that he was Sauron's principal adversary: "The Third Age was my age. I was the Enemy of Sauron; and my work is finished. I shall go soon. The burden must lie now upon you and your kindred." (*LotR*, 1007)

4.7. Frodo and Sam: journey to the end of the Third Age

The way Frodo integrates and assimilates different traditions, and later puts them in writing (being the narrator of the main part of *The Lord of the Rings*), is in part a consequence of the special sensitivity that the Ring gives him. In Moria and Lórien, and at Amon Hen, his awareness is gradually heightened – so much that even Galadriel acknowledges the fact:

> "[...] as Ring-bearer and as one who has borne it on finger and seen that which is hidden, your sight is grown keener. You have perceived my thought more clearly than many that are accounted wise. You saw the Eye of him that holds the Seven and the Nine. And did you not see and recognize the ring upon my finger?" (*LotR*, 385-386)

Frodo becomes more and more attached to the Ring as the story progresses, and this, in turn, makes him intimately related to the end of the Third Age, of which he is one of the main protagonists. Before Amon Hen, the tradition that has dominated the descriptions of the journey has been the novel, tinged with romance. This combination is able to host the different traditions, as represented by the different members of the Fellowship, without much friction, romance and novel being both flexible forms. After the episode at Amon Hen, when the Fellowship splits up, the narrative describing the travels of Aragorn, Legolas and Gimli will be marked by a *mélange* of epic, novel and romance, turned into a dialogue with romance as they approach Fangorn, as we have seen, while the captured hobbits will relate their story using a basically novelistic discourse. Here, all the elements of the situational level intervene: the action, theme, characters, physical space and focalization.

With Frodo and Sam, the theme is different. As Frodo carries the Ring and tells the story of the journey, this part of the narrative is the one that most clearly reflects the end of the Third Age, and with it, the different traditions that co-exist at this stage of the history of Middle-earth, some of which will disappear with the beginning of the Fourth. The following analysis attempts to explain how the narrative incorporates a wide range of the Western narrative traditions, while at the same time creating a link to twentieth-century history and culture, during the final part of the journey to Mount Doom.

The adventure novel

The journey of Frodo and Sam starts off in the novel tradition. As they cross the mountains of Emyn Muil, the narrative is dominated by detailed descriptions of the geography and marked by the colloquial dialogue between Frodo and Sam:

> [...] Once in milder days there must have been a fair thicket in the ravine, but now, after some fifty yards, the trees came to an end, though old broken stumps straggled on almost to the cliff's brink. The bottom of the gully, which lay along the edge of a rock-fault, was rough with broken stone and slanted steeply down. [...] When they came at last to the end of it, Frodo stooped and leaned out.
>
> [...] 'It would be a big jump still,' said Frodo. 'About, well' – he stood for a moment measuring it with his eyes – 'about eighteen fathoms I should guess. Not more.'
>
> 'And that's enough!' said Sam. 'Ugh! How I do hate looking down from a height! But looking's better than climbing.' (*LotR*, 630)

The narrator then dedicates several pages to describing the details of the descent, but little by little, he also introduces several romance elements that produce a *mélange* with this tradition, such as the sudden darkness of a thunderstorm (controlled by Sauron) that makes Frodo blind, the call of a *nazgûl* and an elf-rope that unties itself to follow the hobbits once they have climbed down. This *mélange* is close to the narrative dynamics of the adventure novel, especially as a result of the interaction between the characters.

This is the first time that the particular relationship between Frodo and Sam is fully portrayed, mainly because of the fact that they have not been alone until now.[258] Both of them are quite aware of their roles: Frodo is the master,

---

[258] So far, we have only seen glimpses of this relationship, especially in the first stage of the journey, but then the presence of Pippin ensured a more humorous treatment, much in the vein of Jerome K. Jerome, that eclipsed the narrative dynamics of the adventure novel in Frodo and Sam's interaction.

Sam the servant. Tolkien's treatment of this relationship comes close to the interaction between the hero of the British adventure novel of the nineteenth century, and the helper-friend that aids him in the adventure.[259]

Seen in this context, Sam can be identified, up to a certain point, with the type of friend that Toda Iglesia (2002:27) defines as the servant with the skills that are necessary to the hero in difficult situations. As for the hero of the adventure novel, "he does not fight against his own society but, like the epic hero, the hostility comes from the forces of nature or from enemy societies represented by nature" (Toda Iglesia 2002:31), and he represents aristocratic values that are reconciled with bourgeoise values because of the presence of the friend, who is "practical, skilful, less limited by his social background" (Toda Iglesia 2002:32).[260] Hence, the pragmatic friend of the hero may indulge in morally questionable and indecorous acts, but, because of the hero's reproaches, he never exceeds the limits of what is morally permitted.[261]

The relationship between Frodo and Sam clearly corresponds to this scheme, especially when Gollum enters the scene. This character provides Frodo with an opportunity of showing that he has understood the essence of his mission, and this is reflected in his behaviour, which is motivated by strong feelings of compassion and mercy.

Sam, breaking the moral code of 'fair play', jumps onto Gollum from behind, but Frodo, when given the opportunity, forgives Gollum instead of killing him, remembering Gandalf's words about the need to show pity and mercy. He then asks Gollum to pay his debt by guiding them to Mordor. This sequence – Sam transgressing the limits of fair play in his interaction with Gollum, Frodo correcting him and thereby bringing out the best of what good there ever was in the corrupt creature – will be repeated several times during the journey.

---

259 See also Nelson (1989).
260 All quotations taken from this study are my translations.
261 "[...] since the friend has a different social background, his upbringing is different [...] no prejudice prevents him from [...] questioning the ritual's validity [and] challenging the values of fair play." (Toda Iglesia 2002:59). Toda Iglesia also highlights the friend's tendency to act like a tempter that proposes other models of conduct that the hero must reject. (Toda Iglesia 2002:121)

Gollum as a character simultaneously embodies several different narrative traditions.[262] His speech and behaviour are novelistic in that they show the effects of a disturbed mind;[263] he possesses strange romance powers, such as the longevity conferred to him by the the Ring; he helps the hobbits in an epic mission and he plays a fundamental role in the mythic end of the Third Age, falling with the Ring into the fire. His appearance also establishes a heroic epic triad, which, according to Miller (2000:106-108), consists of "a pair of heroic figures, each with a specific valence or talent, [...] joined by a third figure whose powers are drawn from a manifestly different, usually supernatural, source."

This is also more or less what happens at Emyn Muil: Frodo, a hero with fundamentally internal (spiritual and moral) powers, and Sam, with practical skills, are joined by Gollum, a five-hundred year old creature whose powers are directly derived from a magic object. Before the narrative is finished, however, the text will have subverted both the schemes of the adventure novel and those of the heroic triad, as we shall see.

The dystopic romance of the Great War

At this stage of the journey, the intertraditional dialogue is centered on the *mélange* of novel and romance standards combined with the applicability to contemporary concerns. This particular combination can be seen in the descriptions of the "Waste Land" that dominates the slopes of the mountains of Mordor, which find a clear echo both in the prose romances of William

---

[262] Gollum first appears in *The Hobbit*. For this reason, apart from the general narrative traditions, he also belongs to Tolkien's own tradition, as an *autotextual* reference (Segura 2004:144-145).

[263] Rosebury (2003:215) argues that Gollum is predominantly novelistic, because his characterization implies "a novelistic degree of psychological realism." Perhaps for this reason, Tucev (2005:87-105) finds it so easy to interpret the relationship between Frodo and Gollum in the light of Jung's concept of the "Shadow". Day (2003:144), for his part, highlights the split personality in the character of Gollum with references to novelistic predecessors such as Stevenson's *Dr Jekyll and Mr Hyde* and Dickens's *The Mystery of Edwin Drood*. We may also add James Hogg's *Confessions of a Justified Sinner*, a work belonging to the romantic strain of the gothic novel, and some of Poe's tales. It is interesting to notice that these nineteenth-century narratives about psychological disorders roughly belong to the same era that produced the British adventure novel, which informs the treatment of Frodo and Sam's interaction, and the gothic scenes that take place in Shelob's Lair and Cirith Ungol, which will be discussed a little further on.

Morris, and in the devastated landscapes of the battlefields of the Great War:[264]

> The gasping pools were choked with ash and crawling muds, sickly white and grey, as if the mountains had vomited the filth of their entrails upon the lands about. High mounds of crushed and powdered rock, great cones of earth fire-blasted and poison-stained, stood like an obscene graveyard in endless rows, slowly revealed in the reluctant light. (*LotR*, 657)

The hobbits rest in a crater, infested with "a foul sump of oily many-coloured ooze lay[ing] at its bottom" (*LotR*, 657-658), before they continue their journey toward the Black Gate as night falls. The similarities with the effects of the grenades and bombs on the landscape, with craters full of mud and petrol, earth and rocks poisoned and smashed beyond recognition, and the soldiers' passive wait for the active night-duty, are evident. Compared with the episode taking place at Isengard, the narrative voice of which is controlled and distanced as it describes the wrecked landscape, the treatment of Frodo and Sam's journey comes closer to a first-hand testimony, with detailed descriptions of the horrors and fears felt by those who actually walked these bizarre sceneries. Therefore, Isengard can be more readily compared to the vision of the "Waste Land" as exposed by the poets who did not take part in the conflict but used the devastated landscapes as a symbol to elucidate the horrors of modern life, while the Dead Marshes and the foothills of the mountains of Mordor are more directly experienced and share more features with the approach to myth and romance shown in the works of the war poets.[265]

An example of this is the arrival at the Black Gate, which the narrator describes with images similar to the ones used by the war poets, highlighting the subhuman characteristics of the Enemy:

> Beneath the hills on either side the rock was bored into a hundred caves and *maggot-holes*: there a host of Orcs lurked, ready at a signal to *issue forth like black ants* going to war. (*LotR*, 662)[266]

---

264 Tolkien himself says that "The Dead Marshes and the approaches to the Morannon owe something to Northern France after the battle of the Somme. They owe more to William Morris and his Huns and Romans, as in *The House of the Wolfings* or *The Roots of the Mountains*" (*Letters*, 303). See also Keith Brace's interview with Tolkien in *Birmingham Post*, 23rd of May, 1968. Tolkien participated in the battle of the Somme with the Lancashire Fusiliers.
265 See section 3.1. (p. 75).
266 My italics. The description of the guards as "evil-eyed and fell" (*LotR*, 663) is also painted with heavy strokes of what Fussell terms the *versus habit*.

The Black Gate: Epic rejected

These descriptions are followed by a novelistic dialogue between Sam and Gollum about the impossibility of entering Mordor this way. That Sam should focalize this dialogue seems to be a necessary condition for Frodo to assume an attitude and speech proper to the epic hero:

> His face was grim and set, but *resolute*. He was filthy, haggard, and pinched with weariness, but *he cowered no longer, and his eyes were clear*. 'I said so, because I purpose to enter Mordor, and I know no other way. Therefore I shall go this way. I do not ask anyone to go with me.' (*LotR*, 663)[267]

This determination, and the noble physical appearance produced by it, are similar to the effects we saw in Aragorn during his epic moments at Amon Hen. There are more parallels. The mission that Frodo has agreed to undertake is not a strictly epic one either,[268] though the fortune of the global conflict depends on its results, and as in Aragorn's hunt for the hobbits, the success depends more on moral qualities than on physical prowess, though the latter also plays an important role. This shows a double affinity to both epic (Northern courage in the face of hopelessness, and deeds based on spectacular action) and romance (Christian virtues, the interior journey, moral tests) standards, which is the trademark of Tolkien's heroes. In the scene in front of the Black Gate, Frodo shows an unbreakable faith and determination, in spite of the fact that the possibilities of success are nonexistent.

What motivates this invitation to epic standards is, above all, the intimate relationship between the physical space (the Black Gate) and Frodo's mission (the quest to destroy the Ring). It is interesting to notice that Sam now controls the focalization, because the effect is that the epic is not allowed to enter the dialogue with the main narrative paradigm, based on a combination of novel and romance, but is rejected.

Frodo recovers the focalization some pages later, after a conversation with Gollum, as he ponders the use of the first-person perspective in the creature's

---

267 My italics.
268 For a discussion of the concept of the quest in *The Lord of the Rings*, see Auden (1968). Auden argues that Tolkien's work subverts the classical notions of the quest due to the fact that the mission consists of eliminating something rather than finding it, and because of the characteristics of the protagonists (a mélange of public and private characters).

discourse and its possible relationship to the veracity of his words. This implies a reasoning based on an empiric observation of reality – "For one thing, he noticed that Gollum used I, and that seemed usually to be a sign [...] that some remnants of old truth and sincerity were for the moment on top" (*LotR*, 669) –, and it is also an observation derived from an active interest in the psychological processes of a disturbed mind, which is sufficiently novelistic to justify the devolution of the focalization to his person at that moment. After this, Frodo thinks about the road they must take, and this gives rise to nostalgic memories of the Shire that highlight the difference between the idyllic life of the past and the present situation. The idea of 'Time Before' and 'Time After' also corresponds to one of the effects of the Great War reflected in the works of the war poets, the treatment of which closely resembles Frodo and Sam's visions of the pastoral bliss of the past as they delve deeper into the horrors of Mordor.

The section that portrays the journey to the end of the Third Age is dominated by hobbits, and a narrative standard too far removed from a hobbit perception of reality is difficult to integrate in the dialogue, at least at this stage. It would seem as if any invitation to other traditions, such as the epic, must not deviate too much from the fusion of the novel and romance if it is to be accepted.

Fusion: adventure novel and dystopic romance of the Great War

As the hobbits and Gollum enter the forest of Ithilien, the narrative becomes a *mélange* between the adventure novel and the dystopic romance of the Great War, describing the place as a *potential* paradise,[269] wounded by the presence of Sauron's forces. The combination of the eternal, healing forces of nature and the malign and penetrating influence of modernity is crystallized in the image of the remnants of a cruel sacrificial rite, presumably perpetrated by orcs, where the skulls and bones of the victims are already being hidden by

---

[269] "Ithilien, the garden of Gondor now desolate kept still a dishevelled dryad loveliness." (*LotR*, 676) The expression "garden of Gondor" says something about this potentiality, the garden being, of course, symbolically related to the idea of Paradise (De Paco 2003:288). Shippey (2002: 206) compares Ithilien with the current situation of our own world, partially destroyed but still showing certain vestiges of the garden it once was.

the luxuriance of some wild flowers. This type of imagery emphasizes the consolation that lies in nature's power to mitigate the wounds inflicted by man (or, in this case, by a race of a similar destructive capacity), which is a trait of the poetry of the Great War.[270]

Another prominent feature of the poetry of the Great War is the so-called 'homoeroticism'[271] – a sincere, fraternal love, not necessarily sexual, which was presented as something natural. According to Graves (2000:39), this disposition was triggered in the boarding schools, which, because of the values of the Victorian Age, imposed a strict separation between the sexes, so that there was not much room for informal interaction between young men and women before adulthood. The affective relationships between the young men were not approved of by the institutional authorities, but looked upon as something 'inevitable'. Given the cultural context of the Victorian and the Edwardian adventure novels, homoeroticism is also present in these narratives (if more implicitly), especially in the relationship between the hero and his friend, who represents "his first affectionate relationship outside the family, which is often inexistent or far away. The friend offers unconditional loyalty and warm feelings" (Toda Iglesia 2002:60).

The scene that shows Sam's devotion and love for Frodo implies an interlacement of both traditions[272] and well fits the general narrative dialogue:

> The early daylight was only just creeping down into the shadows under the trees, but he saw his master's face very clearly, and his hands, too, lying at rest on the ground beside him. [...] He shook his head, as if finding words useless, and murmured: 'I love him. He's like that, and sometimes it shines through, somehow. But I love him, whether or no.' (*LotR*, 678)

The picture of Frodo and Sam as two soldiers of the Great War, moving through a no-man's-land marked by the devastating effects of the conflict, is perfectly compatible with the idea of Frodo and Sam as two Victorian adventurers exploring a remote and hostile corner of the British Empire,

---

270 See chapter 3, p. 76.
271 See Featherstone (1995:104-115). Saxey (2005) discusses Tolkien's application of the concept to different male couples in *The Lord of the Rings*.
272 At the same time it should be noted that the theme is not foreign to epic narratives of Classical Antiquity. The most well-known example is the friendship between Achilles and Patroclus in the *Iliad*, but examples abound in other epic narratives as well, such as the *Argonautica*.

and one of the things that link both interpretations is the treatment of their friendship.[273]

Pseudomedieval romance

With the apperance of Faramir and his men, the soldiers and adventurers are forced to enter the world of the nineteenth-century 'pseudomedieval' prose romance, which is present in the works of writers such as Walter Scott and William Morris. The *invitation* on behalf of the physical space, the characters and the action takes us there without much friction, partly because of the context of the adventure novel, that has prepared us for the inclusion of nineteenth-century narrative romance traditions, partly perhaps due to the fact that, as Fussell (1975:135) says, "[f]or most who fought in the Great War, one highly popular equivalent [to the soldier's experience] was Victorian pseudomedieval romance."

The romance coincidence implied by the apparently gratuitous appearance of Faramir and his men is reduced to novelistic credibility by the explanation that they were attracted by the smoke of Sam's fire. Their language shows a novelistic adaptation of medieval diction, not far from Walter Scott, an analogue extended to the description of the newcomers, who communicate by whistling and use camouflage for their guerrilla-like warfare much in the same way as Robin Hood and his band of thieves do.[274]

Shippey (2003:129-130) writes that the contrast between Faramir and Éomer shows two different stages in a cultural evolution: the men of Rohan represent a much more primitive civilization compared to that of the Gondorians. The statement is interesting, because it also seems to highlight the difference between

---

273 Another similarity can be found in the episode that shows Sam's skills as a cook. Sam prepares a dish which is as close as possible to the traditional cooking of the Shire (and, implicitly, of England) – fish and chips. In the British adventure novel, the need to preserve the values and habits of the British civilization in spite of the hostile setting is frequently expressed (Toda Iglesia 2002:26), while nostalgia for the old England (of the times before the Great War) was common in the poetry of the Great War. See chapter 3, p. 76ff.

274 See, for example, Gilbert's (1998, first published 1912) rendering of the legend. Faramir's characterization also largely corresponds to the Robin Hood-figure: he is a nobleman with a keen sense of justice, well-educated and intelligent; he leads a self-imposed life in the woods where he ambushes the representatives of an enemy that threatens the liberty of the natives; he is extremely bold but always protected by his good fortune and his cunning, unconventional warfare. One difference is Faramir's austerity, perhaps because of his allegiance to the epic tradition, which he will display later on in the tale, compared to Robin Hood's jocularity.

a character firmly rooted in the epic and *chanson de geste* traditions (Éomer), and a character informed by standards of romance and the novel, showing a much more nuanced world-view, as in Faramir's case.

Before dinner, Sam shows his provincial rudeness as he sticks his whole head into a bowl of water, causing remarks of disapproval among Faramir's men, and Faramir instructs the hobbits in the Gondorian ritual of turning West (where Númenor used to be) in silence, which makes Frodo feel "strangely rustic and untutored." This is followed by a description of the meal, which consists of "pale yellow wine, cool and fragrant, and [...] bread and butter, and salted meats, and dried fruits, and good red cheese." (*LotR*, 703)[275]

Both the emphasis on the knight's education, of which good manners is a prominent component, and the detailed descriptions of objects apparently insignificant for the argument, are inherent to the world-view of medieval romance,[276] and, judging from the way Sam talks about Galadriel after the meal, it would seem as if he had assimilated something of the romance tradition, and learnt a little about the proper attitude of a servant,[277] though in his own way:

> '[...] I am only a hobbit, and gardening's my job at home, sir, if you understand me, and I'm not much good at poetry [...] so I can't tell you what I mean. [...] But I wish I could make a song about her. [...] Beautiful she is, sir! Lovely! Sometimes like a white daffadowndilly, small and slender like. Hard as di'monds, soft as moonlight. Warm as sunlight, cold as frost in the stars. Proud and far-off as a snow-mountain, and as merry as any lass I ever saw with daisies in her hair in springtime. But that's a lot o' nonsense, and all wide of my mark.' (*LotR*, 706)

Sam's discourse shows a sincere wish to adapt his language and attitude to Faramir's demands. In a submissive tone, he admits that his social position is

---

[275] The description of the dishes is also very detailed: "round platters, bowls and dishes of glazed brown clay and turned box-wood, smooth and clean [...] a cup or basin of polished bronze; and a goblet of plain silver." (*LotR*, 701)

[276] According to Beer (1970:3), "it's typical of romance to be occupied with the everyday paraphernalia of the world it creates. Clothes and feasts, dogs and towels give body to its ideal world." The emphasis on the knight's education and the 'everyday paraphernalia' is very much present in several of the most representative works of medieval and late-medieval romance, such as Chrétien's *Perceval, the Story of the Grail*, and Malory's *Le Mort d'Arthur*. See also chapter 2, p 43ff, of the present study.

[277] Faramir has previously rebuked Sam for his insolent and outspoken attitude in front of his master: "'Do not speak before your master, whose wit is greater than yours. [...] Sit by your master, and be silent!'" (*LotR*, 691)

humble and, implicitly, that his limited poetic skills are a consequence of this. This is also typical of medieval romance (which is very conscious of, and even dependent upon, the primacy of the aristocracy), as is the theme of idealistic reverence for a lady and the use of poetic similes taken from the natural world to describe her. At the same time, Sam's colloquial speech, consistent with his previous characterization, shows a clear adherence to the novel tradition, whereby the narrative never moves further up the formal scale than the *pseudo*medieval romance would allow for.

At the end of the episode, the narrative returns to the original *mélange*, beginning shortly after the hobbits say good-bye to Faramir, as a mysterious darkness prevents the coming of the new day and prepares us for the particular natural symbolism, proper to the dystopic romance of the Great War, that we have seen as they entered Ithilien. Now, shortly before they leave the forest, the narrator describes how the sun comes through the clouds in the West beyond Gondor, before descending in a still immaculate sea. The last sunrays illuminate the figure of a noble king – a stone statue profaned by the graffiti of the orcs – whose head rests among the bushes on the ground. However, the king has been redeemed by nature:

> The eyes were hollow and the carven beard was broken, but about the high stern forehead there was a coronal of silver and gold. A trailing plant with flowers like small white stars had bound itself across the brows *as if in reverence for the fallen king*, and in the crevices of his stony hair yellow stonecrop gleamed.
>
> 'They cannot conquer for ever!' said Frodo. And then suddenly the brief glimpse was gone. (*LotR*, 729)[278]

From my point of view, this is the image that best clarifies the meaning of Frodo and Sam's experience in Ithilien, and the relationship between this place and the modern world. The description underscores the idea that the world is a potentially beautiful place, even when stained by rude, vulgar and cruel manifestations of the forces that are hostile to peaceful co-existence and beauty, and that it is worth the while fighting for its redemption. However, it also shows Tolkien's ambivalence towards the passing of time – on the one hand, the eternal natural cycles may give us solace in times of destruction and

---

278 My italics.

crisis, but on the other hand, the same cycles are relentless as regards Man's earthly existence and will erase the marks he has left when he disappears from the face of the Earth.

The gothic novel

While the narrator explored the limits of the influence of the epic tradition on the *mélange* that dominates Frodo and Sam's journey in the episode at the Black Gate, and Ithilien brought an invitation to the nineteenth-century pseudomedieval prose romance, the road passing by Minas Morgul, Shelob's Lair and Cirith Ungol takes the dialogue straight into the territory of the gothic novel.

The hobbits enter this realm as they approach Minas Morgul, the fortress of the Witch-king of Angmar, which is presented as a sinister castle, the stones of which seem to have a will of their own:

> Paler indeed than the moon ailing in some slow eclipse was the light of it now, wavering and blowing like a noisome exhalation of decay, a corpse-light, a light that illuminated nothing. In the walls and tower windows showed, like countless black holes looking inward into emptiness; but the topmost course of the tower revolved slowly, first one way and then another, a huge ghostly head leering into the night. (*LotR*, 730)

The descriptions of the physical space are completed with a bridge adorned with bestial figures, cold vapour rising from the water and white flowers, beautiful but rotten, that cover the fields on both sides of the road. The motif of the gothic hero (or heroine) approaching a ghostly castle inhabited by a perverse and evil, and, in some ways, monstruos man,[279] is as frequent in the gothic novel as the conception of old buildings as personified guardians of secret vice.[280] As in the case of Minas Morgul, this oppressive and sombre gothic space, usually located in some remote and isolated place, is

---

279 Some typical examples of this figure appear in novels such as Walpole's *The Castle of Otranto*, Reeve's *The Old English Baron*, Radcliffe's *The Italian*, and Stoker's *Dracula*.
280 We come across this phenomenon in works as diverse as Lewis's *The Monk*, Poe's *The Fall of the House of Usher*, and Stoker's *Dracula*, just to mention three well-known examples. It is also significant that the original cover illustration for Isak Dinesen's (Karen Blixen's) collection *Seven Gothic Tales* (1963, first published 1934), which was supposed to reflect the gothic spirit and ambience, shows a mounted hero approaching a medieval-looking castle dramatically situated on a mountain top.

also the setting of supernatural events that inspire hysterical reactions in the protagonists.[281]

As the army of the Witch-king of Angmar marches out of Minas Morgul, a phantasmal light hits the overhanging clouds in response to Sauron's sign. At this moment of almost uncontrolled fear, Frodo is comforted by Galadriel's phial much in the same way as a desperate gothic hero would look for solace by holding up a crucifix, or some other sacred object, between his person and the supernatural enemy.

The influence of the gothic novel is firmly established as the hobbits progress up the narrow stairway to Cirith Ungol and enter the cave of Shelob. Here, the hobbits are left to die in an isolated, dark, oppressive and threatening place indeed. More than the subtle terror of Radcliffe or Reeves, the episode at Shelob's Lair offers a tale of explicit horror in the vein of M.G. Lewis or H.P. Lovecraft, in which no details are missing as the monster's viscous substances and corporeal corruption are described.[282]

Frodo – pure, innocent and virtuous like the gothic heroines – is the object of the transgression, being penetrated by the spider's needle and later carried to Cirith Ungol, another gothic fortress in Sauron's service. Sam, for his part, takes on the role of the hero that rescues the maiden. However, Sam's characterization makes an identification with this role almost impossible, because his firm adherence to the tradition of the realist novel hampers a romance-oriented focalization, and while Frodo remains unconscious, it is Sam who must focalize the events.

While Sam carries out the tasks proper to the friend of the hero in the adventure novel, he is comfortable: he courageously wounds Shelob,[283] but after

---

[281] For an outline of the features of the gothic novel, see p. 57ff of chapter 2.
[282] Burns (2006:117-118) connects Shelob to a wide array of possible sources, such as Ayesha (or She) of Haggard's *She*, the mother of Grendel in *Beowulf*, Sin of Milton's *Paradise Lost*, and Errour of Spenser's *Faerie Queene*. However, the narrative treatment of the episode is much closer to the gothic novel (especially M.G. Lewis's *The Monk* and H.P. Lovecraft's tales of Cthulhu) than to the romance-epic mélange of Spenser or the Christian epic of Milton.
[283] Toda Iglesia (2002:174) highlights the solidarity and altruism of the hero's friend in the confrontations with hostile nature such as caves and subterranean spaces, or in fights against wild animals.

this he becomes much less confident about the course of action. Both in the adventure novel and in the gothic novel, it is the 'aristocratic' hero who must assume leadership and make the most important decisions about the mission, and now it is up to Sam to do so.

The intertraditional dialogue now explores the limits of Sam in this context, showing his difficulties in undertaking and accomplishing the two possible missions required by the cicumstances – to take the Ring and carry on toward Orodruin on his own, or to rescue Frodo from the tower of Cirith Ungol. When Sam puts on the Ring, says good-bye to the presumably dead body of Frodo and sets out to finish the mission, the narrator underscores that this is against his natural inclination:

> 'I've made up my mind,' he kept saying to himself. But he had not. Though he had done his best to think it out, what he was doing was altogether *against the grain of his nature*. 'Have I got it wrong?' he muttered. 'What ought I to have done?'
>
> [...] For a moment, motionless in intolerable doubt, he looked back. [...] Then at last he turned to the road in front and took a few steps: the heaviest and the most reluctant he had ever taken. (*LotR* 760-761)[284]

When Sam realizes that he has made a mistake and that Frodo is alive, he also understands that he must change his current mission for something which, given the dynamics of the intertraditional dialogue in this part of the narrative, may well be compared to the gothic rescue of the heroine trapped in the castle. Sam shrinks back, with some enthusiasm, to the friend-role, ready to renounce the heroic decorum in order to carry out the mission. His actions are motivated by altruism and solidarity, without doubt noble sentiments, but he lacks the gothic hero's extravagance and sophisticated manners – while it is true that he finally manages to finish off the enemies and save Frodo, his *modus operandi* is rather unorthodox, to say the least.

To begin with, Sam's heroic presence is so limited that his enemies do not even notice that he is there:

---

[284] My italics. Sam's comment when he realizes that Frodo is still alive reinforces the possibility of identifying him with the hero's friend of the gothic novel or the British adventure novel: "'I got it all wrong!' he cried. 'I knew I would. [...] Never leave your master, never, never: that was my right rule. And I knew it in my heart. May I be forgiven! [...].'" (*LotR*, 769)

> Sam yelled and brandished Sting, but his little voice was drowned in the tumult. No one heeded him.
>
> The great doors slammed to. Boom. The bars of iron fell into place inside. Clang. The gate was shut. Sam hurled himself against the bolted brazen plates and fell senseless to the ground. (*LotR*, 770)

When he finally enters the fortress, he discovers that the orcs have done most of the job for him, killing each other. Two of them remain. Sam manages to frighten one of them because of the influence of Galadriel's phial, that makes him look like a terrible elf warrior. However, the narrator quickly reduces Sam's heroic stature by comparing him to a dog: "Never was any dog more heartened when its enemy turned tail than Sam at this unexpected flight." (*LotR*, 938)

The other orc moves up the stairs to the topmost quarters of the tower, where he begins to abuse Frodo with a whip. Sam attacks him with his sword before he is able to react. He cuts off one of the orc's hands, a heroic deed mitigated by the following clumsy maneouver, when Sam fails to hit his target and falls to the ground. The only thing that saves him is his enemy's lack of dexterity, as the orc stumbles on a ladder, falls down the trapdoor and breaks his neck.

Apart from the gothic novel, there are also images and metaphors close to the dystopic romance of the Great War present in the episode of Cirith Ungol. The description of Sam entering the tower recalls the explorations of a soldier who penetrates the dark trenches of the enemy, invaded after a fierce battle and full of corpses and the smell of fear and death.[285] In that dark, in the midst of his despair, Sam sings a song to dispel the fear. The lyrics evoke the rural idyll and pastoral scenery of the Shire and the lands of the West, and the poetic images are similar to the ones used by the war poets.[286]

---

[285] See Sassoon's poem 'The Rear-guard' (Driver 1996:61-62).
[286] Apart from the nostalgia for an idyllic past and the use of natural images that appeal to the eternity of natural cycles as a means of consolation, the song is also strangely similar to Brooke's 'The Soldier', a poem that expresses the idea that solace can be found in thinking of England as a place unharmed by the war, with the argument that the English soldier dying in far lands will retain part of his homeland's immaculate distinction. Shippey (2003:191) says that Sam's song represents "a closeness to immediate context reaching out simultaneously to myth," because the words are given to him as some sort of divine inspiration to accompany the melody he is humming and this is what makes him find Frodo, who answers Sam's words from the tower. Shippey's description would also be fitting for much of the war poetry.

The meeting between Frodo and Sam in the tower, offering another example of homoeroticism, enhances the dialogue with the *mélange* of the dystopic romance and the adventure novel:

> '[...] I'd given up hope, almost. I couldn't find you.'
>
> 'Well, you have now, Sam, dear Sam,' said Frodo, and he lay back in Sam's gentle arms, like a child at rest when night-fears are driven away by some loved voice or hand.
>
> Sam felt that he could sit like that in endless happiness; but it was not allowed. It was not enough for him to try and find his master, he had still to try to save him. (*LotR*, 944-945)

The presence of the gothic novel gradually fades and diappears altogether as the pragmatic Sam decides to dress them up like orcs in order to escape unnoticed from the fortress. Frodo answers jokingly that he hopes that Sam has found some suitable inns on the road to Orodruin.

In the adventure novel, the friend of the hero is usually skilled in putting to good use the resources offered by the territory of adventure (Toda Iglesia 2002:129), while the hero, who is in charge of preserving the ethics and customs of the British gentleman, makes sure that the friend does not exceed the limits of acceptable behaviour. Frodo makes it clear that he only agrees to do what Sam says because of the exceptional circumstances: if the world had been different, he would have made civilized stops at the inns along the road, but given the current state of affairs, he is forced to accept the indecorous methods proposed by his servant.

Towards the mythic end of the Third Age

In the chapter 'The Land of Shadow', the novelistic descriptions of the geography are balanced by the increasingly insistent use of natural images that recall the dystopic romance of the Great War, such as the unexpected discovery of a small stream that loses all of its fertilising potential as the water is absorbed by the sterile earth of Mordor;[287] the omnipresence of thorny bushes that

---

[287] Water symbolizes the origin of all life in most cultures, and, in Biblical symbolism, the springs in the desert save the Hebrews (De Paco 2003:104). Wilfred Owen's outraged protest against the futility of beauty and creative powers in the face of modern warfare expresses a similar sense of transgressive desacralization, as the poet contemplates the features of a dead brother-in-arms: "Oh what made fatuous sunbeams toil / To break earth's sleep at all?" (Driver 1996:57)

recall the barbed wire so frequently used in the Great War; the solitary star that brings hope to Sam; the sight of the desert plains of Mordor,[288] and so on. The treatment of the Enemy as a subhuman force dominated by brutish impulses is evident in the descriptions of two orcs that fight, and in the epsiode in which Frodo and Sam join a company of orcs headed for a military camp.

The following chapter, 'Mount Doom', shows how Sam struggles to overcome his growing despair, and how he remains determined to continue with the mission in spite of the tempting nostalgic images of the idyllic past that make him consider a return:

> [...] through all his thoughts there came the memory of water; and every brook or stream or fountain that he had ever seen, under green willow shades or twinkling in the sun, danced and rippled for his torment behind the blindness of his eyes. He felt the cool mud about his toes as he paddled in the Pool at Bywater with Jolly Cotton and Tom and Nibs, and their sister Rosie. 'But that was years ago,' he sighed, 'and far away. The way back, if there is one, goes past the Mountain.' (*LotR*, 974)

This natural symbolism, together with the nostalgia for the past and the treatment of the enemy, reinforce the presence of the dystopic romance of the Great War, while the narrative, at the same time, begins to engage in a dialogue with mythic paradigms. The symbolism of the natural images mingles consolation with despair[289] (appealing to the creative forces of natural cycles while evoking the destructive nightmare scenery of the Great War), and the theme of the British soldier of humble origins who rises above himself in the

---

288 In Sale's (1968) opinion, Mordor represents the most modern landscape on Middle-earth: "it is a landscape fashioned by the imagination of this century; the wasteland, the valley of ashes, the nightmare cities of Birkin and Joseph K."

289 Frye (1971:147) argues that the demonic symbology describes "the world as it is before human imagination begins to work at it," something which in the mineral world will take the shape of "deserts, rocks, cities of destruction, ruins of pride" (Frye 1971:150). This would be consistent with the landscape of Mordor. Shippey (2003:217) also believes that the details and the symbolism of this part of the narrative are given a romance -treatment, highlighting "the extent and nature of Tolkien's moralisations from landscape in such passages". Kocher (1974:108) also underscores the moral dimension of the journey, affirming that the moment when Frodo throws off his armour means that "for [Frodo], struggles for the right must hereafter be waged only on the moral plane." See also Savater (2005:165). The narrative strategies that make the moral interpretation of Frodo and Sam's journey possible are important to take into account in our analysis of the intertraditional dialogue, especially as they pave the way for a dialogue between the romance of the Great War and myth.

face of inevitable death,[290] are combined with an internal dialogue in which it seems as if the Devil himself is trying to avert Sam from his path:

> '[...] It's all quite useless [...] You could have lain down and gone to sleep together days ago, if you hadn't been so dogged. But you'll die just the same, or worse. You might just as well lie down now and give it up. You'll never get to the top anyway.'
>
> 'I'll get there, if I leave everything but my bones behind,' said Sam. 'And I'll carry Mr. Frodo up myself, if it breaks my back and heart. So stop arguing!'
>
> At that moment Sam felt a tremor in the ground beneath him, and he heard or sensed a deep remote rumble as of thunder imprisoned under the earth. (*LotR*, 974-975)

The furious response to Sam's stubborn insistence on destroying the Ring (and thereby overthrowing Sauron, Ilúvatar's enemy) comes from a hot subterranean Underworld, with a clear analogue to the Hell of Christian iconography. This narrative combination of motifs from the dystopic romance of the Great War with mythic symbolism causes the narrative to loosen its ties to the novel, something which can be appreciated in the increasingly blurred descriptions of the geography (though its presence is not altogether obliterated, mainly because of Sam's focalization).

The narrator's announcement that the last day has come coincides with the proximity of the central mythic elements of the narrative: Orodruin is the *physical space* where the destruction of the Ring, and the ensuing regeneration of the world, will take place; the *action* of throwing the Ring into the fire is the culmination of Frodo's epic/mythic mission; the *characters* of Sam, Frodo, Gollum and Sauron represent different degrees of the moral corruption derived from the Ring, which is the central *theme* of the myth that describes the end of the Third Age.

Frodo, at this moment, is as intimately related to the end of the Third Age as the Ring, and seems to acquire a Ring-like appearance himself. This transformation takes place after Gollum's penultimate attack, when he is elevated above his normal height until resembling a figure with supernatural powers:

---

[290] Tolkien admired the privates and batmen of his unit in the First World War for their courage, and acknowledged them as being a source of inspiration for the character of Sam (Carpenter 2000:89).

> [...] a figure robed in white, but at its breast it held a wheel of fire. Out of the fire there spoke a commanding voice.
>
> 'Begone, and trouble me no more. If you touch me ever again, you shall be cast yourself into the Fire of Doom.' (*LotR*, 979)

The moment is described as a 'vision' of Sam, that disappears after a few moments, but the premonition[291] comes true shortly afterwards, as Gollum bites off Frodo's finger and falls into the fire with the Ring. When Frodo puts the Ring on his finger, Sauron is suddenly treated, for the first time, as a character, not as a mere symbol of Evil; we now see a person who is able to feel fear and despair in the face of his imminent destruction. This, I believe, is an immediate consequence of the mythic characteristics of this part of the narrative.[292] Now, Sam – without the aid of Galadriel's luminous phial, which is quenched by the evil forces that control the place – focalizes the final battle between Frodo and Gollum, the outcome of which has seismic effects as Sauron falls, and this is followed by apocalyptic visions of Mordor's destruction. As we can see, even Sam is affected by the overwhelming presence of mythic paradigms in this epsiode.

The journey of Frodo, Sam and Gollum is thus marked by Frodo's growing assimilation of different narrative traditions – the adventure novel, dystopic romance of the Great War, epic, pseudomedieval romance, gothic novel and myth. Frodo reflects this assimilation in writing, being the chronicler of the events. The Ring is the most potent symbol of the end of the Third Age, and Frodo becomes one with it towards the end of his mission. In this way, from the point of view of the intertraditional dialogue, Frodo comes to embody Tolkien's particular approach to ironic myth, describing with his example and in his narrative a circular movement from the novel and back towards myth, incorporating in the process other narrative traditions of the past with great fluency while at the same time yielding space to twentieth-century concerns.

---

291 Frodo has already warned Gollum at the Black Gates that this will be his fate if he tries to steal the Ring. After the second warning the prophecy is fulfilled.
292 In mythic paradigms, the gods are usually personified.

4.8. Back to the Shire: dismantling the intertraditional dialogue

The Field of Cormallen marks the point where the intertraditional dialogue comes to an end and pseudomedieval prose romance takes over without any need for previous transitions. The end of the dialogue is particularly clear in the three main protagonists. Frodo has finished his heroic evolution at Orodruin and returns to his original state, with the important difference that his intimate association with the Ring and the end of the Third Age makes him virtually disappear from the narrative – he has lost both his spirits and his capacity to dialogue with the other traditions in Middle-earth. Aragorn, when he assumes the role of King, is reborn with the Fourth Age but becomes too firmly rooted in the romance tradition to be able to take part in the intertraditional dialogue, and Gandalf also reaches the zenith of his particular trajectory at Mount Mindolluin, when he shows Aragorn the sapling. Then he returns to the role of the benevolent wizard, though in a rather flatter (he now lacks the previous irritability, for instance) state than before.

From this moment on, the general movement shows a descent through the hierarchy of narrative traditions, which is accompanied by the physical movement of the protagonists, who leave the romance scenarios of Minas Tirith, stop briefly at the epic stronghold of Edoras and little by little continue the descent by way of Isengard and Rivendell until they reach the novel at Bree. The progressive physical and generic return is also measured by the farewells and conversations with different characters. At Edoras, they say good-bye to Éomer and Éowyn, and to the body of Théoden; at Isengard they stop to talk to Treebeard; near the Misty Mountains they meet Saruman, and the hobbits begin to talk in a more novelistic way. When they finally reach Rivendell, the hobbits dominate the narrative completely, and the elvish element is reduced to a minimum – in this version, Rivendell might as well have been any old rural mansion to which Bilbo has decided to retire.

In this way, as the hobbits complete the different stages of the journey home, they disencumber the narrative of the characters and the sceneries that used to imply changes in the intertraditional dialogue, until they reach Bree, where we are back in the old narrative nineteenth-century *mélange* that marked the

Shire of the first chapters. That only Gandalf accompanies the hobbits all the way to Bree is consistent with the general dismantlement of the intertraditional dialogue, Gandalf being fully compatible with the less lofty diction required of this narrative zone.

Generally speaking, during the return trip, while we see traces of romance in Minas Tirith and of epic at Edoras, the dialogue is practically non-existent. In part, this is due to the loss of intertraditional flexibility in the three main protagonists as soon as they reach their heroic zenith, in part because of the fact that the narrator does not need a novelistic focalization and description of the world to make it credible, given that the characters and places the hobbits come across during the return trip are already known to the reader, and the events are reduced to successive farewells. The result is a much flatter narrative, resembling a regular prose romance, in which the epic and mythic elements practically disappear from the tale.

The dialogue between novel and romance continues in the Shire, which the hobbits now must redeem on their own, without the help of Gandalf who, like Frodo, belongs mainly to the Third Age and does not take active part in the action anymore.[293] Pippin, Merry and Sam mobilize the hobbits against Sharky, Saruman's new alias, and after overthrowing his ephemeral totalitarian regime, they restore fertility to the region. Sam, portrayed as the main rejuvenating force, plants trees, marries, breeds children and is elected mayor of Hobbiton.[294] That year the harvest is extremely abundant and more children are born than usual.

---

[293] Flieger (1981:61) writes that Frodo, during the return trip, symbolizes "the passing of the old." Tolkien himself says that the limited presence of Frodo in the last part of the tale is a result of his discomfort at not being able to find himself (*Letters*, 327-328). The passive attitude of Frodo during the scouring of the Shire is also typical of the patient Christian hero. In this, Frodo's late role is not far from that of the heroes of Milton's *Paradise Regained*, whose triumphs are spiritual rather than physical. The only real triumph of Frodo is his spiritual and moral authority over Saruman in Hobbiton, as he forgives the former wizard and spares his life, and Saruman admits that he has "grown". (*LotR*, 1057)

[294] With this ending, one of the basic conventions of the British adventure novel is torn apart: in *The Lord of the Rings*, it is not the hero who is reintegrated in society upon his return, and it is definitely not the friend who becomes alienated and bereft of "money, matrimony and social integration" as a sign of his subordination (Toda Iglesia 2002:228), but, quite ostensibly, exactly the other way around. This is yet another example of how the intertraditional dialogue in this work invalidates any interpretation based on conventions from a single genre.

The narrative treatment of this event is necessarily different from that of the renaissance of Minas Tirith after the war: while the latter episode was deeply rooted in medieval romance, the fertilisation of the Shire owes much more to the nineteenth-century blend of fairy tale and prose romance. From this point of view, the return trip also illustrates an evolution of the romance tradition, that begins in the medieval tradition and becomes more and more 'dilluted' as the hobbits draw nearer to Bree, until it is merged with the nineteenth-century novel in the Shire.

Romance, as we have seen in the second chapter, is a very flexible narrative tradition that infiltrates any other tradition with relative ease, and it frequently accompanies the novel, which has been consistently used for the descriptions of the physical space as the travellers discover new parts of Middle-earth. The intertraditional dialogue is usually spun around this double thread, sticky as the web of a spider – myth and epic have almost consistently required the presence of romance elements as a starting point for the dialogue with the novel. For this reason, it is only natural that Tolkien should use the prose romance as the main narrative vehicle when the intertraditional dialogue ends, since this neutral medium may incorporate the more rigid epic tradition (as in the farewell sequence at Edoras) without much friction or need for carefully prepared transitions.

Chapter 5

The Meta-Narrative Myth of Hope for the Twentieth Century

As we have seen in the fourth chapter, the four main Western narrative traditions are all very much present in *The Lord of the Rings*. At the same time, the analysis of the situational level has provided us with possible explanations for several apparent inconsistencies, inherent to the treatment of the five dialoguemes – the physical space, the characters, the action, the themes and the focalization. By referring to the dynamics of the intertraditional dialogue, we may explain the anachronism of the Shire within the larger context of Middle-earth; Aragorn's shifting stances during his journey from Bree to Minas Tirith; the apparent redundancy of the Old Forest, Tom Bombadil and the Barrow-downs; the profound *mélange* of Christian and pagan ideals that permeates most of the story, and the continuous shifts in focalization between Frodo and Sam in the narrative zone of the Black Gate, to mention only a few examples.

The analysis of the transitional level reveals that the prepared transitions are infinitely more numerous than the unprepared. This means that the narrative does not explore the limits of the intertraditional dialogue arbitrarily, putting different traditions together and making them clash or merge at will, but the incorporation of a new tradition is usually prepared for by the more or less subtle presence of mediating elements that help to integrate it in the narrative context. It does not always work, as we can see by the occasional presence of *rejected invitations*, and it is not necessarily the outcome of a conscious process, but it indicates the author's profound, if perhaps 'only' intuitive, knowledge of the characteristics and limits of the different traditions that he incorporated in the text.

We must also emphasize the fact that among the prepared transitions, the *dialogue* and the *mélange* are by far the most common. This means that the dialogue normally operates within the limits of functionality, and this provides it with an element of invisibility: the reader hardly perceives the immense complexity of the web of interrelated traditions that is hidden beneath the adventure story, whereby the tale becomes much more accessible to the average reader than the works of modernist literature we have studied in chapter three. This invisibility, generated by narrative functionality, may be part of the reason why *The Lord of the Rings* has not been previously studied in the context of ironic myth. At the same time, it may also provide us with a plausible reason for the enormous labour of reconstruction Tolkien carried out in order to successfully incorporate the new elements of the narrative as they appeared in his imagination, seemingly from nowhere, as indicated by the four volumes of the study of the successive revisions of the narrative, *The History of The Lord of the Rings*. Tolkien, in short, incorporated the main Western narrative traditions on a simultaneous level, working over many years to give narrative fluency to the dialogue. Quite obviously, these narrative traditions are not automatically compatible, and the functionality of the dialogue is the result of a meticulous and skilful analysis, whether intuitive or consciously elaborated, of its limits and feasibility.

Because of the insistent dialogue between these traditions, it is impossible to attribute any given genre to the narrative. The novel is used as the main narrative vehicle for the author's almost obsessive desire to situate the reader in space and time during most of the journeying, and for the particular distribution of information with dramatic intentions, which causes the reader to make assumptions that he or she must modify as more information is provided. Furthermore, the text is marked by a very insistent polyphony, which Bakhtin (1989:117-148) considers one of the main traits of the novel genre, by the use of several narrators and focalizers that bring many different points of view and cultural expressions to the text.

However, the text is also heavily informed by romance standards. Many events seem to take place gratuitously, and the improbable coincidences are many (eucatastrophe as such may be said to adhere more easily to romance than to any other narrative paradigm). There is a constant mélange of Christian and pagan motifs that offers an apparently secular alternative to the contemporary audience, and we frequently come across visual images that are used to express the essence of the experience (the fallen King redeemed by nature in Ithilien, the stream in the rock in Mordor, etc.). Sometimes, usually coinciding with narrative zones set in forests, space and time are portrayed with the blurred lens of romance, making the exactness of spatial and temporal relationships redundant.

At the same time, the epic is very much present in the narrative. *The Lord of the Rings* is the story of the end of the Third Age and the main action spans two years, but the text compresses and sums up the main historical events and the artistic legacy of several thousand years of the history of Middle-earth, which are almost encyclopaedically incorporated in the text. As in the epic tradition, this information is transmitted by means of digressions, generated by the contents of the main action, but also by regular catalogues in the appendices, which must be seen as an internal part of the narrative.

Furthermore, Aragorn, who on the epic level at least is the most conspicuous protagonist of the tale (*Letters*, 180), is a complete and exemplary representative of his community, and his feats give coherence to the story. Like the epic heroes, he is neither purely mythic nor completely human, being of a lineage related to the gods. As in the epic tales, the story is set in a remote past which is a mixture of historical and primordial time: Tolkien considered that the events take place in this world, but that "the historical period is imaginary" (*Letters*, 239). At the same time, he provided this pseudohistorical past with a proper cosmogony and a pantheon of gods, though they are not frequently referred to in the text.

Another thing that makes the tale similar to the epic is that its internal logic and coherence does not depend on a realist kind of verisimilitude, but neither is it a dreamlike world without reference to space and time. In *The Lord of the Rings* we find a very obvious intention of giving the world a considerable spatial and temporal coherence – more so, I would say, than in most realist novels – by means of constant references to distances and dates, in spite of the presence of supernatural elements.

The influence of myth in *The Lord of the Rings* is more difficult to state with concrete examples, this type of narrative paradigm being much more elusive compared to the other three. However, if we look at Cupitt's (1997:5) list of what he takes to be the basic features of all myths – they are about supernatural beings with human form and supernatural powers; the action takes place outside historical time or in a supernatural world; there may be irruptions between this world and the supernatural world; they express the fragmented logic of a dream, and they explain and legitimate the action they describe –, *The Lord of the Rings* incorporates almost all of them up to a certain point at one moment or another in the narrative (with the possible exception of the fragmented logic of a dream, though there are hundreds of dreams described in the story, and several dream visions).[295]

These conclusions point to the more profound reasons why Tolkien created such a particular alternative to ironic myth. In this work, the *revelation* of the secondary world is prior to the development of the plot, the characters, the themes, etc., given that these elements seem to emerge *as a result* of the revelation. The analysis of the intertraditional dialogue clearly shows that as Tolkien discovered more and more of the world, he had to adapt the characters, the plot and the themes to be able to portray the different narrative zones that composed the world with narrative fluency. This may be a result of the author's known ambition to create a context (in turn related to real cultural contexts) for his invented words, in which these words and languages would make sense. From this plurilingual and multicultural starting point comes the need to use a dialogue capable of integrating them in one universe, and in one literary work, on a simultaneous level.

The result is a narrative that transmits, while updating and renewing, the narrative legacy of our own past. This ambition is similar to that of modernists such as Eliot, Pound and Joyce, but Tolkien invests the tale with coherent, well-contextualized references to the internal history of the secondary world – what Segura (2004:144) calls *autotextualidad* (in English autotextuality) – instead of using elitistic and ironic juxtapositions that depend on the reader's familiarity with the sources for a proper understanding, due to the particular characteristics of his secondary world. The desire to transmit a message of hope to the modern world by writing a tale set in a remote past (instead of portraying modernity from the defeatist perspective, that centered on the most obviously negative aspects of modernity) also makes Tolkien's work very different from the modernists'. In *The Lord of the Rings*, the particular

---

[295] For a discussion of the dream visions in *The Lord of the Rings*, see Amendt-Raduege (2006).

treatment of the literary and historical sources, within the framework of the secondary world, gives rise to a vast applicability that reaches from old myths to the modernist literature of the twentieth century; from historical events that took place thousands of years ago to the devastating effects of the two World Wars in modern times. I believe that it is in the skilful conjunction of these elements, which, taken together, constitute what we may call a meta-narrative myth of hope for the twentieth century, that we find one of the major attractions of Tolkien's best-known work.

Bibliography

Primary Sources

Beowulf: A Verse Translation, 1973 (translated from Old English and edited by M. Alexander), Harmondsworth: Penguin.

APPOLONIUS RHODIUS, 1986, *Las Argonáuticas* (ca. 250-240 B.C.E. Translated to Spanish by M. Brioso Sánchez) Madrid: Cátedra.

ARIOSTO, L., 2002, *Orlando Furioso* (first published 1532. Translated to Spanish and edited by M. Muñiz Muñiz) Madrid: Cátedra.

CONRAD, J., 1995, *Heart of Darkness* (first published 1899) Harmondsworth: Penguin Books.

COOPER, J. F., 1998, *The Last of the Mohicans* (first published 1826), Oxford: Oxford University Press.

DE TROYES, C., *El Cuento del Grial* (ca. 1182. Translated to Spanish and edited by C. Alvar, 1999), Madrid: Alianza.

DICKENS, C., 2003, *The Posthumous Papers of the Pickwick Club* (first published in a serialized version 1836-1837), London: Penguin.

DINESEN, I., 1963, *Seven Gothic Tales*, Harmondsworth. Penguin.

DRIVER, P. (ed.), 1996, *Early Twentieth-Century Poetry* (first edition 1995), London: Penguin.

ELIOT, T.S., 1970, *The Complete Poems and Plays of T.S. Eliot* (first edition 1969), London: Faber and Faber.

1999, *The Waste Land and Other Poems* (first published in *Collected Poems* 1940) London: Faber and Faber.

FEATHERSTONE, S. (ed.), 1995, *War Poetry: An Introductory Reader*, London: Routledge.

GILBERT, H., 1998, *Robin Hood* (first published 1912), Here, Hertforeshire: Wordsworth.

GRAHAME, K., 1993, *The Wind in the Willows* (first published 1908), Ware, Herefordshire: Wordsworth.

GRAVES, R., 1917, *Goliath and David*, London: Chiswick Press.

2000, *Good-bye to All That* (first published 1929, revised edition 1957), London: Penguin.

HAMER, R. (ed.), 1970, *A Choice of Old English Poetry* (translated from Old English by R. Hamer), London: Faber and Faber.

HARDY, T., 2000, *Far From the Madding Crowd* (first published 1874), London: Penguin Books.

HAWTHORNE, N., 1986, *The House of the Seven Gables* (first published 1851), Harmondsworth: Penguin.

HAYWARD, J., 1956, *The Penguin Book of English Verse*, London: Penguin.

HOMER, 1983, *Odisea* (translated to Spanish and edited by J. L. Calvo Martínez), Madrid: Editora Nacional.

1999, *Ilíada*, (translated to Spanish and edited by J. Alarcón Benito) Madrid: Edimat.

JOYCE, J., 1998, *Ulysses* (first published 1922), Oxford: Oxford University Press.

MALORY, T., 1986, *Le Mort D'Arthur* (ca. 1485), Harmondsworth: Penguin.

MORRIS, W., 1996, *The Well at the World's End* (first published 1896), Phoenix Mill: Alan Sutton Publishing Limited.

ORWELL, G. 2000, *Homage to Catalonia* (first published 1938), London: Penguin Classics.

POUND, E., 1977, *Selected Poems* (expanded reprint, first edition 1975), London: Faber and Faber.

REEVE, C., 1967, *The Old English Baron: A Gothic Story* (first published 1777), London: Oxford University Press.

REEVES, J. (ed.), 1968, *Introduction to Georgian Poetry*, (first edition 1962), Harmondsworth: Penguin Books.

SILKIN, J. (ed.), 1979, *The Penguin Book of First World War Poetry*, Harmondsworth: Penguin Books.

TOLKIEN, J.R.R., 1993, *The Lord of the Rings* (first edition 1954-1955), London: HarperCollins.

2000, *The Letters of J.R.R. Tolkien* (edited by H. Carpenter with the assistance of C. Tolkien, first edition 1981), Boston: Houghton Mifflin.

VIRGIL, P., 2002, *La Eneida* (18 B.C.E. Translated to Spanish and edited by A. Cuatrecasas, first edition 1998), Barcelona: Espasa Calpe.

WALPOLE, H., 1998, *The Castle of Otranto* (first published 1764), Oxford: Oxford University Press.

WOOLF, V., 1996, *To the Lighthouse* (first published 1927), London: Penguin Books.

Secondary Sources

Literary genres, concrete works and literary theory

ALARCÓN BENITO, J., 1999, *Prólogo*, in Homer (1999), pp. 5-23.

ALEXANDER, M., 1973, *Introduction*, in *Beowulf: A Verse Translation:* 9-49.

ALLEN, W., 1991, *The English Novel* (first edition 1958), Harmondsworth: Penguin Books.

ARISTOTLE and HORACE, 1991, *Artes Poéticas* (translated to Spanish and edited by A. González, first edition 1987), Madrid: Taurus.

ATTEBERY, B., 1980, *The Fantasy Tradition in American Literature: From Irving to LeGuin*, Bloomington, IN: Indiana University.

AUERBACH, E., 1979, *Mímesis: la representación de la realidad en la literatura occidental* (first Spanish edition 1950. Translated to Spanish by I. Villanueva and E. Ímaz. Original title: *Dargestelle Wirklichkeit in der Abendländischen Literatur* 1944), México: Fondo de Cultura Económica.

BAKHTIN, M., 1989, *La Teoría y Estética de la Novela* (Translated to Spanish by H. Kriúkova and V. Cazcarra), Madrid: Taurus.

BARFIELD, O., 1973, *Poetic Diction: A Study of Meaning* (first published 1928), Middletown, CT: Wesleyan University Press.

BEER, G., 1977, *The Romance* (first edition 1970), London: Methuen.

BEYE, C., 1993, *Ancient Epic Poetry: Homer, Apollonius, Virgil*, Ithaca, NY: Cornell University Press.

BOBES NAVES. C., 1993, *La Novela*, Madrid: Síntesis.

BRIOSO SÁNCHEZ, M., 1986, *Introducción*, in Appolonius of Rhodes (1986), pp. 9-35.

BROWN, S., 1992, *The History of European Fairy Tales*, New York: Macmillan.

BROWNLEE, K. y M. BROWNLEE SCORDILIS (ed.), 1985, *Romance: Generic Transformation from Chrétien de Troyes to Cervantes*, Hanover, NE, and London: University Press of New England.

BULLEN, J.B., 1989, 'The Gods in Wessex Exile: Thomas Hardy and Mythology', in BULLEN, J.B. (ed.), 1989, *The Sun is God: Painting, Literature and Mythology in the Nineteenth Century*, Oxford: Clarendon Press, pp. 181-198.

CAMPBELL, J., 1997, *El Héroe de las Mil Caras: Psicoanálisis del Mito* (first Spanish edition 1959. Original title: *The Hero With a Thousand Faces*, 1949), México: Fondo de Cultura Económica.

CLAUSS, J., 1992, *The Best of the Argonauts: The Redefinition of the Epic Hero in Book 1 of Apollonius' Argonautica*, Berkeley: University of California Press.

CLERY, E.J., 1995, *The Rise of Supernatural Fiction, 1762-1800*, Cambridge, NY: Cambridge University Press.

1998, *Introduction*, in Walpole (1998), pp. vii-xxxiii.

CORUGEDO, S. and J.L. CHAMOSA, 2001, *Introducción*, in Wordsworth, W. and S.T. Coleridge, 2001, *Baladas Líricas* (first Spanish edition 1990. Translated to Spanish and edited by S. Corugedo and J.L. Chamosa. Original title: *Lyrical Ballads* 1798), Madrid: Cátedra, pp. 9-23.

COUPE, L., 1997, *Myth*, London: Routledge.

CUATRECASAS, A., 1998, *Introducción*, in Virgil (2002), pp. 9-35.

DAVIDSON, H.R., 1964, *Gods and Myths of Northern Europe*, London: Penguin.

DAY, A., 1996, *Romanticism*, London: Routledge.

DUMÉZIL, G., 1977, *Mito y Epopeya* (Translated to Spanish by E. Trías. Original title: *Mythe et epopée I* 1968), Barcelona: Seix Barral.

ELIADE, M., 2000, *Aspectos del Mito* (Translated to Spanish by L. Gil Fernández. Original title: *Aspects du mythe* 1963), Barcelona: Paidós.

FEATHERSTONE, S., 1995, *War Poetry: An Introductory Reader*, London: Routledge.

FORD, A., 1993, *Homer: The Poetry of the Past*, Ithaca, NY: Cornell University Press.

FORSTER, E. M., 1983, *Aspectos de la Novela* (translated to Spanish by G. Lorenzo. Original title: *Aspects of the Novel*, 1927), Madrid: Editorial Debate.

FRYE, N., 1971, *Anatomy of Criticism: Four Essays* (first edition 1957), Princeton: Princeton University Press.

1976, *The Secular Scripture: A Study of the Structure of Romance*, Cambridge: Harvard University Press.

GADAMER, H-G., 1997, *Mito y Razón* (Translated to Spanish by J-F. Zúñiga. Compilation of essays published in *Gesammelte Werke, vol. VIII, Ästhetik und Poetik I, Kunst als Aussage*, 1993), Barcelona: Paidós.

GARCÍA GUAL, C., 1974, *Primeras Novelas Europeas*, Madrid: Istmo.

1985, *Mitos, Viajes, Héroes* (first edition 1981), Madrid: Taurus.

1987, *La Mitología: Interpretaciones del Pensamiento Mitológico*, Barcelona: Montesinos.

1988, *Los Orígenes de la Novela* (first edition 1972), Madrid: Istmo.

GREENE, T., 1963, *The Descent From Heaven: A Study in Epic Continuity*, New Haven: Yale University Press.

HAINSWORTH, J., 1991, *The Idea of Epic*, Berkeley: University of California Press.

HARDIE, P., 1993, *The Epic Successors of Virgil: A Study in the Dynamics of a Tradition*, Cambridge, NY: Cambridge University Press.

HAWTHORNE, N. 1851, *Preface*, in Hawthorne (1986), pp. 1-3.

HEGEL, F., 1975, *Aesthetics* (Translated to English by M. Knox. Original title: *Vorlesungen über die Asthetik*, 1832), vol. 2, Oxford: Oxford University Press.

HERNADI, P., 1978, *Teoría de los Géneros Literarios* (Original title: *Beyond Genre: New Directions in Literary Classification*, 1972), Barcelona: Antoni Bosch.

JACKSON, R., 1981, *Fantasy, the Literature of Subversion*, London: Routledge.

JEWERS, C., 2000, *Chivalric Fiction and the History of the Novel*, Gainesville: University Press of Florida.

KERÉNYI, C., 1997, *The Heroes of the Greeks* (first edition 1959), London: Thames and Hudson.

KING, K., 1987, *Achilles: Paradigms of the War Hero From Homer to the Middle Ages*, Berkeley: University of California Press.

KNIGHT, V., 1995, *The Renewal of Epic: Responses to Homer in the Argonautica of Apollonius*, Leiden: E.J. Brill.

KRUGER, S. F., 1993, *Dreaming in the Middle Ages* (first edition 1992), Cambridge: Cambridge University Press.

LANDOW, G., 'And the World Became Strange' in Schlobin (1982), pp. 105-140.

LATACZ, J., 2005, *Troy and Homer: Towards a Solution of an Old Mystery*, New York: Oxford University Press.

LAWLOR, J., 1969, *Introduction*, in Malory (1986), pp. vii-xxxi.

LEWIS, C.S., 1988, *The Allegory of Love: A Study in Medieval Tradition* (first edition 1936), Oxford: Oxford University Press.

LOVECRAFT, H.P., 2002, *El Horror Sobrenatural en la Literatura* (Translated to Spanish by J. Álvaro Garrido. Original title: *The Supernatural Horror in Literature*, 1927), Madrid: Edaf.

MANLOVE, C.N., 1978, *Modern Fantasy: Five Studies* (first edition 1975), Cambridge: Cambridge University Press.

1982, 'On the Nature of Fantasy', in Schlobin (1982), pp. 16-35.

1983, *The Impulse of Fantasy Literature*, London and Basingstoke: Macmillan Press.

MATHEWS, R., 2002, *Fantasy: The Liberation of Imagination* (first edition 1997), New York: Routledge.

MENDELSON, E., 1976, 'Encyclopedic Normatives: from Dante to Pynchon', in *Modern Language Notes*, 9, 1976.

MILLER, D.A., 2000, *The Epic Hero*, Baltimore: John Hopkins University Press.

MORETTI, F., 1996, *The Modern Epic: The World System From Goethe to García Márquez*, London: Verso.

QUINT, D., 1985, 'The Boat of Romance and Renaissance Epic', in Brownlee and Brownlee (1985), pp. 178-202.

RABKIN, E., 1976, *The Fantastic in Literature*, Princeton, NJ: Princeton University Press.

REEVE, C., 1778, *Preface to the Second Edition*, in Reeve (1967), pp. 3-6.

RICOEUR, P., 1987, *Tiempo y Narración II*, (translated to Spanish by A. Neira. Original title: *Temps et Récit* 1983), Madrid: Ediciones Cristiandad.

SCHLAUCH, M., 1967, *English Medieval Literature and its Social Foundations* (first edition 1956), Warszaw: PWN.

SCHLOBIN, R., (ed.), 1982, *The Aesthetics of Fantasy Literature and Art*, Indiana: University of Indiana Press.

SEGRE, C., 2002, *Introducción* (translated to Spanish by M. Muñiz), in Ariosto (2002), pp. 9-75.

STEADMAN, J.M., 1969, *Milton and the Renaissance Hero* (first edition 1967), London: Oxford University Press.

STEVENS, J., 1973, *Medieval Romance: Themes and Approaches*, London: Hutchinson University Library.

SWINFEN, A., 1984, *In Defense of Fantasy: A Study of the Genre in English and American Literature Since 1945*, London: Routledge & Kegan Paul.

TODA IGLESIA, M., 2002, *Héroes y Amigos: Masculinidad, Imperialismo y Didactismo en la Novela de Aventuras Británica, 1880-1914*, Salamanca: Ediciones Universidad de Salamanca.

TOLKIEN, J.R.R., 1966, *The Tolkien Reader*, New York: Ballantine Books.

TOOHEY, P., 1992, *Reading Epic: an Introduction to Ancient Narratives*, London: Routledge.

VINAVER, E., 1984, *The Rise of Romance* (first edition 1971), Cambridge: D.S. Brewer.

VON FRANZ, M., 1993, *Érase Una Vez* (Translated to Spanish by C. Quintana. Original title: *L'Interprétation des Contes de Fées*, 1970), Barcelona: Luciérnaga.

WATSON, J. and M. FRIES (ed.), 1989, *The Figure of Merlin in the Nineteenth and Twentieth Centuries*, New York: Edwin Mellen Press.

WATT, I., 1983, *The Rise of the Novel: studies in Defoe, Richardson, and Fielding* (first published 1957), Harmondsworth: Penguin.

WEBER, G.W., 1983, 'History and Heroic Tale: the Authority of the Poet. Some Synthesizing Abstractions', in *History and Heroic Tale: A Symposium*, 1985, Odense: Odense University Press, pp. 223-238.

ZANGER, J., 1982, 'Heroic Fantasy and Social Reality', in Schlobin (1982), pp. 226-236.

Poetry of the Great War, Modernism and the Twentieth Century

AIKEN, C., 1923, 'An Anatomy of Melancholy' in Cox and Hinchcliffe (1968), pp. 91-99.

BERGONZI, B., 1993, *Wartime and Aftermath: English Literature and Its Background, 1939-1960*, Oxford: Oxford University Press.

BERIAIN, J., 2000, *La Lucha de los Dioses en la Modernidad: Del Monoteísmo Religioso al Politeísmo Cultural*, Barcelona: Anthropos.

BOOTH, A., 1996, *Postcards From The Trenches: Negotiating the Space Between Modernism and the First World War*, New York: Oxford University Press.

BRADBURY, M., 1976, 'The Name and Nature of Modernism', in Bradbury and MacFairlane (1976), pp. 19-56.

— and J. MACFAIRLANE (ed.), 1976, *Modernism*, Harmondsworth: Penguin.

BRIGGS, A., and P. CLAVIN, (ed.), 1997, *Historia Contemporánea de Europa 1789-1989*, (translated to Spanish by J. Ainaud. Original title: *Modern Europe 1789-1989*, 1997), Barcelona: Crítica.

BROOKS, C., 1939, 'The Waste Land: Critique of the Myth', in Cox and Hinchcliffe (1968), pp. 128-161.

CANO ECHEVARRÍA, B., 2002, *En los Límites del Modernismo: La Poesía de Guerra de Wilfred Owen*, Valladolid: Universidad de Valladolid.

CANTOR, N.F., 1988, *Twentieth-Century Culture: Modernism to Deconstruction*, New York: Peter Lang.

COX, C.B., and A.P. HINCHCLIFFE, (ed.), 1968, *T.S. Eliot: The Waste Land*, London: Macmillan.

CRAIG, D., 1960, 'The Defeatism of The Waste Land', in Cox and Hinchcliffe (1968), pp. 200-215.

EKSTEINS, M., 1990, *Rites of Spring: The Great War and the Birth of the Modern Age* (first edition 1989), New York: Anchor Books.

ELIOT, T.S., 1919, 'Tradition and the Individual Talent', in Eliot (1966), pp. 13-22.

'Ulysses, Order, and Myth', Dial LXXV.5, November 1923.

1966, *Selected Essays* (first edition 1933, 3rd expanded edition 1951), London: Faber & Faber.

FEATHERSTONE, S. (ed.), 1995, *War Poetry: An Introductory Reader*, London: Routledge.

FERGUSON, N., 1999, *The Pity of War*, (first edition 1998) New York: Basic Books, Perseus Book Group.

FILMER, K. and D. JASPER (ed.), 1992, *Twentieth-Century Fantasists: Essays on Culture, Society and Belief in Twentieth-Century Mythopoeic Literature*, New York: St. Martin's.

FUSSELL, P., 1975, *The Great War and Modern Memory*, Oxford: Oxford University Press.

GROSS, J., 1974, *Joyce* (translated by M. Covián. Original title: *Joyce* 1970), Barcelona: Ediciones Grijalbo.

JAIN, M., 2002, *A Critical Reading of the Selected Poems of T.S. Eliot*, (first published 1991), New Delhi: Oxford University Press.

JOHNSON, J., 1998, *Explanatory Notes*, in Joyce (1998), pp. 763-980.

JONES, D., 1937, *Introduction*, in Featherstone (1995), pp. 239-241.

KERMODE, F., 1968, *The Sense of an Ending* (first edition 1967), London: Oxford University Press.

LEAVIS, F.R., 1972, *New Bearings in English Poetry: A Study of the Contemporary Situation*, Harmondsworth: Penguin Books.

LLOYD, T., 1993, *Empire, Welfare State, Europe: English History 1906 – 1992*, Oxford: Oxford University Press.

LODGE. D., 1983, *The Modes of Modern Writing* (first edition 1977), London: Edward Arnold.

MACFAIRLANE, J., 'The Mind of Modernism', in Bradbury and MacFairlane (1976), pp. 71-94.

MARDONES, J. M., 2000, *El Retorno del Mito: La Racionalidad Mito-Simbólica*, Madrid: Síntesis.

MAY, R., 1992, *La Necesidad del Mito: la Influencia de los Modelos Culturales en el Mundo Contemporáneo* (translated to Spanish by L. Botella García del Cid. Original title: *The Cry For Myth* 1991), Barcelona: Paidós.

MENDELSON, E., 1976, 'Encyclopedic Normatives: from Dante to Pynchon', *Modern Language Notes*, 9, 1976.

MURRAY, P., 1994, *T.S Eliot and Mysticism: The Secret History of Four Quartets*, (first edition 1991), New York: St Martin's Press.

PETERSON, R. F., 1992, *James Joyce Revisited*, New York: Twayne.

PICÓ, J., 1999, *Cultura y Modernidad: Seducciones y Desengaños de la Cultura Moderna*, Madrid: Alianza.

REEVES, J., 1968, *Introduction to Georgian Poetry* (first edition 1962), Harmondsworth: Penguin.

RUBINSTEIN, W. D., 1994, *Capitalism, Culture and Decline in Britain* (first edition 1993), London: Routledge.

SILKIN, J., 1979, *The Penguin Book of First World War Poetry*, Harmondsworth: Penguin.

SPENGLER, O., 2006, *The Decline of the West* (English abridged edition translated by Charles Francis Atkinson. Original title: *Untergang des Abendlandes*, 1918), New York: Vinatge Books.

SYMONS, J., 2000, *Introduction*, in Orwell (2000).

TRAVERSI, D., 1978, *T.S. Eliot: The Longer Poems* (first edition 1976), London: The Bodley Head.

WATSON, J. and M. FRIES (ed.), 1989, *The Figure of Merlin in the Nineteenth and Twentieth Centuries*, New York: Edwin Mellen Press.

WITEMEYER, H., 1981, *The Poetry of Ezra Pound: Forms and Renewal 1908 – 1920* (first edition 1969), Berkeley: University of California Press.

Monographs and studies on Tolkien and his works

AMENDT-RADUEGE, A. M, 'Dream Visions in J.R.R. Tolkien's The Lord of the Rings', in Anderson et al. (ed.) (2006), pp. 45-56.

ANDERSON, D. (ed.), 2000, *El Hobbit Anotado* (first Spanish edition 1990. Translated to Spanish by M. Figueroa and R. Masera. Original title: *The Annotated Hobbit* 1988), Barcelona: Minotauro.

— et al. (ed.), 2005, *Tolkien Studies: An Annual Scholarly Review*, Vol. II, Morgantown, VI: West Virginia University Press.

— et al. (ed.), 2006, *Tolkien Studies: An Annual Scholarly Review*, Vol. III, Morgantown, VI: West Virginia University Press.

AUDEN, W. H., 1968, 'The Quest Hero', in Isaacs and Zimbardo (2004), pp. 31-51.

BASNEY, L., 'Myth, History, and Time in *The Lord of the Rings*', in Isaacs and Zimbardo (1981), pp. 8-18.

BATES, B., 2003, *The Real Middle-earth: Exploring the Magic and Mystery of the Middle Ages, J.R.R. Tolkien and "The Lord of the Rings"*, Houndmills: Palgrave Macmillan.

BATTARBEE, K., (ed.), 1993, *Scholarship and Fantasy: Proceedings of the Tolkien Phenomenon, Anglicana Turkuensia* 12, Turku: University of Turku.

BLUMBERG, J.L., 2002, 'The Literary Backgrounds of *The Lord of the Rings*', in West (2002), pp. 53-81.

BRACE, K., interview with J.R.R. Tolkien, *Birmingham Post*, May 23, 1968.

BUCHS, P. and T. HONEGGER (ed.), 1997, *News from the Shire and Beyond – Studies on Tolkien*, Zürich and Bern: Walking Tree Publishers.

CANTOR, N.F., 1993, *Inventing the Middle Ages: The Lives, Works, and Ideas of the Great Medievalists of the Twentieth Century* (first edition 1991), New York: William Morrow and Company.

CARPENTER, H., 2000, *J.R.R. Tolkien: A Biography* (first edition 1977), Boston and New York: Houghton Mifflin.

CARRETERO, M., 1997, 'A Utopian Reading of J.R.R. Tolkien's *The Lord of the Rings*', in GOMIS, A. and M. MARTÍNEZ (ed.), 1997, *Dreams and Realities, Versions of Utopia in English Fiction From Dickens to Byatt*, Almería: Universidad de Almería, pp. 25-56.

— 1997, *Fantasía, Épica y Utopía, en* The Lord of the Rings*: Análisis temático y de la Recepción* (tesis doctoral), Granada: Universidad de Granada.

1998, '*The Lord of the Rings*: A Myth for Modern Englishmen', *Mallorn* 36, 1998, pp. 51-57.

CARTER, L., 2002, *Tolkien: el Origen de El Señor de los Anillos* (translated to Spanish by M.A. Menini. Original title: *A Look Behind The Lord of the Rings* 1969), Barcelona: Ediciones B.

CHANCE, J. and D. DAY, 1991, "Medievalism in Tolkien: Two Decades of Criticism in Review", *Studies in Medievalism* 3, 1991, pp. 375-387.

CHANCE, J., 1986, 'Tolkien and His Sources', in Miller, M.Y., (ed.), 1986, *Approaches to Teaching Sir Gawain and the Green Knight*, New York: Modern Language Association of America, pp. 151-155.

2001, '*The Lord of the Rings*: Tolkien's Epic', in Isaacs and Zimbardo (2004), pp. 195-232.

(ed.), 2004, *Tolkien And the Invention of Myth*, Lexington, KY: The University Press of Kentucky.

CLARK, G., and D. P. TIMMONS (ed.), 2000, *J.R.R. Tolkien and His Literary Resonances: Views of Middle-earth*, Westport, CT: Greenwood.

CROFT, J.B., 2004, *War and the Works of J.R.R. Tolkien*, Westport, CT: Praeger.

CURRY, P., 1997, *Defending Middle Earth,* London: HarperCollins.

DAY, D., 1994, *Tolkien's Ring*, London: HarperCollins.

2003, *The World of Tolkien: Mythological Sources of The Lord of the Rings*, London: Mitchell Beazley.

DEYO, S. M., 1988, 'Wyrd and Will: Fate, Fatalism and Free Will in the Northern Elegy and J.R.R. Tolkien', *Mythlore* 14, 1988, pp. 59-62.

DICKERSON, M., 2003, *Following Gandalf: Epic Battles and Moral Victory in The Lord of the Rings*, Grand Rapids, MI: Brazos Press.

DUBS, K. E., 1981, 'Providence, Fate, and Chance: Boethian Philosophy in *The Lord of the Rings*,' in Chance (2004), pp. 133-142.

DUFAU, J-C., 2005, 'Mythic Space in Tolkien's Work', in Honegger (2005), pp. 107-128.

DURIEZ, C., 2003, *Tolkien and C.S. Lewis: The Gift of Friendship*, Mahwah, NJ: HiddenSpring.

EAGLESTONE, R. (ed.), 2005, *Reading The Lord of the Rings: New Writings on Tolkien's Classic*, London and New York: Continuum.

FENWICK, M., 1996, 'Breastplates of Silk: Homeric Women in *The Lord of the Rings*', *Mythlore* 21, 1996, pp. 17-23.

FLIEGER, V., 1981, 'Frodo and Aragorn: the Concept of the Hero', in Isaacs and Zimbardo (1981), pp. 40-62.

1997, *A Question of Time: J.R.R. Tolkien's Road to Faërie*, Kent, OH: The Kent State University Press.

2002, *Splintered Light: Logos and Language in Tolkien's World* (revised edition, first edition 1983), Kent, OH, and London: The Kent State University Press.

2005, *Interrupted Music: The Making of Tolkien's Mythology*, Kent, OH, and London: The Kent State University Press.

and C. HOSTETTER (ed.), 2000, *Tolkien's Legendarium, Essays on the History of Middle-earth*, Westport, CT: Greenwood Press.

FORD, J.A., 2005, 'The White City: *The Lord of the Rings* as an Early Medieval Myth of the Restoration of the Roman Empire', in Anderson et al. (2005), pp. 53-74.

FOSTER, W., interview with J.R.R. Tolkien, *Scotsman*, March 25, 1967.

GARTH, J., 2003, *Tolkien and the Great War: The Threshold of Middle-earth*, Boston: Houghton Mifflin.

GASQUE T. J., 1968, 'Tolkien: the Monsters and the Critters', in Isaacs and Zimbardo (1968), pp. 151-163.

GONZÁLEZ,. L., 1999, *La Lengua de los Elfos*, Barcelona: Minotauro.

GREENE, D., 1992, 'Higher Argument: Tolkien and the Tradition of Vision, Epic and Prophecy', in Reynolds and Goodknight (1996), pp. 45-52.

GREENMAN, D., 1992, 'Aeneidic and Odyssean Patterns of Escape and Return in Tolkien's "The Fall of Gondolin" and *The Return of the King*', *Mythlore* 18, 1992, pp. 17-23.

GYMNICH, M., 2005, 'Reconsidering the Linguistics of Middle-earth', in Honegger (2005), pp. 7-30.

HABER, K. (ed.), 2003, *La Tierra Media: Reflexiones y Comentarios* (translated to Spanish by E. Gutiérrez. Original title: *Meditations on Middle-earth* 2001), Barcelona: Minotauro.

HAMMOND, W.G., 1996, 'The Critical Response to Tolkien's Fiction', in Reynolds and Goodknight (1996), pp. 226-232.

and C. SCULL (ed.), 2000, *J.R.R. Tolkien: Artist and Illustrator* (first edition 1995), Boston: Houghton Mifflin Company.

HARGROVE, G., 1986, 'Who Is Tom Bombadil?', *Mythlore* 13, 1986, pp. 20-24.

HEIN, R., 1998, *Christian Mythmakers*, Chicago: Cornerstone Press.

HOLMES, J.R., 2004, 'Oaths and Oath Breaking: Analogues of Old English Comitatus in Tolkien's Myth', in Chance (2004), pp. 249-261.

HONEGGER, T., (ed.), 1999, *Root and Branch – Approaches Towards Understanding Tolkien*, Zürich and Bern: Walking Tree Publishers.

2005, 'Tolkien Through the Eyes of a Mediaevalist', in Honegger (2005), pp. 45-66.

(ed.), 2005, *Reconsidering Tolkien*, Zürich and Bern: Walking Tree Publishers.

2006, 'The Passing of the Elves and the Arrival of Modernity: Tolkien's "Mythical Method"', in Weinreich and Honegger (2006), pp. 211-232

HOPKINS, C., 'Tolkien y lo inglés', in Segura and Peris (2003), pp. 171-178.

HUGHES, D., 1981, 'Pieties and Giant Forms', in Isaacs and Zimbardo (1981), pp. 72-86.

HUTTAR, C.A., 1992, 'Tolkien, Epic Traditions, and Golden Age Myths', in Filmer, K. and D. Jasper, (ed.), 1992, *Twentieth Century Fantasists: Essays on Culture, Society and Belief in Twentieth Century Mythopoeic Literature*, New York: St Martin's, pp. 92-107.

ISAACS, N., and R. ZIMBARDO (ed.), 1968, *Tolkien and the Critics: Essays on J.R.R. Tolkien's The Lord of the Rings*, Notre Dame, IN: Notre Dame Press.

1981, *Tolkien: New Critical Perspectives,* Lexington, KY: The University Press of Kentucky.

2004, *Understanding The Lord of the Rings*, Boston: Houghton Mifflin.

JEFFERY, R., 1999, 'Árbol y Hoja: Desarrollo de los Escritos de Tolkien', in Pearce (2001), pp. 163 – 178.

JONES, L. E., 2002, *Myth and Middle-earth: Exploring the Legends Behind J.R.R. Tolkien's The Hobbit & The Lord of the Rings*, New York: Cold Spring Press.

KAUFMANN, U. M., 1975, 'Aspects of the Paradisiacal in Tolkien's Work', in Lobdell (1975), pp. 143-152.

KOCHER, P., 1972, 'Middle-earth: An Imaginary World?', in Isaacs and Zimbardo (2004), pp. 146-162.

1974, *Master of Middle Earth: The Achievement of J.R.R. Tolkien* (first edition 1972), Harmondsworth: Penguin.

KRANTZ, G., 'Der Heilende Aragorn', *Inklings: Jahrbuch für Literatur und Asthetik* 2, 1984, pp. 11-24.

LAWHEAD, S., 1992, 'J.R.R. Tolkien: Señor de la Tierra Media', in Pearce (2001), pp. 179-196.

LEWIS, A., and E. CURRIE, 2002, *The Uncharted Realms of Tolkien*, Oswestry: Medea Publishing.

LEWIS, C. S., 'El Señor de los Anillos, de Tolkien', in Segura and Peris (2003), pp. 207-214.

1955, 'The Dethronement of Power', in Isaacs and Zimbardo (2004), pp. 11-15.

LIBRÁN MORENO, M., 2005, 'Parallel Lives: The Sons of Denethor and the Sons of Telamon', in Anderson et al. (2005), pp. 15-52.

LOBDELL, J., (ed.), 1975, *A Tolkien Compass*, La Salle, IL: Open Court.

LOBDELL, J., 2004, *The World of the Rings: Language, Religion, and Adventure in Tolkien* (revised edition, first edition 1981: *England and Always: Tolkien's World of the Rings*), Chicago and La Salle, IL: Open Court.

LYONS, M., 2004, *There and Back Again: In the Footsteps of J.R.R. Tolkien*, London: Cadogan Guides.

MADSEN, C., 1988, 'Light From an Invisible Lamp: Natural Religion in *The Lord of the Rings*', in Chance (2004), pp. 35-47.

MATHEWS, R., 2002, chapter 3 in Mathews (2002), pp. 54-84.

MILLER, M.Y., 1989, 'J.R.R. Tolkien's Merlin: An Old Man with a Staff: Gandalf and the Magus Tradition', in Watson and Fries (1989), pp. 121-142.

1991, '"Of sum mayn meruayle, that he myyt trawe": The Lord of the Rings and Sir Gawain and the Green Knight', *Studies in Medievalism* 3, 1991, pp. 345-365.

MOORMAN, C., 1968, 'The Shire, Mordor, and Minas Tirith', in Isaacs and Zimbardo (1968), pp. 201-217.

MORTIMER, P., 2005, 'Tolkien and Modernism', in Anderson et al. (2005), pp. 113-129.

MORSE, D. E., 1986, *The Evocation of Virgil in Tolkien's Art: Geritol for the Classics*, Oak Park: Bolchazy-Carducci.

NELSON, C. W., 1989, 'Courteous, Humble, and Helpful: Sam as Squire in *The Lord of the Rings*', *Journal of the Fantastic in the Arts*, 2, 1989, pp. 53-63.

NELSON, D., 'Little Nell and Frodo the Halfling', in Anderson et al. (2005), pp. 145-149.

NOEL, R. S., 1977, *The Mythology of Middle-earth*, Boston: Houghton Mifflin.

1980, *The Languages of Tolkien's Middle-earth*, Boston: Houghton Mifflin.

OBERTINO, J., 1993, 'Moria and Hades: Underworld Journeys in Tolkien and Virgil', *Comparative Literature Studies* 30, 1993, pp. 153-169.

ODERO, J. M., 1987, *J.R.R. Tolkien: Cuentos de Hadas. La Poética Tolkiniana como Clave Para una Hermenéutica Sapiencial de la Literatura de Ficción*, Pamplona: EUNSA.

PEARCE, J., 1999, 'Tolkien y el Renacimiento Literario Católico', in Pearce (2001), pp. 122-143.

(ed.), 2001, *J.R.R. Tolkien: Señor de la Tierra Media* (translated to Spanish by A. Quijada. Original title: *Tolkien: A Celebration* 1999), Barcelona: Minotauro.

2003, *Tolkien: Hombre y Mito*, (first Spanish edition 2000. Translated to Spanish by E. Gutiérrez. Original title: *Tolkien: Man and Myth* 1998), Barcelona: Minotauro.

QUELLA KELLY, M., 'The Poetry of Fantasy: Verse in *The Lord of the Rings*', in Isaacs and Zimbardo (1968), pp. 170-200.

REILLY, R. J., 1963, 'Tolkien and the Fairy Story', in Isaacs and Zimbardo (2004), pp. 93-105.

1971, *Romantic Religions: A Study of Barfield, Lewis, Williams, and Tolkien*, Athens, GA: University of Georgia Press.

REYNOLDS, P. 1993, 'Funeral Customs in Tolkien's Fiction', *Mythlore* 19, 1993, pp. 45-53.

and G. GOODKNIGHT (ed.), 1996, *J.R.R. Tolkien Centenary Conference 1992*, Milton Keynes/Tolkien Society.

ROSEBURY, B., 2003, *Tolkien: A Cultural Phenomenon* (revised and expanded edition, first edition 1992: *Tolkien: A Critical Assessment*), Houndmills: Palgrave.

RYAN, J.S., 1984, 'Uncouth Innocence: Some Links between Chretien de Troyes, Wolfram von Eschenbach and J.R.R. Tolkien', *Inklings: Jahrbuch für Literatur und Asthetik* 2, 1984, pp. 25-41.

1991, 'By 'Significant Compounding We Pass Insensibly into the World of Epic', *Mythlore* 17, 1991, pp. 45-49.

SALE, R., 1968, 'Tolkien and Frodo Baggins', in Isaacs and Zimbardo (1968), pp. 247-288.

SALO, D., 2004, *A Gateway to Sindarin: A Grammar of an Elvish Language from J.R.R. Tolkien's The Lord of the Rings*, Utah: University of Utah Press.

SANTOYO, J.C., and J. M. SANTAMARÍA, 1983, *Tolkien*, Barcelona: Barcanova.

SAVATER, F., 1983, chapter 10, 'En Compañía de las Hadas', in *La Infancia Recuperada*, 2005, Madrid: Alianza/Taurus, pp. 157-173.

SAXEY, E., 2005, 'Homoeroticism', in Eaglestone (2005), pp. 124-137.

SEGURA, E., 2002, *Tolkien, el Mago de las Palabras*, Barcelona: Magisterio Casals.

2003, 'Tolkien, el Narrador de Historias: La Evolución de la Voz Narrativa desde El Hobbit a El Señor de los Anillos', in Segura and Peris (2003), pp. 217-237.

and G. Peris (ed.), 2003, *Tolkien o La Fuerza del Mito*, Madrid: Libroslibres.

2004, *El Viaje del Anillo*, Barcelona: Minotauro.

SHIPPEY, T., 2002, *J.R.R. Tolkien: Author of the Century* (first published 2000), Boston and New York: Houghton Mifflin.

2003, *The Road to Middle-earth* (revised and expanded edition, first edition 1982), Boston and New York: Houghton Mifflin.

SLY, D., 2000, 'Weaving Nets of Gloom: Darkness Profound in Tolkien and Milton', in Clark and Timmons (2000), pp. 109-119.

SPACKS, P. M., 1959, 'Power and Meaning in *The Lord of the Rings*', in Isaacs and Zimbardo (2004), pp. 52-75.

STANTON, M. N., 2001, *Hobbits, Elves, and Wizards. Exploring the Wonders and Worlds of J.R.R. Tolkien's The Lord of the Rings*, New York and Houndmills: Palgrave Macmillan.

ST CLAIR, G., 1996, 'An Overview of the Northern Influences on Tolkien's Works', in Reynolds and Goodknight (1996), pp. 63-67.

THOMAS, P. E., 2000, 'Some of Tolkien's Narrators', in Flieger and Hostetter (2000), pp. 161-181.

THORPE, D., 1996, 'Tolkien's Elvish Craft', in Reynolds and Goodknight (1996), pp. 315-321.

TINKLER, J., 'Old English in Rohan', in Isaacs and Zimbardo (1968), pp. 164-169.

TOLKIEN, J.R.R., 1997, 'Beowulf: The Monsters and the Critics' (originally the Sir Israel Gollancz Memorial Lecture to the British Academy read on 25 November 1936; first published 1939), in Tolkien, J.R.R., *The Monsters and the Critics and Other Essays*, (edited by C. Tolkien), London, Harper Collins, pp. 5-48.

2000, *The Return of the Shadow: The History of The Lord of the Rings*, (Vol. 1, edited by C. Tolkien, first edition 1988), Boston and New York: Houghton Mifflin.

TOLLEY, C., 1992, 'Tolkien and the Unfinished', in Battarbee (1993), pp. 151-164.

TOYNBEE, P., 'Dissension Among the Judges', *The Observer*, August 6, 1961, p. 19.

TUCEV, N., 2005, 'The Knife, the Sting and the Tooth: Manifestations of Shadow in *The Lord of the Rings*', in Honegger (2005), pp. 87-105.

VELDMAN, M., 1994, *Fantasy, the Bomb, and the Greening of Britain: Romantic Protest, 1945-1980*, Cambridge: Cambridge University Press.

VEUGEN, C., 2005, '"A Man, Lean, Dark, Tall": Aragorn Seen Through Different Media', in Honegger (2005), pp. 171-209.

WEINREICH, F., and HONEGGER, T., 2006, *Tolkien and Modernity*, Zurich and Berne: Walking Tree Publishers.

WEST, J. G. (ed.), 2002, *Celebrating Middle-earth: The Lord of the Rings as a Defense of Western Civilization*, Seattle: Inkling Books.

WEST, R.C., 1975, 'The Interlace Structure of *The Lord of the Rings*', in Lobdell (1975), pp. 77-94.

WILSON, E., 1956, 'Oo, those Awful Orcs!', in WILSON, E., 1965, *The Bit Between My Teeth: A Literary Chronicle of 1950-1965*, New York: Farrar, pp. 326-332.

WOOD, R.C., 2003, *The Gospel According to Tolkien: Visions of the Kingdom in Middle-earth*, Louisville and London: Westminster John Knox Press.

Dictionaries

Encyclopaedia Britannica, 1992, Vol. 10 (fifteenth edition), University of Chicago.

DE PACO, A., 2003, *Diccionario de Símbolos*, Barcelona: Editorial Optima.

Index

A
Aeneid 35–39, 51, 68
    and *Beowulf* 41
Aiken, C. 81
Aithiopis 34
alêtheia 24, 25, 66
Alexander, Lloyd 106
Alexander, M. 39, 41
Alice in Wonderland 122
allegory
    and applicability 190
    Christian 53, 78
    Tolkien's dislike for 93
Allen, W. 122
Alvar, C. 47
Apollonius Rhodius 29–35, 43
applicability 102, 183–190
Argonautica 29–35, 37
    and *Beowulf* 41
Ariosto, Ludovico 43, 50, 51, 53
Arthurian legend 44, 48
    Le Mort D'Arthur 50, 113
    Perceval, the Story of the Grail 46
    Sir Gawain and the Green Knight 45, 48, 133
Austen, Jane 59, 136

B
Bakhtin, M. 16, 110, 111, 182, 222
Baudelaire, Charles 91
Beer, G. 45, 48, 65
Beowulf 17, 23, 39–42, 69, 167, 168, 193
Beriain, J. 105

Beye, C. 21, 31, 35, 39
Blunden, Edmund 86
Boiardo, Matteo Maria 50, 53
de Boron, Robert 48
Brioso Sánchez, M. 34
Broceliande, Forest of 141
Brontë, Emily 135
Brooke, Rupert 73, 76, 89, 95, 96
Brooks, C. 81
Bunyan, John 78
Burns, M. 104, 198
'Burnt Norton' (poem) 92

C
Callimachus 29, 30
Campbell, J. 67, 104, 146
Cantar del Mío Cid 48, 49
The Cantos 74, 81, 82, 83
Carroll, Lewis 122
The Castle of Otranto 57, 58, 59, 70
de Cervantes, Miguel 55
chanson de geste 48–53, 54, 55, 69, 114, 159, 163, 164, 182, 208
Le Chanson de Roland 48, 84, 113, 163
Chaucer, Geoffrey 44
de Troyes, Chrétien 43, 44, 46, 47, 55
Christianity
    Christian allegory 53, 78
    Christian dogma, references in Tolkien 104, 197
    Christian duty and Northern courage 197
    Christian virtues 161, 164, 167, 168, 190, 191, 193–199, 204

combination of pagan with
    Christian motifs 45, 160,
    179, 189–190, 193–199, 222
Hell of Christian iconography 216
in *Beowulf* 40
in Renaissance literature 52
manifestation of God in nature 45
swords in Christian tradition 160
The Chronicles of Narnia 106
Clery, E.J. 57, 58
Coupe, L. 69
Craig, D. 82, 86, 87
Croft, J.B. 74
Cupitt, D. 68
Curry, P. 104

D
Dante 50, 79, 91, 100
David and Goliath (biblical) 197
Day, D. 189
Defoe, Daniel 56, 70, 84
De Paco 141, 161, 189, 198
'De Profundis' (poem) 77
de Troyes, Chrétien 43, 44, 46, 47, 55
Dickens, Charles 19, 119–122, 153
Divine Comedy 50
Don Quijote de la Mancha 53, 55, 120
A Dream of John Ball 64
Driver, P. 77, 95, 97
'The Dry Salvages' (poem) 92
Dunsany, Lord 65, 105

E
The Earthsea Trilogy 106
'East Coker' (poem) 91
Edda 84
Eddison, E.R.R. 65, 105
Eksteins, M. 76, 79, 84
Eliade, M. 67, 68, 146
Eliot, George 121
Eliot, T.S. 74, 79–83, 85, 87–93, 100–102, 104, 224

enargês 24
Enlightenment 56, 62
Epic romance and the novel 54–59
escapism 87, 93, 98, 103
von Eschenbach, Wolfram 48
eucatastrophe 132, 222

F
The Faerie Queene 52, 53
fairy tales 60, 62, 63, 65, 103, 122, 137
Far From the Madding Crowd 121, 134
Featherstone, S. 77, 87–89, 90
First World War. See Great War
Les Fleurs du Mal 91
Flieger, V. 73, 74, 94, 140, 146, 159, 181
Ford, D. 24
Forster, E.M. 135
Four Quartets 87–93, 101, 105
Frankenstein 60
Frye, N.
    ironic myth 75, 80, 84
    literary modes 15, 16, 78, 84, 86, 109, 151
    literary treatment of romance 60, 62, 71
Fussell, P. 76–79, 86, 207

G
García Gual, C. 30, 46, 49, 69
Garth, J. 73
Gaskell, Elizabeth 121
Gasque, T.J. 127, 129, 136, 138
Sir Gawain and the Green Knight 45, 48, 133
German Romantics 62
Gerusalemme Liberata 50, 52, 54
'Goliath and David' (poem) 197
The Good Soldier Svejk 84
gothic novel 57–59, 60
Grahame, Kenneth 123, 136

Le Grand Cyrus 55
Graves, Robert 73, 76, 86, 87, 197, 206
Great War 75–82
   disillusionment after 85, 98, 197
   experiences in 87
   homoeroticism in 206
   literary influences of 83, 88, 89, 207
   and *The Lord of the Rings* 74, 93–99, 184, 203, 205–207, 213–215, 217
   recovery from 199
   rural England before 119
   Tolkien as soldier in 73, 93
   war poets. See main entry for war poets
Greene, T. 24, 35, 51, 52
Grenfell, Julian 76
Gross, J. 81
Gurney, Ivor 76, 77, 89

H

Hainsworth, J. 19, 20, 26, 28, 30, 35, 38, 51, 52
Hamer 168
Hardy, Thomas 89, 121, 134, 135, 136
Hasek, Jaroslav 84
Hawthorne, Nathaniel 43, 61, 62, 135
The Hobbit 100
   characters from *The Lord of the Rings* 123, 124, 176–178
   The Lord of the Rings as sequel of 119, 122, 127, 137
   The Lord of the Rings breaking with 175, 176, 178, 185
hobbit poetry 95
The Hollow Land 63
Homer 24–29, 79
   and Apollonius 30–32, 35
   appreciation of 30, 68
   homeric heroes 163
   influence on fantasy novels 66
   and Joyce 81
   and Pound 81
   romance traits 43, 84
   and Virgil 37, 38, 51
homoeroticism 206, 214
Hour of the Dragon 105
The House of the Seven Gables 61
The House of the Wolfings 64
Howard, Robert E. 105
Hrolf Kraki Saga 40
Hughes, D. 191
Hugh Selwyn Mauberley 88

I

Iliad 21, 25–29, 35–37
Iliou persis 34
Inferno 91
'Into Battle, Flanders, April 1915' (poem) 76
In Parenthesis 87–93, 101, 105
ironic myth 15, 16, 75, 80, 82–111, 139, 190, 217, 222, 224
The Italian 58
Italian romance-epics 50–53

J

Jackson, Peter 179
Jerome, Jerome K. 121, 136, 170
Jewers, C. 44, 45, 54, 55, 142
Jones, David 87–93, 101, 102
Joyce, James 79–84, 87, 99, 100–102, 104, 139, 224

K

Kafka, Franz 84
Kalevala 63
Kermode, F. 84, 85
King, K. 163
Kocher, P. 166
Kypria 34

L

Landow, G. 64
Lang, Andrew 122
Lawlor, J. 50
Les Fleurs du Mal 91
Lewis, C.S. 15, 106
   on Spenser 53
Lewis, Matthew Gregory 58, 211
Le Chanson de Roland 48, 84, 113, 163
Le Guin, Ursula K. 15, 65, 106
Le Mort D'Arthur 50, 113
Le Roman de Troie 43, 163
Lindsay, David 105
'The Little Dog's Day' (poem) 95, 97
'Little Gidding' (poem) 92, 93
Little Iliad 34
Lloyd, T. 76
Lobdell, J. 73, 113, 114
Lönnroth, Elias 63
The Lord of the Rings
   connecting invented world to our own 138
   contemporary literary context 74, 75
   critical approaches to 13
   criticism of 16
   epical elements 223
   escapism 87
   Frye's literary modes 109, 151. See also Frye
   genres in 14, 15, 19, 150
   genre of 15, 73, 106
   and the Great War 74, 93–99
   and *The Hobbit*. See *The Hobbit*
   internal logic and coherence of 75, 119, 143, 178, 223
   intertraditional literary dialogue 16, 93, 113–220
   invented world, use of to create narrative universe 67
   ironic myth 15, 73–111, 222
   languages, as a context for 100
   literary and historical sources 71, 73, 74, 100, 101, 224
   modernism 99–102
   mythical features in 224
   mythical influence in 189, 223
   narrative traditions 15, 16, 19, 113, 137, 221
   quest for a meaningful context 13–17
   re-entchantment of world in 105
Lovecraft, H.P. 211

M

MacDonald, George 62–67, 71, 105, 122
The Magic Fishbone 122
Malory, Sir Thomas 43, 50, 51, 53
Manlove, C.N. 63, 126, 143
Mardones 104
Martorell, Joan 54
Mathews, R. 63, 64, 66
Maturin, Charles 60
medieval Romance 43–48
Melmoth the Wanderer 60
'The Merry Old Inn' (song) 96
meta-text 100
Metamorphoses 113
Miller, D.A. 141, 153, 154, 168, 172, 174, 202
Milton, John 100
Modernism 99–102
   modernist literature 75, 83, 85–88, 92, 99
   modernist movement 79
   Tolkien compared to modernist works 74, 100, 102, 139, 222
modern novel 56–67
Moll Flanders 56, 84
The Monk 58, 59
of Monmouth, Geoffrey 44
Moorcock 65
Moore, G.E. 76
Moore, George 121

Morris, William 15, 43, 62–67, 71, 78, 105, 132, 137, 203, 207
Mortimer, P. 74
The Mysteries of Udolpho 58, 59

N

News From Nowhere 64
Nibelungenlied 40, 48
Njal 196
Norse mythology 40, 42, 104, 189, 198
Northanger Abbey 59, 136
Northern courage 196, 197, 204
Nostoi 34

O

Odyssey 25–29, 48, 113
  and *Aeneid* 35, 37
  and *Argonautica* 31, 33, 34
  and *chanson de geste* 48
  and Joyce's *Ulysses* 81
  and Pound's *Cantos* 81
The Old English Baron 58, 59
On Fairy-Stories 102
Orlando Furioso 50, 54
Orlando Innamorato 50, 54
Ovid 113
Owen, Wilfred 73, 76, 78

P

pagan courage and Christian virtues 160, 193–199
Pamela 56, 58
Paradise Lost 100
Parzival 48
Pearl 133
Perceval, the Story of the Grail 46
Phantastes 63
The Pickwick Papers 119, 120, 121, 122, 153
The Pilgrim's Progress 78
A Portrait of the Artist as a Young Man 81

Potter, Beatrix 122, 123
Pound, E. 74, 79–83, 85, 88, 100, 102, 104, 224
The Princess and the Goblin 122, 185
The Prince of Elfland's Daughter 105
Prince Prigio 122
The Prydain Chronicles 106

Q

Quentin Durwood 59
Quint, D. 52, 54, 55, 150

R

Rabkin, E. 59
Radcliffe, Ann 58, 60, 211
Reeve, Clara 58, 211
Renaissance epic 48–53
Richardson, Samuel 56, 58
Ricoeur, P. 85
Rider Haggard, Henry 120
The Rise of the Novel 56
Rites of Spring: The Great War and the Birth of Modern Age 79
'Roads' (poem) 96
'The Road Goes Ever On' (song) 97
Robinson Crusoe 56, 70
Roman de Troie, Le 43, 163
The Roots of the Mountains 64
Rosebury, B. 74, 138, 139, 151
The Rose and the Ring 122

S

de Sainte-Maure, Benoît 43, 163
Saint Clair, G. 196
Sassoon, Siegfried 73, 76, 86, 87
Schlauch, M. 41
Scott, Walter 59, 207
Segura, E. 73, 100, 224
The Selfish Giant 122
She 120
Shelley, Mary 60, 62
Shippey, T.
  on Black Riders 126

on contrast between Faramir and
	Éomer 207
on Denethor's failure 196
on the Old Forest 138
on Frye's literary modes 15, 109
on genre 73
on pseudomedieval romance 207
on Tolkien's significance 74
The Silmarillion 100
Sir Gawain and the Green Knight 45,
	48, 133
Sir Orfeo 133
Sophocles 30
Spenser, Edmund 52, 53
Stevens, J. 44, 45, 47
*The Story of the Glittering Plain or the
	Land of Living Men* 64
'Strange Meeting' (poem) 78
Sturlusson 84
supernatural fiction 57–59
swords in Christian tradition 160

T

Tasso, Torquato 50, 51, 52, 53
Telegony 34
Thackeray, William Makepeace 63,
	122
The Fall of Gil-galad 101
Thomas, Edward 73, 76, 89, 96
Thorpe, D. 142
Three Men in a Boat 121, 135
Tirant lo Blanc 54
Toda Iglesia 120, 157, 201, 206, 214
Tolkien's interpretation of
	Beowulf 40
Tolley, C. 106
Toohey, P. 23, 25
Traversi, D. 92, 100
Troilus and Criseyde 44
Trojan War
	compared to *Beowulf* 42
de Troyes, Chrétien 43, 44, 46, 47,
	55

U

Ulysses 74, 81, 82, 83, 100, 139

V

Veugen, C. 151
Vinaver, E. 142
Virgil 35–39, 51, 79
	and *Beowulf* 41, 42
	and Homer 51
	in the Renaissance 51, 69
A Voyage to Arcturus 105

W

Walpole, Horace 43, 57, 70
war poets 76–79, 82, 83, 85
	and Frye's literary modes 86
	compared to Tolkien 74, 98, 99
	literary imagination of 75
	and *The Lord of the Rings* 94,
		203, 205, 213
	Tolkien's rebuttal of 197
	See also entries for Owen,
		Sassoon, Thomas, Gurney,
		Grenfell and Grave
The Waste Land 74, 82, 83, 86, 88,
	90, 100, 139
The Water of the Wondrous Isles 64
Watt, I. 56
Webster, John 91
The Well at the World's End 64–66,
	71, 78, 95, 132
White Devil 91
Wilde, Oscar 121, 122
The Wind in the Willows 136
Witemeyer, H. 81
The Wood Beyond the World 64
The Worm Ouroboros 105

Y

Yeats, W.B. 80, 84

Z

Zanger, J. 64, 65, 106

Walking Tree Publishers

Walking Tree Publishers was founded in 1997 as a forum for publication of material (books, videos, CDs, etc.) related to Tolkien and Middle-earth studies. Manuscripts and project proposals can be submitted to the board of editors (please include an SAE):

Walking Tree Publishers
CH-3052 Zollikofen
Switzerland
e-mail: info@walking-tree.org
http://www.walking-tree.org

Cormarë Series

The *Cormarë Series* has been the first series of studies dedicated exclusively to the exploration of Tolkien's work. Its focus is on papers and studies from a wide range of scholarly approaches. The series comprises monographs, thematic collections of essays, conference volumes, and reprints of important yet no longer (easily) accessible papers by leading scholars in the field. Manuscripts and project proposals are evaluated by members of an independent board of advisors who support the series editors in their endeavour to provide the readers with qualitatively superior yet accessible studies on Tolkien and his work.

News from the Shire and Beyond. Studies on Tolkien
Peter Buchs and Thomas Honegger (eds.), Zurich and Berne 2004, Reprint, First edition 1997 (Cormarë Series 1), ISBN 3-9521424-5-X

Root and Branch. Approaches Towards Understanding Tolkien
Thomas Honegger (ed.), Zurich and Berne 2005, Reprint, First edition 1999 (Cormarë Series 2), ISBN 3-905703-01-7

Richard Sturch, *Four Christian Fantasists. A Study of the Fantastic Writings of George MacDonald, Charles Williams, C. S. Lewis and J.R.R. Tolkien*
Zurich and Berne 2007, Reprint, First edition 2001 (Cormarë Series 3), ISBN 978-3-905703-04-7

Tolkien in Translation
Thomas Honegger (ed.), Zurich and Berne 2003 (Cormarë Series 4), ISBN 3-9521424-6-8

Mark T. Hooker, *Tolkien Through Russian Eyes*
Zurich and Berne 2003 (Cormarë Series 5), ISBN 3-9521424-7-6

Translating Tolkien: Text and Film
Thomas Honegger (ed.), Zurich and Berne 2004 (Cormarë Series 6), ISBN 3-9521424-9-2

Christopher Garbowski, *Recovery and Transcendence for the Contemporary Mythmaker. The Spiritual Dimension in the Works of J.R.R. Tolkien*
Zurich and Berne 2004, Reprint, First Edition by Marie Curie Sklodowska, University Press, Lublin 2000, (Cormarë Series 7), ISBN 3-9521424-8-4

Reconsidering Tolkien
Thomas Honegger (ed.), Zurich and Berne 2005 (Cormarë Series 8),
ISBN 3-905703-00-9

Tolkien and Modernity 1
Frank Weinreich and Thomas Honegger (eds.), Zurich and Berne 2006 (Cormarë Series 9), ISBN 978-3-905703-02-3

Tolkien and Modernity 2
Thomas Honegger and Frank Weinreich (eds.), Zurich and Berne 2006 (Cormarë Series 10), ISBN 978-3-905703-03-0

Tom Shippey, *Roots and Branches. Selected Papers on Tolkien by Tom Shippey*
Zurich and Berne 2007 (Cormarë Series 11), ISBN 978-3-905703-05-4

Ross Smith, *Inside Language. Linguistic and Aesthetic Theory in Tolkien*
Zurich and Berne 2007 (Cormarë Series 12), ISBN 978-3-905703-06-1

How We Became Middle-earth. A Collection of Essays on The Lord of the Rings
Adam Lam and Nataliya Oryshchuk (eds.), Zurich and Berne 2007 (Cormarë Series 13), ISBN 978-3-905703-07-8

Myth and Magic. Art According to the Inklings
Eduardo Segura and Thomas Honegger (eds.), Zurich and Berne 2007 (Cormarë Series 14), ISBN 978-3-905703-08-5

The Silmarillion - Thirty Years On
Allan Turner (ed.), Zurich and Berne 2007 (Cormarë Series 15),
ISBN 978-3-905703-10-8

Martin Simonson, *The Lord of the Rings and the Western Narrative Tradition*
Zurich and Jena 2008 (Cormarë Series 16), ISBN 978-3-905703-09-2

Beyond Middle-earth: Tolkien's Shorter Works. Proceedings of the 4th Seminar of the Deutsche Tolkien Gesellschaft & Walking Tree Publishers Decennial Conference
Margaret Hiley and Frank Weinreich (eds.), Zurich and Jena 2008 (Cormarë Series 17)

Constructions of Authorship in and around the Works of J.R.R. Tolkien
Judith Klinger (ed.), Zurich and Jena, forthcoming

Tolkien's The Lord of the Rings: Sources and Inspirations
Stratford Caldecott and Thomas Honegger (eds.), Zurich and Jena, forthcoming

Rainer Nagel, *Hobbit Place-names. A Linguistic Excursion through the Shire*
Zurich and Jena, forthcoming

Tales of Yore Series

The *Tales of Yore Series* grew out of the desire to share Kay Woollard's whimsical stories and drawings with a wider audience. The series aims at providing a platform for qualitatively superior fiction with a clear link to Tolkien's world.

Kay Woollard, *The Terror of Tatty Walk. A Frightener*
CD and Booklet, Zurich and Berne 2000 (Tales of Yore Series 1),
ISBN 3-9521424-2-5

Kay Woollard, *Wilmot's Very Strange Stone or What came of building "snobbits"*
CD and booklet, Zurich and Berne 2001 (Tales of Yore Series 2),
ISBN 3-9521424-4-1

Ossie felt the back of his neck go prickly....

www.ingramcontent.com/pod-product-compliance
Lightning Source LLC
Chambersburg PA
CBHW070731160426
43192CB00009B/1400